Political and Constitutional Transitions in North Africa

The transformations which are taking place in the Arab world are dynamic processes characterized by a number of variables that one can refer to as *actors* and *factors*.

The implications of the Arab uprisings are important for the world at large; the Arab world's successes, and failures, at this crucial moment may well serve as a model for other nations. *Political and Constitutional Transitions in North Africa* focuses on five Northern African countries: Tunisia, Egypt, Morocco, Libya and Algeria, examining specific institutions and actors participating in the political upheavals in North Africa since 2011, and placing them in a comparative perspective in order to better understand the processes at work. This book addresses issues pertinent to North African and Middle Eastern Studies, comparative constitutional law, political science and transitional studies and it contains contributions by experts in all these fields.

Providing a significant contribution to the understanding of events that followed the immolation of Mohamed Bouazizi in Tunisia, this book is a valuable contribution to North African Studies, Middle Eastern Studies, Comparative Constitutional Law and Transitional Studies.

Justin O. Frosini is Assistant Professor of Public Law at the Bocconi University in Milan, Director of the Center for Constitutional Studies and Democratic Development (CCSDD) in Bologna and Adjunct Professor of Constitutional Law at the Johns Hopkins University SAIS Europe. He is the author of *Constitutional Preambles: At a Crossroads between Politics and Law* (2012) as well as several articles and book chapters in the field of comparative constitutional law with particular attention for federalism, regionalism and devolution, constitutional justice and forms of government.

Francesco Biagi is a postdoctoral research fellow at the University of Bologna's School of Law and researcher at the Center for Constitutional Studies and Democratic Development (CCSDD). He is the author of several articles and book chapters focusing on transitions to democracy, constitution-building, constitutional justice and electoral justice. In 2012 his research on "Constitutional Courts in Democratic Transitions: The Cases of Italy, Spain and the Czech Republic" was awarded best Ph.D. thesis in Constitutional Law at the University of Ferrara by the Istituto Universitario di Studi Superiori (IUSS).

Routledge Studies in Middle Eastern Democratization and Government

Edited by Larbi Sadiki

University of Exeter

This series examines new ways of understanding democratization and government in the Middle East. The varied and uneven processes of change, occurring in the Middle Eastern region, can no longer be read and interpreted solely through the prism of Euro-American transitology. Seeking to frame critical parameters in light of these new horizons, this series instigates reinterpretations of democracy and propagates formerly 'subaltern,' narratives of democratization. Reinvigorating discussion on how Arab and Middle Eastern peoples and societies seek good government, *Routledge Studies in Middle Eastern Democratization and Government* provides tests and contests of old and new assumptions.

Revolution, Revolt and Reform in North Africa
The Arab Spring and Beyond
Edited by Ricardo René Larémont

Informal Power in the Greater Middle East
Hidden Geographies
Edited by Luca Anceschi, Gennaro Gervasio and Andrea Teti

Crowds and Politics in North Africa
Tunisia, Algeria and Libya
Andrea Khalil

Egypt's Long Revolution
Protest Movements and Uprisings
Maha Abdelrahman

Sectarianism in Iraq
The Making of State and Nation Since 1920
Khalil F. Osman

Sufism and Politics in Morocco
Activism and Dissent
Abdelilah Bouasria

Political and Constitutional Transitions in North Africa
Actors and Factors
Justin O. Frosini and Francesco Biagi

Political and Constitutional Transitions in North Africa

Actors and Factors

Edited by
Justin O. Frosini and Francesco Biagi

Routledge
Taylor & Francis Group
LONDON AND NEW YORK

First published 2015
by Routledge
2 Park Square, Milton Park, Abingdon, Oxon OX14 4RN

and by Routledge
711 Third Avenue, New York, NY 10017

First issued in paperback 2017

Routledge is an imprint of the Taylor & Francis Group, an informa business

British Library Cataloguing in Publication Data
A catalogue record for this book is available from the British Library

Library of Congress Cataloging-in-Publication Data
Political and constitutional transitions in North Africa : actors and factors / edited by Justin Frosini & Francesco Biagi.
pages cm. – (Routledge studies in Middle Eastern democratization and government ; 7)
Includes bibliographical references and index.
1. Africa, North–Politics and government–21st century. 2. Arab countries–Politics and government–21st century. 3. Democratization–Africa, North. 4. Democratization–Arab countries. 5. Constitutional law–Africa, North. 6. Constitutional law–Arab countries. 7. Arab Spring, 2010- I. Frosini, Justin Orlando, editor of compilation. II. Biagi, Francesco, editor of compilation.

JQ3198.A58P64 2014
320.961–dc23
2014021703

ISBN 13: 978-0-8153-4888-7 (pbk)
ISBN 13: 978-1-138-81638-1 (hbk)

Typeset in Times New Roman
by Taylor and Francis Books

Contents

Contributors

Francesco Biagi is a postdoctoral research fellow at the University of Bologna's School of Law and researcher at the Center for Constitutional Studies and Democratic Development (CCSDD). Biagi obtained a Ph.D. in constitutional law from the University of Ferrara after graduating in law from the University of Bologna. In 2012 his research on "Constitutional Courts in Democratic Transitions: The Cases of Italy, Spain and the Czech Republic" was awarded best Ph.D. thesis in Constitutional Law at the University of Ferrara by the Istituto Universitario di Studi Superiori (IUSS). He is the author of articles and book chapters focusing on transitions to democracy, constitution-building, constitutional justice, electoral justice and federalism. He is currently coordinating a project on the constitutional transitions in North Africa. His latest publications include: "The 2011 Constitutional Reform in Morocco: More Flaws than Merits," *Jean Monnet Occasional Papers*, Institute for European Studies (Malta), no. 7/2014; "Will Surviving Constitutionalism in Morocco and Jordan Work in the Long Run? A Comparison with Three Past Authoritarian Regimes," *Cambridge Journal of International and Comparative Law*, vol. 3 (3), 2014 (forthcoming); "Three Generations of European Constitutional Courts in Transition to Democracy," *Diritto pubblico comparato ed europeo*, no. 2, 2014 (forthcoming).

Nathan J. Brown is Professor of Political Science and International Affairs at George Washington University and non-resident senior associate at the Carnegie Endowment for International Peace. Brown's scholarly work over the years has focused on Egypt, Islamist movements, Palestinian politics, Arab law, and constitutionalism. In 2009, Brown was named a Carnegie scholar by the Carnegie Corporation of New York. For the 2009–10 academic year, he was a fellow at the Woodrow Wilson International Center for Scholars. In 2013 he was named a Guggenheim fellow. Brown is the author of six books, among them *When Victory is Not an Option: Islamist Movements in Arab Politics* (Cornell University Press, 2012), *Resuming Arab Palestine* (University of California Press, 2003), *Constitutions in a Non-Constitutional World: Arab Basic Laws and Prospects for Accountable Government* (SUNY Press, 2001), and *The Rule of Law in the Arab World: Courts in Egypt and the Arab States of the Gulf* (Cambridge University Press, 1997).

John P. Entelis is Professor and Chair of the Department of Political Science and Director of the Middle East Studies Program at Fordham University. He received his Ph.D. from New York University and studied Arabic in Cairo, Harvard, and Princeton. He has been awarded several Fulbright awards including a US Department of Education Fulbright-Hays Doctoral Dissertation Research Abroad Fellowship to conduct research in Lebanon, a Senior Fulbright Professorship at the University of Algiers and one at the University of Tunis, and a Fulbright Regional Research Award to Morocco, Algeria, and Tunisia. Professor Entelis is the author or co-author of numerous scholarly publications on the comparative and international politics of the Middle East and North Africa including *Algeria: The Revolution Institutionalized*, *Culture and Counterculture in Moroccan Politics*, *State and Society in Algeria*, and *Islam, Democracy, and the State in North Africa*. Professor Entelis is president of the American Institute for Maghrib Studies (AIMS) and former editor-in-chief of its scholarly journal, *The Journal of North African Studies.*

Justin O. Frosini is Assistant Professor of Public Law at the Bocconi University, Milan, Adjunct Professor of Constitutional Law at the Johns Hopkins University SAIS Europe and Director of the Center for Constitutional Studies and Democratic Development (CCSDD). He is the author of several articles and book chapters and has published widely in English and Italian in the field of comparative constitutional law with particular attention for federalism, regionalism and devolution, constitutional justice and forms of government; some of his works have been translated into Spanish, Serbo-Croat, and Ukrainian. His fields of interest are comparative constitutional law, democratic development, constitutional adjudication, devolution, and federalism and his publications include *Constitutional Preambles: At a Crossroads Between Politics and Law* (Maggioli, 2012); *Democracy With (out) Nations. Old and New Foundations for Political Communities in a Changing World* (Universidad del País Vasco, 2011, edited with I. Filibbi and N. Cornago); *Analytic Report of the Consultation Draft of the Constitution of the Somali Republic*, in IDLO 2012 (with T. Ginsburg and J. Chiebub); "A Constitutional Paradox? Ghana's Peaceful Democratic Transition," *Percorsi costituzionali*, no. 2/3, 2011.

Eric Knecht is a journalist and translator based in Cairo. He was formerly a fellow at the American University in Cairo's Center for Arabic Study Abroad (CASA), and a Fulbright grantee in Egypt, where as a freelance journalist he covered post-revolution politics in the Nile Delta. He has authored or co-authored numerous reports and publications on Libya, including "POMED Backgrounder: Previewing Libya's Elections," and "Post-revolutionary Politics in Libya: Inside the General National Congress." He formerly worked as a research assistant at the Rafik Hariri Center for the Middle East, where he contributed research and analysis on Libya's political transition. His work has appeared in *US World News*,

Jadaliyya, *Egypt Independent*, *Tripoli Post*, and elsewhere. He received his B.A. in economics and history from Rutgers University.

Karim Mezran is a senior fellow at the Atlantic Council's Rafik Hariri Center for the Middle East and Adjunct Professor at the School of Advanced International Studies (SAIS), Johns Hopkins University. In addition to teaching at SAIS, Karim Mezran was an assistant professor of political science at the John Cabot University and acted as a visiting professor at the Libera Università per gli Studi Sociali (LUISS) in Rome (2002). He has been the director of the Center for American Studies (Rome). He received his Ph.D. in international relations at SAIS. He also holds a J.D. in comparative law from the University of Rome "La Sapienza" (Italy), a L.L.M. in comparative law from George Washington University (US), a M.A. in Arab studies from Georgetown University (US), and a B.A. in management from Hiram College (US). His most recent publications are: "Libya in Transition: From Jamahiriya to Jumhuriyya?," in *The New Middle East: Protest and Revolution in the Arab world*, F. Georges (ed.), London, January 2014; "Power Shifts in the Arab Spring: A Work in Progress," *Bologna Center Journal of International Affairs*, vol. 15, 2012 (with Alice Alunni); *Libia. Fine o rinascita di una nazione?* (Donzelli Editore, 2012, ed. with Arturo Varvelli); "Libya's wars," *The American Interest*, September/October 2011; *Negotiation and Construction of National Identities* (Martinus Nijhoff Publishers, 2007).

Duncan Pickard is a non-resident fellow at the Rafik Hariri Center for the Middle East. He has worked on electoral and constitutional politics in North Africa and Yemen since the start of the Arab revolutions. He was country director in Libya for Democracy Reporting International, and he has worked in Tunisia on projects through Harvard Law School and the International Foundation for Electoral Systems. His writings on Tunisia and Libya have appeared in the *Journal of Democracy*, the *Journal of North African Studies*, *Mediterranean Politics*, and *Good Governance Africa*. Pickard holds degrees from Tufts University and the Harvard Kennedy School, and is currently pursuing his law degree at Stanford University.

Preface

This book is the result of a three-year research project on "Transitional Law and the Challenge of the Arab Spring" conducted by the Center for Constitutional Studies and Democratic Development (CCSDD) with the support of the George Lawrence Abernethy Endowment, a fund established by Robert J. Abernethy to honor the memory of his father. Part of the results of this project were presented at the international conference "Constitutional Transformations in the Arab World following the Arab Spring: Comparative Models" which took place at the Johns Hopkins University's School of Advanced International Studies in Bologna on February 7–8, 2013.

Three of the five original papers were presented at this conference and we then added the remaining two with the aim of presenting an exhaustive analysis of the political and constitutional transitions in North Africa. The final chapter draws together the five case studies in order to examine the actors and factors of these transitions in a comparative perspective.

We would like to express our gratitude to CCSDD researchers Sara Pennicino and Čarna Pištan for their precious advice and critical observations, and to CCSDD interns for their invaluable research assistance. Special thanks go to colleague and friend Karim Mezran for believing in this project from the very outset. His suggestions were of the utmost importance in ameliorating the conduct of this research. We are very grateful to our authors for their contributions, which all provide a unique insight into the Arab upheavals. Our appreciation also extends to the editor of the series Larbi Sadiki and to Joe Whiting and Kat Rylance at Routledge.

Finally we are indebted to Bob Abernethy: without his ceaseless support this book would never have gone to print.

Justin O. Frosini and Francesco Biagi
Bologna, May 2014

Introduction

Justin O. Frosini and Francesco Biagi

"Egypt, the Arab world's most populous nation and for so long its cultural beating heart, does not have long to go. The situation there is 'explosive' and sooner or later the Muslim Brotherhood will take over." As surprising as it might seem, this statement, rendered public by WikiLeaks, was made by none other than Zine el-Abidine Ben Ali, president of Tunisia, in a comment to a visiting secretary of state. Ben Ali further demonstrated his skills as a seer by underlining that "Muammar Qaddafi of Libya was not a normal person," predicting that he would also soon be ousted from power. Ben Ali's prophecies, however, proved to be decidedly less accurate when he added with self-satisfaction that he was glad Tunisia was in the Maghreb not the Levant—part of stable North Africa, not the fractious Middle East. Little was he aware that at the beginning of 2011 the immolation of Mohamed Bouazizi, a street vendor from the small town of Sidi Bouzid, would bring an end to his 23-year "reign" and spark off a series of events that we commonly refer to as the Arab Spring.

It would be far too easy, however, to take a pot shot at Ben Ali for getting his predictions on Tunisia so wrong. Indeed, the truth of the matter is that at the time it was far from easy to foresee any of the revolutions that have taken place and, on the contrary, there were strong reasons for arguing that the autocracies in the region would still have a long duration.

Even after the break out of the Jasmine Revolution it was reasonable to think that Tunisia would not have a domino effect on the rest of the region. As Richard Spencer, *The Daily Telegraph*'s Middle East correspondent, stated in early January 2011 "the coup in Tunisia sent shockwaves throughout the Arab world. But don't expect it to herald an era of democratic reform," and of course one cannot forget the skepticism expressed by Harvard University's professor of international affairs Stephen Walt. In fact, with regard to the idea that the overthrow of Ben Ali would become the catalyst for a wave of democratization throughout the Arab world as occurred in Central and Eastern Europe after the fall of the Berlin Wall, he stated in his *Foreign Policy Blog*: "In fact, the history of world revolution suggests that this sort of revolutionary cascade is quite rare, and even when some sort of revolutionary contagion does take place, it happens pretty slowly and is often accompanied by overt foreign invasion."

In many respects, three and a half years since the Jasmine Revolution, one has to stress the fact that Walt highlighted a series of problematic issues related to the Arab uprisings that we are still addressing today. Certainly, he did not predict such a rapid fall of the Mubarak and Qaddafi regimes (though the latter was indeed "accompanied by overt foreign invasion") but, as the following chapters of this book will demonstrate, the transition in Tunisia is very different to the transitions taking place in Egypt and Libya (not to mention the maintaining of power of the *ancien régimes* in Morocco and Algeria) and, for now at least, it appears highly inappropriate to talk of a new wave of democratization in the MENA region. Indeed to paraphrase Walt's concluding paragraph "anyone who was expecting to see a rapid transformation of the Arab world in the wake of the Jasmine Revolution, is likely to have been disappointed."

Bearing in mind the great difficulty in understanding, on the one hand, the dynamics of the Arab world, and on the other the full dimension of transitions from authoritarian rule, the *raison d'être* of this volume is not to provide an exhaustive overview of the political and constitutional transformations occurring in North Africa, but rather to analyze specific variables that are relevant to the country and meaningful in a comparative perspective, so as to better comprehend these processes.

In particular, with regard to Tunisia, Egypt and Morocco, a single actor is examined (i.e. Al-Nahda, the Supreme Constitutional Court and the king respectively), while in the cases of Libya and Algeria several variables are the object of analysis.

Duncan Pickard, in his chapter on Tunisia—"Al-Nahda: Moderation and Compromise in Tunisia's Constitutional Bargain"—examines the role played by the moderate Islamic party Al-Nahda in the constitution-making process. Pickard shows that Al-Nahda's goals for the constitution have at all times advocated compromise (for example regarding the role of Islam in society, the distribution of executive powers and the end of the constitution-making process), and that this approach to compromise is a distinguishing feature with respect to other constitution-making processes.

In the chapter on Egypt—"Egypt: A Constitutional Court in an Unconstitutional Setting"—Nathan J. Brown analyses the role played by the Egyptian Supreme Constitutional Court. Brown examines well-known and lesser-known judgments issued by the Court that deeply affected the process of transition in Egypt, and argues that there is no similar revolutionary setting in which constitutional judges proved to be as significant a player as generals, politicians, or leaders of security forces.

In the chapter on Morocco—"The Pilot of *Limited* Change: Mohammed VI and the Transition in Morocco"—Francesco Biagi focuses on the role played by King Mohammed VI. In particular, he argues that the king has not guaranteed Morocco a transition to a fully democratic country. In fact, although the adoption of the 2011 Constitution is effectively a sign of greater democratization of the country, for the time being Morocco continues to be a hybrid regime, in which the king remains the fulcrum of the political and institutional system.

In the chapter on Libya—"Actors and Factors in Libya's Revolution"—Karim Mezran and Eric Knecht analyze the major actors and factors (both internal and external) that influenced the direction of the Libyan transition. In particular, Mezran and Knecht examine how Western engagement and "reform" ushered in by Saif al-Islam Qaddafi, the late-dictator's second eldest son, and the resultant actors, networks and ideas that emerged in the decade before the revolution, set the stage for a revolt that involved a significantly large share of the international community with a Libyan population that was determined to change the regime.

The case of Algeria stands alone since, unlike the other Northern African countries, it has remained to a large extent immune to the Arab uprisings. In his chapter "Algeria: The Outlier State?" John P. Entelis argues that Algeria constitutes an "outlier" in the Arab world explained by a combination of factors (such as the absence of a regime "culprit," abundant hydrocarbon resources, matters of political geography, a policy of cooptation of the Islamist idiom, etc.) that serve to immunize it, in the short- and intermediate-term at least, from sudden mass-based overthrow.

Why we decided to focus on the abovementioned actors and factors is because they represent crucial variables not only in the country under examination, but also in other countries involved in the Arab upheavals as well as in other past and present transitions. In other words, each of these actors/factors is indicative of specific *trends* taking place in North Africa and in the Middle East. Al-Nahda in Tunisia is an example of one of the Islamist parties that came to power following the Arab uprisings, and that now have to face a number of sensitive and difficult challenges; the Egyptian Supreme Constitutional Court is indicative of the trend consisting of the emergence and strengthening of constitutional courts following the Arab upheavals; the role played by Mohammed VI in Morocco reflects the resistance of Arab monarchies to the wind of change; the key role played by external actors in Libya highlights that the outcome of the processes of transition not only depends on internal variables; the case of Algeria shows that despite the profound changes taking place in the MENA region, there are numerous and heterogeneous factors that hinder reform processes. Given the significance of these actors and factors, the five case studies are followed by a final chapter that draws all these variables together and analyses them from a comparative constitutional standpoint.

Bologna, May 2014

1 Al-Nahda: Moderation and compromise in Tunisia's constitutional bargain

Duncan Pickard

Introduction

The new Tunisian constitution is the first in the Arab world written outside the influence of a dictator or foreign power. It is difficult to exaggerate the influence that the members of the National Constituent Assembly, the body responsible for drafting the constitution, have had on the democratic transition in Tunisia and the fate of Middle Eastern democracy. Like all, albeit few, free elections in the modern Arab Middle East, the plurality party in the National Constituent Assembly has an explicit Islamic tendency. The Party of the Al-Nahda Movement (*hizb al-harakat an-nahdha*) is a moderate Islamic party whose president and founder, Rached Ghannouchi, for decades has been in the vanguard of Islamic democrats. Al-Nahda as a political party is Islamic not only because it tries to achieve religious objectives through the political process, framing international principles of democracy in Islamic terms; Al-Nahda also preaches Islam as a guide for society at large. The activities of both the party and the movement of Al-Nahda are deliberately linked.

Al-Nahda's success in the 2011 elections for the National Constituent Assembly presented an opportunity to put theories of Islamic democracy into practice, and to model the leadership of an Islamic party over a democratic constitution-making process. How has Al-Nahda conducted itself, what has been Al-Nahda's vision for the Tunisian constitution, and how can we evaluate its leadership in the transition to democracy? The defining characteristics of Al-Nahda's leadership in the constitution-making process have been compromise, cooperation, and moderation, as well as loyalty among party leaders across a broad ideological spectrum. Al-Nahda has had the most succinct and thoughtful position on constitutional issues, but its members have also been among the first to make concessions in the interest of consensus. Indeed, it has been Al-Nahda's compromises that have driven Tunisia's constitutional bargain, such as in its omission of Islamic *sharia* from the draft constitution and its acceptance of a semi-presidential system.

The commitment to consensus from all parties makes Tunisia distinct from other experiences with constitution-making in the Arab Spring. Egypt drafted two new constitutions after its revolution, each adopted and ratified rapidly (in a matter of days) without real public input, and under threat of judicial shutdown and military coup. Yemen has not yet had meaningful constitutional reform, and conditions of widespread illiteracy and single-party rule make such a development unlikely in the short to medium term. Syria is in the midst of civil war. Libya faces daunting security challenges that will threaten stability throughout the work of its constituent assembly. In contrast, Tunisian political leaders have envisioned a new constitution to represent the new democratic order and have orchestrated a constitution-making process to work toward that order.

No single feature of an emerging democracy makes a greater contribution to political stability than a well-formed constitution. Constitutions lay out rules that solve conflicts, establish the rule of law, and enable peaceful transfers of power. While no constitution can guarantee stability, stability is not possible without a good one. But constitutions are meant to do much more than frame balanced structures of power and establish the rule of law. Tunisians expect their constitutions to stand for the values of their revolutions. The constitution should represent society, accounting for the characteristics of each country and reflecting the shared imagination of the values and meaning of the state. It is in some ways strange to entrust one party, especially one with a particular religious ideology, with leading the process of drafting a document that has such broad obligations to fulfill.

The constitution-making process in Tunisia provides a forum for debate around the critical questions of how to balance executive constraint with political stability, and how to embody the dignity of citizens violated by dictatorship. These questions are not new to democratic transitions. Tunisia does, however, present a rare opportunity to explore complex questions facing democratic development, especially in the Arab Middle East. Tunisia's is the first democratic constitution written with an Islamist party in the driver's seat.

This chapter proceeds in three parts to describe Al-Nahda's role in the constitution-making process, and in particular the compromises it has made along the way. First is a background on Al-Nahda, including its history, the ideology of Rached Ghannouchi, its internal structure, and some of the governance challenges the party faces in post-revolution Tunisia. Second, the chapter describes the constitution-making process in Tunisia, including the internal structure of the National Constituent Assembly, a timeline, and the approval process. The section also describes Al-Nahda's role in the constitution-making process, the formal characteristics of its leadership, and some information on Al-Nahda assemblypersons. The third section looks at compromises Al-Nahda has made on three critical issues in the constitutional debate: the role of Islam in society, the distribution of executive powers, and the end of the constitution-making process. The chapter concludes with some thoughts on Al-Nahda's approach to compromise as a distinguishing feature from other constitution-making processes.

History and ideology of Al-Nahda

The ideology of Rached Ghannouchi

Al-Nahda stands out among Islamic parties in the Arab world for its emphasis on moderation and synthesis with democracy. The precedent for Al-Nahda's moderate platform can be traced to the writings of Rached Ghannouchi, the movement's president and founder. Ghannouchi had perceived of a "Tunisian specificity" (*al-khususiyah at-tunsiyah*), an idea that he developed while studying the work of founding thinkers in political Islam, including Muhammad Iqbal, Mawdudi, Sayyid Qutb, Hassan al-Banna, and Malik Bennabi (whom he studied under personally). The Salafi orientation of many of these thinkers could not fit Tunisia, he argued, due to the profound European influence on Tunisian law and society. Ghannouchi first tried to explain the Tunisian specificity through European philosophers of economic justice. He saw compatibilities between Marx and the Qur'an in the eternal fight for social and economic justice, inspiring him to change his worldview: from a total rejection of Western philosophy in exchange for a better path offered in Islam, to an "objective interaction" between the two philosophies.[1]

Ghannouchi's political views evolved similarly, taking tenets of Islamic thought to apply critiques of the "Western model of democracy." His central critique is that the unit of political participation is the nation-state, that boundaries and governments are required to promulgate democracy, tending toward nationalism and even racism. The Western nation-state—arrived at, in Ghannouchi's view, via the theories of Darwin, Hegel, Nietzsche, and Weber—guarantees democracy as a virtue of citizenship in one nation, not as an inherent value of humankind. As evidence, Ghannouchi points to the brutal crimes of colonialism perpetrated by some of the world's most revered democracies. His choice example is Tunisia, where he argues that a traditional Islamic society was first corrupted by colonialism and later by its offspring, the modern nation-state. Ghannouchi envisions countering the despotic nation-state with a new political order grounded in noble and humanistic values that preserve dignity and humanity.[2]

Ghannouchi sees Islamic faith in God as the right spiritual foundation for such an order but concedes that no plausible alternative to the Western model currently exists. Indeed, writing in the 1990s, he calls for a Western-style democracy in Tunisia as the best of all plausible options. Amid his critiques, he wholeheartedly endorses the mechanisms of Western democracy, including elections, parliaments, and the separation of powers. He sees these as excellent methods for operationalizing the Qur'anic concept of *shura,* or consultation of those who are affected by decisions. Ghannouchi firmly believes in a civilian authority that embodies the values of Islam but is answerable only to the public. There is no room for theocracy in Islamic democracy, therefore, since the public can and should criticize government policies only on the grounds of their practical soundness.[3]

Another feature of a Western democratic system that Ghannouchi endorses is the power of the law to constrain executive power, a role filled by the Islamic *sharia.* He, like most scholars of Islamic governance, argue that political leaders cannot disregard Islamic *sharia,* though they are limited in their application of it to the interpretation of the *ulama,* or body of Islamic scholars. Islamic *sharia* and the legal scholars who interpret it serve as a check on executive power, much in the way that courts do in European and North American democracies.[4] His early writing on the role of Islamic *sharia* in an Islamic democracy is what makes him a philosopher of Islam. His party's rejection of Islam in the new Tunisian constitution, as we will see, reflects one of the hard choices that Al-Nahda has made during its leadership of Tunisia.

Some of the difficult choices that Al-Nahda made *vis-à-vis* its Islamic tendency had antecedents in political opinions that Ghannouchi professed while living in exile in the 1980s. Ghannouchi had long criticized Tunisia's personal-status code on the grounds that it outlawed polygamy. He changed his view in the late 1980s, arguing that polygamy is not a central tenet of Islam and therefore can be ignored as a policy priority if advocating for it would harm Al-Nahda's chances of success.[5] Ghannouchi's reversal on the personal-status code foreshadowed his and his party's omission of Islamic *sharia* in the constitution, a striking decision for an Islamic party, both reflecting Ghannouchi's difficulty in balancing his dual role as a political and a philosophical leader. Ghannouchi's duality has gotten him into trouble. Critics of Ghannouchi's philosophy argue that he often emphasizes the best aspects of either Islam or "Western democracy" while ignoring the downsides of each. His political critics take issue with how Ghannouchi emphasizes different themes or approaches to democracy depending on the audience to which he is speaking, both publicly and in private; more than once, he has been accused of contradicting himself across audiences and languages.

Founding of Al-Nahda

As Ghannouchi was developing his philosophies in the 1970s, he and a group of colleagues were quietly building support for an illegal organization they called the Islamic Tendency Movement (MTI), based largely on Ghannouchi's writings. The MTI was a loose coalition that began to have greater significance in national and local politics as the socialist policies of President Habib Bourguiba began to fail. The MTI advocated Islam-based solutions to Tunisia's problems as well as a liberal political system, including parliamentary elections. In 1981, after police discovered the group's founding manifesto, Ghannouchi authorized a referendum among the membership to determine whether the group should release the manifesto publicly. The movement voted 70 percent in favor of going public. The Shura Council certified the referendum, and on June 6, 1981, the MTI released its Founding Manifesto. The manifesto committed the movement to the democratic process, free elections, political pluralism, and the peaceful alternation of power. MTI's Islamic contemporaries, the revolutionaries in Iran, denounced the manifesto as having been infiltrated by Western values.[6] MTI's leaders wanted to model the democratic system of government within their own party and have governed it as a democratic institution since its founding. According to the manifesto, there are four sources of power: the president, the executive committee, the Shura Council, and the general assembly. More than ten members have served as president, who is elected every three years by the general assembly.

Bourguiba legalized political parties beyond his own Neo-Dustour in 1981 after large demonstrations in Gafsa, which shattered his traditional alliance with the national labor union. Bourguiba did not legalize the MTI, however. The MTI's violent demonstrations in protest of Bourguiba's decision gave the government an excuse to arrest hundreds of its members and label it a terrorist organization with ties to Iran. MTI members continued to be arrested throughout the 1980s for their membership in a banned organization. Bourguiba was overthrown in a bloodless coup in 1987, with his prime minister, Zine el-Abidine Ben Ali, taking power. Ben Ali entered office with promises of democracy and released most political prisoners, including 600 MTI members, and later freed all who had been convicted of "crimes against public rights." Ben Ali pardoned Ghannouchi and allowed other members to return from exile.

Ben Ali relaxed other restrictions on political life. He recognized more political parties and extended the freedom of the press. But Ben Ali refused to legalize the MTI, even after it changed its named to Al-Nahda (Renaissance) to comply with Ben Ali's public view that no party should claim to represent Islam since the religion belonged to all Tunisians as Muslims. Ben Ali did allow Al-Nahda members to run as independent candidates for the Chamber of Deputies, the national legislature, in April 1989. These candidates did not win any seats, but did win 14.5 percent of the national vote and as much as 30 percent in the cities of Tunis, Gabes, and Sousse.[7] Al-Nahda's turnout numbers, which might have been officially suppressed, are more impressive when compared with those of the Movement of Democratic Socialists (MDS), a secular coalition that was also allowed to front candidates in the 1989 elections. The MDS won hardly any votes at all, leaving little doubt that the only credible opposition to Ben Ali was Islamic.

The success of Al-Nahda's membership shocked Ben Ali and drove him to place further restrictions on political Islam. In a speech commemorating the second anniversary of his rule, in November 1989, Ben Ali said that the government would not allow any parties to "combine religion and politics." Al-Nahda boycotted the 1990 local elections in response. Nevertheless, many Al-Nahda members ran and thirty-four were elected—the first time that Ben Ali's party did not have absolute control of local councils. Government-Islamist relations worsened over the following years, with student protests, strikes, a new resurrected ban on headscarves in universities, and the closing of *Al-Fajr*, the Al-Nahda newspaper.[8] Hundreds of Al-Nahda members were arrested, with some accused of plots to overthrow the government. Military leaders were imprisoned based on allegations that Islamist forces were infiltrating the government by way of the military. It is estimated that the government hauled in more than 8,000 detainees between 1990 and 1992.[9] Ghannouchi went into exile in London.[10] Throughout its struggle against the Ben Ali regime, Al-Nahda leaders emphasized the ideals of democracy. They tried to fit Al-Nahda within the framework of democracy by participating in party politics and parliamentary elections. Al-Nahda leader Abdelfattah Mourou said in an interview at the time, "We accepted the rules of the game. … We want to act within the framework of democracy."[11]

Tunisian politics began to stabilize by 1992. Economic growth had climbed to above 8 percent and most Al-Nahda members had been arrested, exiled, or scared into hiding. A few members remained, but the organization for "all practical purposes … became an offshore operation sustained by supporters in Europe and North America."[12]

The 2011 revolution

The fact that all of Al-Nahda's senior leaders were abroad meant that they had little role in the revolution that toppled Ben Ali in 2011. The revolution was not driven by Islam; indeed, it was largely secularized youth taking to the streets in Tunis that drove Ben Ali from power. A turning point in the revolution was the general strike called for by the Marxist national labor union, the UGTT—only its second since the Gafsa protests in 1978. The rallying cry of the revolution was a return to dignity, a theme that captured the country's economic distress and political repression. The lack of a rallying point characterized the Arab world until December 2010. Nine Arab presidents ruled at the time, most of them clearly intending to stay for life, others grooming heirs to take power after their death. The most promising chances for political reform came through institutional changes: budding opposition to the candidacies of Gamal Mubarak in Egypt and Ahmed Saleh in Yemen, the sons of the aging presidents, or nudges toward reform in Libya led by Saif al-Islam Qaddafi. All of a sudden, the self-immolation of Mohamed Bouazizi in rural Tunisia sparked popular protests in that country that spread across the region.

The precise reason why that act was so powerful is unclear. Indeed, nearly 200 Tunisians have self-immolated since the revolution began, scarcely making headlines. Scholars have theorized that the psychological cost of concealing true political opinions in the face of harsh penalty builds in persons over time, amplifying the effect of slight surges of opposition. Others have said that Facebook and Twitter lowered the cost of dissent, giving the sense of an overwhelming opposition before demonstrations began, thus emboldening the protestors.[13] Whatever the reason, the rallying point was distinctly non-institutional, and more powerful because of it. Even though Al-Nahda did not drive the revolution, it capitalized on the non-institutional discourse to argue that a return to Islam would fulfill the assault on dignity driven by secular politics of Bourguiba and Ben Ali.

Al-Nahda and the National Constituent Assembly in the constitution-making process

Election of the National Constituent Assembly and Al-Nahda's rise to power

The departure of Ben Ali created a constitutional crisis in Tunisia. There was a question which of two constitutional provisions, neither of which had been employed since 1987, would be used to account for the recent events. The first provision, Article 56, held that the president could be deposed of his power temporarily, in which case the presidency *ad interim* would pass to the prime minister. The second provision, Article 57, was reserved for the permanent removal of the president of the republic, in which case the presidency *ad interim* would pass to the speaker of the Chamber of Deputies, who would organize elections for a new president. His term would be limited to 60 days.

Ben Ali's prime minister, Mohamed Ghannouchi, invoked Article 56 upon Ben Ali's departure on January 14, making Ghannouchi the interim president of the republic. On January 15, the Constitutional Council ruled that Ben Ali's departure fit the requirements of Article 57, and Fouad Mebazaa, speaker of the Chamber of Deputies, assumed the presidency of the republic. Ghannouchi remained as prime minister. On January 17, Ghannouchi announced his new cabinet, comprised of experienced technocrats and some key opposition figures. He also inaugurated the High Commission for Political Reform, which would coordinate the process of constitutional reform within the context of the existing 1959 constitution. The High Commission for Political Reform was led by Yadh Ben Achour, a respected scholar of law and Islam, and comprised of 18 other prominent legal scholars.

As the government and the commissions worked, protestors became impatient with the slow pace of reform. Thousands of Tunisians converged on Tunis, culminating in a sit-in in the Kasbah, a large square next to the prime minister's office. After three days of violent clashes and the death of several protestors, Ghannouchi resigned as prime minister on February 27. President Mebaaza named Beji Caid Essebsi, a former president of the Chamber of Deputies, as interim prime minister. All of Ghannouchi's ministers left with him, but the High Commission for Political Reform remained. Civil-society and professional organizations, and political parties, upset at the slow pace of reform, created the Committee to Safeguard the Revolution to consolidate protestor demands and serve as the street's chief negotiator with the cabinet. Many of the demands—especially the suspension of the 1959 constitution—fell under the purview of the High Commission for Political Reform. On March 15, in a concession to the Committee to Safeguard the Revolution, the Committee and the Commission were merged, and under Ben Achour's leadership were charged with determining the future of the Tunisian constitution. The merged committee was thus called the High Commission for the Realization of the Goals of the Revolution, Political Reform, and Democratic Transition, referred to as the Ben Achour commission. The commission included some 150 members: from political parties (three each, at least one of whom had to be a woman), civil-society groups (two each), the regions (one each), families of the martyrs from the revolution (one each), and several prominent Tunisians, mostly intellectuals and business leaders. The full commission first met on March 17. On March 23, on Ben Anchour's recommendation, Mebaaza suspended the 1959 constitution by decree on the grounds that it did not "guarantee democratic, pluralistic, transparent, and impartial elections." Elections would be held for a constituent assembly to draft a new constitution, and the Ben Achour commission would write the electoral law.

Because seats were distributed in equal numbers to each political party, the three Al-Nahda members were dramatically outnumbered as the only representatives with an Islamic tendency. Al-Nahda had few natural allies in the commission. The Congress for the Republic stood by Al-Nahda in several public declarations, but Al-Nahda members otherwise described deliberations that were frequently adversarial. Farida Labidi, a member of the commission and future member of the National Constituent Assembly from Al-Nahda, said: "High Commission was not representative. All the others were of the same color."[14]

The choice of electoral system for the constituent assembly exemplified the commission's ideological bent. The law called for a system of closed-list proportional representation across 33 districts, with an average district size of 6.6 seats. Votes were assigned to seats according to an electoral formula called the Hare quota with largest remainders. The relatively high district magnitude and particularly the electoral formula were the least favorable choices for Al-Nahda in terms of electoral-system design. Al-Nahda won 37 percent of the votes and 41 percent of the seats in the Assembly. If the Ben Achour commission had chosen the other most common formula of assigning votes to seats—called the d'Hondt divisor—Al-Nahda would have won 69 percent of seats in the Assembly.[15] Furthermore, the law did not include a threshold of votes that a party would have to achieve nationwide, which would have limited the number of small secular parties that won seats. The point was not lost on Al-Nahda, but Al-Nahda did not oppose the electoral system, nor did it propose changes to the system when the National Constituent Assembly considered a permanent electoral law in 2014. "The electoral law was not just," said Labidi, "but it was necessary for the period."[16] Al-Nahda resigned its seat in the Ben Achour commission on June 28, 2011, in protest over the postponement of the elections from June to October and the passage of a controversial law on political finance, both of which Al-Nahda considered to be out of the commission's scope. Elections were held on October 23, 2011.

The Assembly elections were a victory for democracy in the Arab world, despite the challenges parties faced in drafting the law. The elections were credible with more than 90 percent turnout. The elections were conducted according to a system of closed-list proportional representation across 31 constituencies: 27 in Tunisia and four abroad. Al-Nahda won every constituency, with 40 percent of the popular vote and 87 seats out of 217 in the Assembly.

In most constituencies, Al-Nahda won the top two seats based on closed-list proportional representation. The second-place party, Congress for the Republic (CPR), received half as many votes and 20 seats. Al-Nahda emerged from the Assembly elections atop a political system that a year previously had imprisoned or exiled all of its senior leadership. It had emerged from a multiparty, democratic election that it had been advocating for decades. Al-Nahda was able to put into practice the vision for an Islamic democracy.

There are several partial explanations for Al-Nahda's success in the 2011 elections. The first, pragmatic argument is that Al-Nahda had the best field operation of any political party. Al-Nahda was the only party that had headquarters in each of Tunisia's 27 electorates, which understates the sheer number of party offices—numbering the thousands in practically every town across Tunisia. Al-Nahda had the best marketing strategy and most robust field operation of any party in the country. In the words of Abdelhamid Jelassi, a member of the Executive Bureau of Al-Nahda: "Given that we are an old party, we have been able to revive our structures immediately after the revolution in January. Militants who were in prison for a long time started working for the party again, together with those who had operated underground."[17] Al-Nahda did not provide social services in Tunisia in the way that the Muslim Brotherhood did in Egypt, but its political membership did run deep in cities and towns around Tunisia. Ghannouchi was treated as a kind of folk hero during the elections, travelling widely around the country and attracting thousands of Tunisians willing to wait hours to see their country's most prominent political thinker. Al-Nahda quickly reconstituted itself as prominent figures returned from abroad and built up the party's organization in the regions.[18]

Haugbølle and Cavatorta have argued that Tunisian society had prepared the ground for an Al-Nahda victory given the middle class's gradual recommitment to Islam in the final years of the Ben Ali regime, partly in response to the parasitic nature of the Tunisian kleptocracy. The authors describe a Qur'anic association called Riadh Ennasr, founded by six young men in 2007 in a middle-class suburb of Tunis. The men, disappointed in the religious education of the local imam who was a mouthpiece of the regime, found their own Islamic scholars who taught them to read the Qur'an "properly." Within three years, 1,800 persons had signed up for reading classes, including 1,200 women.[19] They continue:

> It would be misleading to draw a solitary bright line of causality between the Qur'anic associations […], on the one hand, and Ennahda's electoral triumph, on the other. But there is a clear resonance between the respective discourses and practices of the social activists and Ennahda, and membership in the two circles overlaps […] It is largely these younger middle-class activists, together with the older generation of militants returning from exile and coming out of prison, who have swollen the ranks of Ennahda and contributed to its success. Their rallying to

Ennahda is not necessarily based on the party's policy statements or past record or on Ghannouchi's leadership, but on the assumption that it is the political actor whose beliefs are closest to their own.[20]

The second category of explanations for Al-Nahda's success is linked to voter preferences and the lack of organization of the secular parties. Al-Nahda faced no opposition in the Islamic spectrum. Al-Nahda was the only viable Islamic party and attracted votes from a range of religiously inclined voters. But Al-Nahda also had a nonreligious appeal as the most prominent opposition group to the Ben Ali regime in an election that was largely about disruption of the past. The non-Islamic dimension was considerably more fractured, with parties representing all views from Marxism and socialism to free-market capitalism.

Al-Nahda officials contribute a third explanation: the party's commitment to consensus. Al-Nahda had signaled from early in the elections its intention to form a governing coalition with one or more secular parties. Human-rights activist Moncef Marzouki, president of the Congress for the Republic, had said that his party would be willing to be that party. Days after the elections, Mustafa Ben Jaafar, president of the socialist Democratic Forum for Labor and Liberties, or Ettakatol, shocked its base and the country for also stating its intent to partner with Al-Nahda. (Ettakatol has plummeted in polls since Ben Jaafar announced the alliance.) The presidents of the three parties met and decided to distribute the top seats among them. Al-Nahda secretary general Hamadi Jebali was named prime minister, Marzouki would be president of the republic, and Ben Jaafar would be president of the Assembly. The powers of each were spelled out in a so-called mini constitution passed by the Assembly in November 2011. The tripartite alliance, known as the Troika, also divided up the ministries that would serve in Jebali's cabinet. Al-Nahda has always wanted to rule in coalition, and in particular with two secular parties, to model the form of multiparty democracy that it envisions for Tunisia. The emphasis on coalition building and consensus is evident in the party's strategy toward policymaking and the drafting of the new constitution.

Al-Nahda's leadership challenges

Al-Nahda's leadership of the interim government strained the constitution-making process; cabinet politics were linked with constitutional politics. One reason for this was that the Assembly was simultaneously a parliament and a constitution-making body, meaning that Assembly members were responsible for passing laws and overseeing the government while also drafting the constitution. Membership in the constitutional committees were assigned according to the distribution of seats in the party as a whole, placing Al-Nahda in the driver's seat.

In addition to intensifying partisanship, the Assembly's legislative function delayed the constitution-making process by dividing members' attention.

The constitutional committees generally met three days a week and the legislative committees for two, but this schedule was often disrupted by pressing concerns. A deadly snowstorm in February 2012, the sacking of the governor of the central bank in July 2012, and economic distress throughout the Assembly's tenure were three legislative issues that demanded members' attention and time from constitution-making, a fact that has been a frequent complaint among members.

Policy challenges facing the Al-Nahda-led government exacerbated partisanship that leaked into the constitution-making process. Its lackluster leadership of economic policy—as evidenced by anemic production and job growth, combined with little visible progress on policy reform—has hurt Al-Nahda's chances of re-election. Increasing security challenges, exacerbated by conflicts and weapons trading in Algeria, Libya, and Mali have increased the specter of violence. Indeed, the challenges of security policy are intimately linked with two of the most divisive issues in Tunisian politics: the rise of Salafism and the response to the assassinations of two prominent secular opposition figures, Chokri Belaid and Mohamed Brahmi. The partisanship inspired by Al-Nahda's approach to Salafism and the assassinations has threatened the constitution-making process.

Al-Nahda is torn between competing interests directly linked to its security policy: secularists who accuse Al-Nahda of accommodating violent extremism when it takes a softer line on security threats, and some Salafi groups that challenge Al-Nahda's leadership and religious credentials when it takes a harder line.[21] Al-Nahda wants both to remain moderate to attract non-religious voters compelled by Al-Nahda's other policy positions while still maintaining its religiously conservative base.[22] A demonstration on March 25, 2012, highlighted the volatility of Al-Nahda's political balance and its relationship the constitution. The demonstration was called in response to Al-Nahda's decision to not support a mention of Islamic *sharia* in the constitution. Salafis had climbed the clock tower in the center of Tunis and raised their black flag. Other Salafis attacked a group of secularist artists nearby. Still others set fire to police stations, courts, and headquarters of opposition parties and the national labor union in Tunis and around the country. Even though much of the Salafis' anger was directed at Al-Nahda, secular parties still accused Al-Nahda of accommodating the protests by waiting several days to call in elite anti-riot police to end the violence.[23] On August 27, 2013, Prime Minister Ali Laarayedh of Al-Nahda declared Ansar al-Sharia, a leading extremist group, a terrorist organization.

Al-Nahda's relationship with the Salafis is ambiguous because its leaders send mixed messages about its policy positions on constitutional issues in a constant balance of appealing to a conservative and moderate electorate. Al-Nahda's rhetorical arbitrage ultimately has favored secularists: Al-Nahda Assembly members have at various times proposed religiously conservative constitutional language, such as unequal inheritance rules for men and women, the criminalization of attacks on religion (a "repugnancy clause"), and a mention of Islamic *sharia* as a source of legislation. Al-Nahda has refuted all of these positions and the final draft constitution includes none of them. Al-Nahda's political arbitrage make sense. Al-Nahda is negotiating on two fronts—with secularists and Salafis—but only the former is represented in the Assembly where the constitutional bargain is ultimately struck.

The disparate nature of Al-Nahda's membership only contributes to its ambiguous positions on questions of constitutional design.[24] Al-Nahda as an opposition movement had a broad and uncoordinated membership. Many longtime leaders in the party were split between exile across Europe and imprisonment in Tunisia. Midlevel members might have evaded imprisonment and worked in Tunisia's professional classes. The return of party leaders and the unification with each other and militants from within Tunisia presented an internal governance challenge with a disparate set of visions for what the party should represent. Yet another current are young members of the party, many conservative, who see Al-Nahda as a tool to reshape Tunisia into their image through the strict exclusion of Ben Ali-era secularist politicians and revitalize Islam. The Salafis are not the only conservative group that Al-Nahda feels compelled to keep under its sphere of influence.[25]

Constitution-making in the National Constituent Assembly

The demonstrations around the country and the challenges of domestic politics occurred in the background of extensive debates in the Assembly around constitutional design. The constitution-making process was coordinated through a series of committees, each with 22 members distributed by political party roughly according to the membership as a whole and organized around a theme. Each committee has a chair and a rapporteur; Al-Nahda holds three chairs, while CPR, Ettakatol, and Modern Democratic Pole, a secular opposition group, each hold one. Each of the chairs also sits on the constitutional coordinating committee, charged with stitching together a coherent draft from the chapters passed to them by the six committees.

Assembly president Ben Jaafar chairs the coordinating committee but plays a largely formal role. The general rapporteur, a lawyer named Habib Kheder, who will take the lead on integrating the committees' drafts, does the day-to-day coordination. Kheder was an Al-Nahda member. While the leadership of the constituent assembly was divided, Al-Nahda was squarely in charge of the constitution-making process. Al-Nahda members lead half of the constitutional committees and dominate the membership of each, and Kheder—a powerful figure with the final say on the shape of constitutional drafts submitted to plenary votes—came from Ghannouchi's inner circle.

The constitutional committees began their work in January 2012, after the state budget and interim constitution were passed in late 2011. The chair of each committee exercised much control over the committees' structure and timeline in the subsequent months. Some committees, such as the first (preamble), began writing almost immediately. Others—including the second

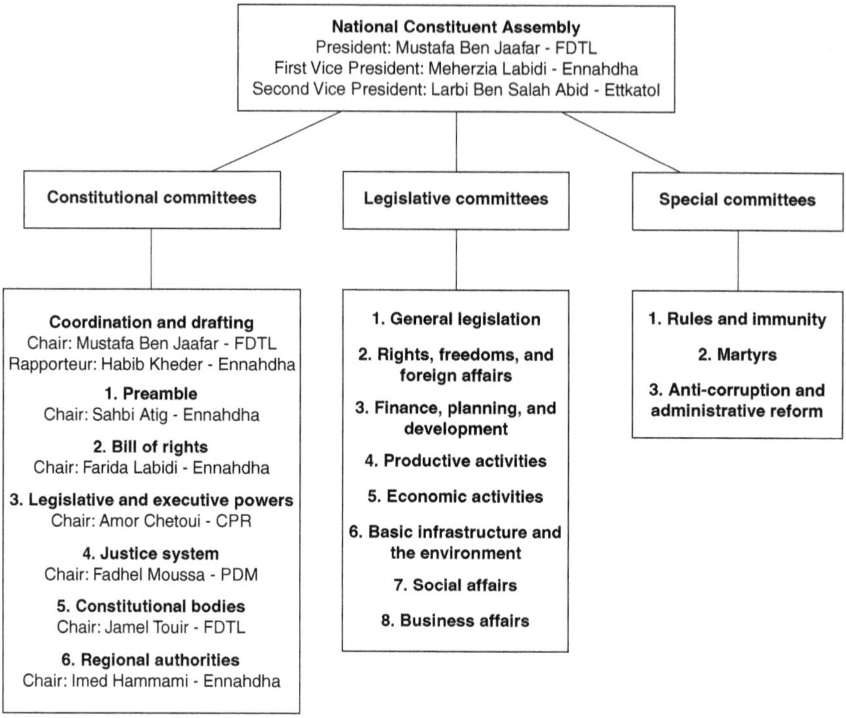

Figure 1

(rights and freedoms) and third (legislative and executive powers)—held long periods of public comment before beginning internal deliberations. The committee chairs invited civil-society groups, international advisors, and legal scholars to their meetings. The committees have a small team of lawyers to support their work, but they perform largely administrative functions and offer little advice on constitutional design.

The coordinating committee submitted its final draft of the constitution to the Assembly on June 1, 2013. Several critical issues—including executive powers, appointment to the Constitutional Court, and amendment procedures—were left undecided. Several months later, the Assembly appointed a 22-member consensus committee to agree on the remaining issues. The membership of the constitutional committee was roughly equivalent to the share of seats in the Assembly, and its decisions were critical to the swift passage of the constitution in the final stages. The Assembly began voting on the constitution in plenary on January 3, 2014. The plenary met nearly daily for the remainder of the month to vote on the constitution and on other legislative issues; the consensus committee met concurrently. The final constitution was adopted on January 26, 2014, the first time the whole text was put to the floor. According to the interim constitution, the Assembly would have two chances to pass the constitution by an absolute two-thirds majority. The Assembly far surpassed that threshold with 200 for, 12 against, and four abstentions: over 92 percent in favor. Farida Labidi, an Al-Nahda member and chair of the committee on rights and freedoms, said: "We voted for the constitution out of admiration, not obligation."[26]

Al-Nahda in the National Constituent Assembly

The Al-Nahda parliamentarians were a diverse group, representing a range of political attitudes, regional backgrounds, and levels of education. Selected for candidacy by local Al-Nahda offices in every constituency in the country, they have deep community roots and strong Islamic credentials. Many Al-Nahda parliamentarians have lived abroad but, unlike many of their secular colleagues, do not idolize the French influence on Tunisian society. They are well-educated, but some do not speak French fluently, instead opting to learn English as their second language. All speak and write fluently in Arabic, which gives them a distinct advantage when it comes to constitutional drafting. Most are longtime members of the Al-Nahda party.

Al-Nahda parliamentarians won a plurality of seats in the foreign constituencies of France, Italy, Germany, and the Americas and Europe (representing Tunisians living abroad). Eight of 16 MPs from foreign constituencies are from Al-Nahda. This means that, while many Tunisians are known for having one foot in France and one in Tunisia, Al-Nahda parliamentarians had the plurality of foreign members in the constituent assembly.

Forty-two of Al-Nahda's 87 members—nearly 50 percent—were women. This was due to the design of the Tunisian electoral system. The closed-list PR system included a vertical zipper, which required that lists alternate between men and women. If the first position on the list is held by a man, then the second must be held by a woman, and so on. Parties were free, however, to determine whom they placed at the head of their lists. Nearly all lists—regardless of party—were led by men, meaning that in order for a woman to get elected, a party had to win two seats on the list; Al-Nahda was the only party that consistently won at least two seats per constituency. The constituent assembly includes 49 women (about 23 percent), only seven of which represent secular parties.

Al-Nahda's women occupy senior leadership positions in the Assembly, including as chair of the constitutional committee on rights and freedoms, as the vice-president of the assembly. Still, women are poorly represented in party leadership: virtually all policymaking positions on Al-Nahda's executive bureau were men. Women's lack of representation party leadership is partially explained by the fact that nearly half of Al-Nahda MPs joined the party only after the revolution; the men, by contrast, all joined before the revolution. Youssef Ben Ismail found that women MPs from Al-Nahda were more highly educated than their male colleagues; there are three times as many female lawyers as male lawyers in the parliamentary group, despite the fact that the women were only a quarter of the group overall. Ben Ismail argues that women had to prove their "competence" as new members of the party, while men were selected according to "old markers of legitimacy, namely time spent in jail and seniority in the movement."[27] Al-Nahda's women rose quickly through the leadership of the party and the Assembly as a result.

The Al-Nahda parliamentarians were the best-organized and most coordinated bloc in the Assembly. Al-Nahda members often caucused before committee meetings, sometimes meeting for strategy sessions after morning prayers before going to the Assembly. Attendance of opposition members in constitutional committee meetings was not as regular, and a caucus of opposition groups before a constitutional committee meeting was rare. According to data from the watchdog group Al Bawsala, Al-Nahda MPs showed up to more plenary votes than all other parliamentary blocs: the average rate of participation among Al-Nahda MPs was 86 percent, compared with 71 percent for the Congress for the Republic and 60 percent for the Democratic Alliance. Of the 49 MPs who participated in more than 90 percent of the votes, 45 of them are from Al-Nahda.

Al-Nahda party structure since the revolution

Al-Nahda parliamentarians took their cues from the party headquarters. The party's governance structure is the same that Al-Nahda has used since its founding, with four centers of decision-making: the general assembly, the president, the executive bureau, and the Shura Council. The general assembly consists of more than 1,000 representatives elected through national constituencies and meets annually to set party priorities and elect new leadership. The 150-member Shura Council is elected from among the general assembly, and it makes more targeted decisions that are not left to the general assembly. The president heads the executive office, which makes decisions in line with general Al-Nahda policy. The executive office meets regularly and is at the forefront of Al-Nahda policymaking. The members of the executive bureau are longtime party leaders close to Ghannouchi, and to each other. The head of the political bureau, for example, is the brother of Ali Laarayedh, the former prime minister.

Some of Al-Nahda's senior and moderate leaders were also members of the Assembly, but most Al-Nahda parliamentarians did not have seats elsewhere in the leadership of the party. Nevertheless, Al-Nahda was distinct among parliamentary groups in the Assembly for the high degree of party loyalty that it enjoys among its members. All 87 members that were elected from Al-Nahda lists in October 2011 remained members of the parliamentary group, an anomaly in the assembly otherwise characterized by shifting alliances and new groups. The Ettakatol parliamentary group, by contrast, dwindled from 20 members at its peak to fewer than ten. Al-Nahda parliamentarians also largely adhered to decisions made by senior party officials. Al-Nahda parliamentarians often spoke of decisions that need to be made by "Montplaisir," the Tunis neighborhood where Al-Nahda headquarters were located. The centralized decision-making structure within Al-Nahda reflected the fact that Al-Nahda parliamentarians were recruited from outside the inner circle of Al-Nahda leadership, a deliberate campaign strategy to select local leaders who could attract votes since most senior leadership had been living abroad. The commitment to decentralization is also seen in the representation of area councils in the executive board. Yet Ghannouchi and other senior leaders still control policymaking through the deputy presidents.

Another feature of the party's leadership structure is the union of the party and the movement, seen also in the organigram (Figure 2 on p. 20), notably in the deputy president in charge of culture, youth, and mosques. The political party is formally the "Party of the Al-Nahda Movement," which reflects a matter of policy that Al-Nahda's social project comes first. Al-Nahda first seeks to recommit Tunisian society to principles of Islam, and provide a platform for those Tunisians who do want to commit themselves to Islam. Personal recommitment and identity might have an influence on political opinion—a choice presented by the party. The debate over whether the party and the movement should be separated is ever-present among Al-Nahda members and leaders. The issue was last taken up at the July 2012 Al-Nahda congress, the party's eighth, representing more than 1,100 representatives elected internally. Perhaps paradoxically, the Al-Nahda's radical, largely younger members support separation; the old guard stands for union. The more radical members want to follow the model of the Justice and Construction Party in Egypt, which is separate from the Muslim Brotherhood. The separation enables the party to seek to Islamize society through law and politics, by advocating, for example, a reference to Islamic *sharia* as a source of legislation in the constitution. To the more moderate members of Al-Nahda who advocate union, achieving that reference means little if the social project is not won first.

The diffuse membership of the party and the various loci of power has made it difficult for Al-Nahda to control its messaging. As we will see, senior members of the parliamentary group have at times expressed personal opinions that have been taken to be Al-Nahda policy, only to be later overruled by the party leadership. Al-Nahda Assembly members adhere to the senior decisions once they have been made, but Al-Nahda has faced accusations of doublespeak given their inability to control messaging in the first instance.[28]

Al-Nahda's moderation and compromise

Al-Nahda's compromises and moderate stances on key issues have driven the crafting of a constitutional bargain in the National Constituent Assembly. After the election and in the early days of constitutional negotiations, battle lines were forming around the role of Islam in the constitution and in society. But Al-Nahda took the air out of that debate in spring 2012 when the Shura Council voted to not to include a reference to Islamic *sharia* in the

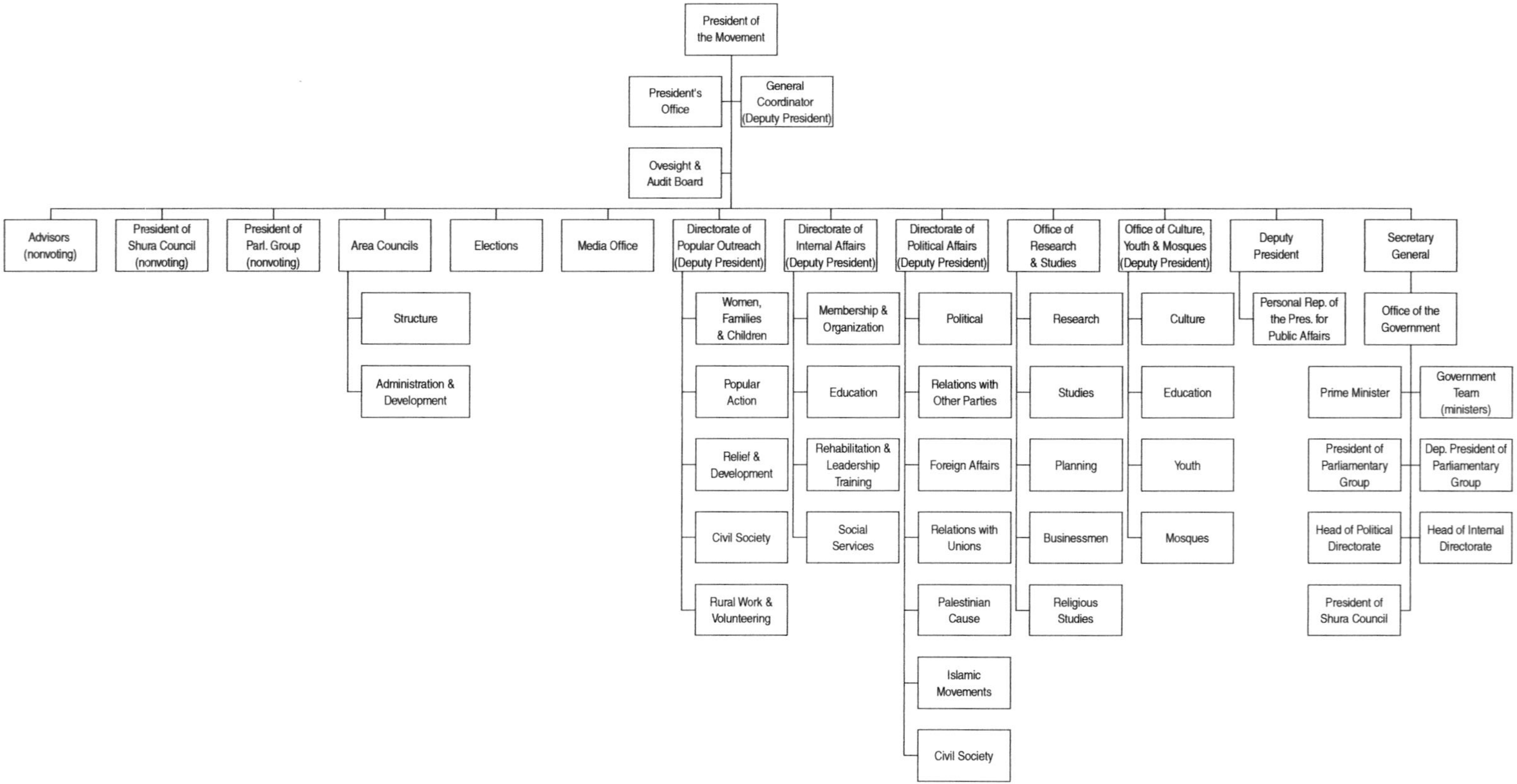
President of the Movement
President's Office
General Coordinator (Deputy President)
Ovesight & Audit Board
Advisors (nonvoting)
President of Shura Council (nonvoting)
President of Parl. Group (nonvoting)
Area Councils
Structure
Administration & Development
Elections
Media Office
Directorate of Popular Outreach (Deputy President)
Women, Families & Children
Popular Action
Relief & Development
Civil Society
Rural Work & Volunteering
Directorate of Internal Affairs (Deputy President)
Membership & Organization
Education
Rehabilitation & Leadership Training
Social Services
Directorate of Political Affairs (Deputy President)
Political
Relations with Other Parties
Foreign Affairs
Relations with Unions
Palestinian Cause
Islamic Movements
Civil Society
Office of Research & Studies
Research
Studies
Planning
Businessmen
Religious Studies
Office of Culture, Youth & Mosques (Deputy President)
Culture
Education
Youth
Mosques
Deputy President
Personal Rep. of the Pres. for Public Affairs
Secretary General
Office of the Government
Prime Minister
Government Team (ministers)
President of Parliamentary Group
Dep. President of Parliamentary Group
Head of Political Directorate
Head of Internal Directorate
President of Shura Council

Figure 2

constitution, usually a *sine qua non* of Islamist parties. The central debate among Assembly members shifted from questions of religion to questions of the distribution of executive powers: how to constrain executive power while avoiding religious or military domination. Al-Nahda members made iterative compromises on draft texts related to executive powers without seeing many reciprocal compromises from secular colleagues. Through evading conflict, Al-Nahda set the agenda of the constitutional debate—by dictating what was left off (Islamic *sharia*) and where it went (tending toward a more powerful president). Al-Nahda's compromises on process design, notably its resignation from the government, were a critical element of success in the final stages as well. This section focuses on those compromises and their implications for the political process.

Islamic Sharia and religion

The constitutional committees presented a draft in August 2013, reflecting months of dissent and compromise. One of the most important issues that had been settled was the extent to which Islamic *sharia* would be mentioned in the constitution. This was the subject of much public debate throughout the spring, with uncertainty as to what position Al-Nahda would take. An internal Al-Nahda draft had been circulated in February that included a reference to Islamic *sharia* as a "source among sources" of legislation. At a public protest on March 16, Al-Nahda parliamentarian Sahbi Atig shouted that Islamic *sharia* would be "the main source of legislation." The crowd chanted in response, "the only source!" Meanwhile, Ben Jaafar declared that he would resign and withdraw Ettakatol from the ruling coalition should the word *sharia* appear in the constitution.

Despite the strong rhetoric from several leaders, Al-Nahda's institutional stance on the issue was not clear until the Shura Council made a formal announcement on March 26. Of the 80 members who voted, only 12 supported some mention of Islamic *sharia*. Al-Nahda was the only parliamentary group that considered including a provision on Islamic *sharia*, and the issue has been dead in the Assembly ever since, despite frequent protests from self-proclaimed Salafi groups and some conservatives within Al-Nahda. Coincidentally, the Al-Nahda parliamentary group held a non-binding straw poll on March 24, before the Shura Council vote. The straw poll came our slightly in favor of mentioning Islamic *sharia* as a source among sources of legislation. The straw poll indicates how sharply divided Al-Nahda was on the issue, and how Al-Nahda parliamentarians adhere to the decisions of party decision-makers. A critique could be lodged against the constitution-making process that the issue of Islamic *sharia* was not debated within the Assembly despite the strong preference for a reference to Islamic law in the constitution by a significant share of the Tunisian public. Subsequent Salafi protests might have been mollified if the issue of Islamic *sharia* were ruled out by the Assembly as a whole.

The role of religion beyond Islamic *sharia* was also a point of contention between Al-Nahda and secular parties. Draft constitutions included a so-called repugnancy clause that would have outlawed speech that violated ill-defined "principles of Islam." The June 2013 removed the repugnancy clause and replaced it with an affirmation that the state "sponsors religion," as well as positive obligations on the state to protect the freedom of belief and the sanctity of religious places. Although secular groups consider this an improvement, they are still concerned about the future implementation of these principles, such as changes to Tunisia's progressive family law and dress requirements in public institutions.

One controversial issue that emerged in the final weeks of the constitutional debate was a new interdiction on *takfir*, the allegation of apostasy in Islam. Assembly members proposed the amendment to Article 6 when Al-Nahda MP Habib Ellouz called MP Mongi Rahoui, an opposition member, an "enemy of Islam." Rahoui had opposed an earlier draft of the article, which had established Islam as the state religion. The prohibition on *takfir* appears to be an exception to the "freedom of opinion, thought, and expression" (Article 30) and the "freedom of conscience and belief" (Article 6) protected elsewhere. It also inspired calls by religious conservatives to include a repugnancy clause that would ban speech that insulted or violated principles of Islam, a measure that previously had been defeated in committee. Article 1 maintains the same formulation from Tunisia's previous constitution, which refers to Islam as the religion of the state but places no obligation on the state to enforce its tenets.

But these articles even taken together do not make the constitution Islamist, or even notably drafted under the aegis of an Islamic party. Secular parties were nervous that Al-Nahda would take advantage of its leadership of the constitution-making process to insert clauses that would give Islamists a foothold in lawmaking in the future, regardless of their performance in subsequent elections. The constitution does not appear to include any such Trojan horses. The constitution does not make a reference to Islamic principles to be used in lawmaking, and it does not establish a role for Islamic institutions in the review or making of laws. By contrast, the Pakistani constitution creates an Islamic court that can nullify laws that violate its interpretation of Islam and the 2012 constitution of Egypt created a consultative role for Islamic scholars in lawmaking.[29]

Executive powers

With Islamic *sharia* off the table, the main feature of the constitutional debate in the Assembly was over the system of government. Al-Nahda favored a parliamentary system with a weak or indirectly elected president, while many secular parties sought a strong president *vis-à-vis* parliament. Ennahda preferred a parliamentary system for several reasons. First, party leaders believed that a parliamentary system is both best suited for Tunisia as an emerging democracy and consistent with the principle of *shura*—or consensus-based decision-making—that is fundamental to Islamic governance.[30] Al-Nahda party leaders also wished to govern in coalition with secular parties that could diffuse some criticism of the party in a country where sharply partisan divides are drawn along religious lines. Furthermore, in a crowded landscape of political parties, Al-Nahda felt confident in its ability to command a plurality of seats in parliament in at least the next few parliamentary elections.

Secular parties pushed for a presidential or semi-presidential system, which they saw as the best way to check Al-Nahda's power. Some CPR parliamentarians sought a semi-presidential system in order to maintain their party's presidency in the Troika. Semi-presidentialism also attracted support from Assembly members who would support a secular president to check the power of an Al-Nahda prime minister. More centrist parliamentarians—such as those from the former Progressive Democratic Party—support a US-style presidential system. They argue that Al-Nahda won only 40 percent of the seats nationwide, which means that 60 percent of Tunisians would support a secular candidate for president. They hold this view despite the fact that secular parties in Tunisia are desperately fractured and would be hard-pressed to capture the support of the entire 60 percent. Regardless of whether electoral predictions are correct, secular parties see the institution of the presidency as a check against Al-Nahda's parliamentary dominance.

The debate over the system of government led to a stalemate in the third constitutional committee, which was responsible for drafting chapters related to executive and legislative powers. In the draft released in mid-August, the committee released two versions of the relevant chapters, one calling for a parliamentary regime and the other for a semi-presidential one with a particularly strong president. The debate in the committee was deadlocked, and the issue was elevated out of the committee to be settled in a plenary session or a grand compromise among leading political parties.

In October 2012, the Troika managed to find a partial compromise on the issue of the presidency. Ettakatol, CPR, and Al-Nahda agreed that the president would be directly elected and that legislative and presidential elections would be held in June 2013. The announcement did not settle all the issues at hand, however, and it is too early to conclude what the executive structure will look like. The Troika did not assign powers to the president and prime minister. In fact, Al-Nahda had considered proposing a weak, directly elected president for several months prior to the announcement by the Troika.[31]

The constitutional coordinating committee presented its third draft to the Assembly on April 22, 2013. It was the first draft that presented a single proposal for executive powers, which can be classified as semi-presidential.[32] Al-Nahda's Shura Council compromised in late April by coming out in favor of the semi-presidential system established in the April 22 draft in an attempt to achieve multi-partisan support for the draft constitution in plenary. Opposition parties did not meet them in the middle. Several days after the Shura Council announcement, Beji Caid Essebsi, the octogenarian politician from the era of Habib Bourguiba who quickly became the vanguard of the secular opposition, announced his candidacy for president. The draft, however, placed an age limit of 75 on presidential candidates. Around the same time, he stated his preference for a strong president, calling the American presidency too weak for his taste. Essebsi was backed by Nida Tunis, the political party that he founded in June 2012, which is quickly becoming the most prominent opposition party in Al-Nahda.

The crisis of summer 2013

Executive powers were not the only unanswered question facing the political transition at the time. The timeline for elections, which was linked with the appointment of the independent elections commission, was also hotly debated. The Assembly had established a committee to select the members of the elections commission. According to one Al-Nahda MP, the committee had met on July 24, 2014, a Wednesday, to name the last member, which would finally achieve a partisan balance on the committee. The next day, Thursday, July 25, Mohamed Brahmi was assassinated.

Brahmi, an outspoken opposition member of the Assembly, drove Tunisia to its most intense political crisis since the removal of Ben Ali. Brahmi was the second secular political leader to be killed since Chokri Belaid was killed in February 2013. Both assassinations led to outrage against the Al-Nahda government from secular opposition figures, ranging from accusations of incompetence to collaboration with the Islamist armed suspected of both killings. Press reports that the US Embassy had warned the Ministry of Interior about a threat against Brahmi fueled the accusations. The Al-Nahda leadership condemned both attacks in the strongest terms. After the Belaid killing, Prime Minister Hamadi Jebali of Al-Nahda called for a technocratic government; the party leadership did not back him, and he resigned his office. Al-Nahda nominated Ali Laarayedh, a party insider, to take his place. After the Brahmi killing, secular protestors, emboldened by the nearly simultaneous *tamarrod* demonstrations that ousted former president Mohamed Morsi in Egypt, called not only for the resignation of Laarayedh but the withdrawal of Al-Nahda from government altogether. Essebsi called for Al-Nahda's immediate resignation in favor of a technocratic government. Al-Nahda agreed to resign, but demanded to complete the constitution first, by October at the latest. The response did not appease opposition MPs, who boycotted the Assembly in August. Ben Jaafar suspended meetings of the Assembly on August 6, over the objections of the Al-Nahda leadership.

A series of high-level negotiations followed the suspension of the Assembly meetings. Remarkably, many of the negotiating parties are unelected. Al-Nahda was represented by Ghannouchi, who signaled willingness to compromise by offering a quick end to the constitution-making process, fast elections, and the appointment of a technocratic government to lead the country through election day. The latter concession was offered after a meeting on August 22 with Houcine Abassi, the president of the UGTT, the most powerful trade union in Tunisia but with no elected members in the Assembly. The backing of UGTT was critical to national stability in the transitional phase: UGTT can bring hundreds of thousands of Tunisians to the street by calling for a general strike, which breathed life into the Tunisian revolution in late 2010.

Another unelected actor in the negotiations is Essebsi's party Nida Tunis. In these negotiations, Nida Tunis demanded the resignation of the Al-Nahda government in favor of technocrats, the dissolution of the National Constituent Assembly, and the appointment of a "committee of experts" to review the draft constitution. The appointment of all the members of the elections commission was also back on the table, despite the agreement already reached in the Assembly committee. Several rounds of negotiations were held between Ghannouchi and Essebsi, including one facilitated by German foreign minister Guido Westerwelle. Nevertheless, Nida Tunis secretary general Tayyib Baccouche countered Ghannouchi's offer from August 22 the day after he made it, calling for nothing less than the end of the draft constitution and dissolution of the Constituent Assembly. Nida sympathizers launched a week of protests on August 24.

Al-Nahda stuck to the "rhetoric of democracy" in the aftermath of the Brahmi assassination, calling for a return to constitutional negotiations within the elected Assembly while offering to resign once a draft was complete.[33] Nida Tunis, by contrast, sought the resignation of Al-Nahda before the constitution was complete in order to start over with its committee of experts. Ghannouchi summarized the situations in a press conference in September: Tunisia is suffering from "*une crise de confiance*" where the secularists "*nous disent, 'Vous ne voulez pas quitter le pouvoir,' et nous leur rétorquons, 'Nous craignons que vous ne preniez le pouvoir et que vous ne le quittiez plus.'*"[34] Al-Nahda was in the uncomfortable position of defending a constitution that resembled little of its ideal of parliamentarism.

The negotiations, and the resumption of meetings of the Assembly on September 10, gave some traction to negotiations between the UGTT and Al-Nahda. On September 19, Al-Nahda agreed in principle to step down in favor of new elections and the completion of the constitution. But three days later, negotiations again stalled when Al-Nahda refused to step down before the constitution was completed. The following week, UGTT called for protests in Tunis against Al-Nahda, raising important questions about whether UGTT had entered negotiations in good faith or whether they wanted to portray Al-Nahda as uncompromising.

President Marzouki called for a National Dialogue between major political actors to resolve the crisis. The National Dialogue first met in late October with the primary purpose of determining the sequencing of the resignation of Laarayedh and the name of the technocrat who would replace him. The two protagonists were Ghannouchi and Essebsi, with mediation from a "quartet" comprising the UGTT, the employers' union, the national bar association, and the Tunisian League of Human Rights. "The train of this crisis is on the tracks, and we are now on the way to finishing our transition to elections," Ghannouchi told reporters on October 25 while reaffirming his party's decision to step down from power.[35] The National Dialogue announced progress incrementally, deciding on the timeline for elections and some key aspects of the electoral law. The National Dialogue averted the crisis finally on December 14 when it announced that Mehdi Jomaa would succeed Laarayedh as prime minister once the constitution was completed. Laarayedh submitted his resignation on January 9, becoming the first Islamist prime minister in the Arab world to step down voluntarily.

Women's rights

After the conclusion of the National Dialogue, the National Constituent Assembly returned to its constitutional work, including several controversial provisions. An earlier draft constitution had granted women the same rights as men in their status, but as man's "complement" in society. Women's advocacy groups and many Tunisians across the country—both secular and religious—were offended by the notion that women derive their rights from men and do not hold equal rights inherently. The debate exemplified the disconnect between political groups in Tunisia, often draw between religious and linguistic barriers; Francophone secularists and Arabophone Al-Nahda supporters often talked past each other. Protests against the article featured signs in opposition to *complémentarité*, which was retranslated into Arabic as *takmila* in the slogan, *muwatinat, la takmilat* (citizens, not complements). In fact, the article used the word *nadheer*, which more closely connotes equality in the sense of "equal" or "counterpart."

Members of the committee responsible for the draft article said that they had agreed upon it under significant pressure to meet the deadline set by the coordinating committee. Nevertheless, secular activists feared that the article was a step from Al-Nahda to abridge Tunisia's progressive laws on women's rights. Article 20 now states that men and women are "equal in rights and duties." Advocates of women's rights remain nervous about Article 7, which defines the family as the "nucleus of society" and could limit divorce rights, and Article 21, which calls sacred the right to life and could be used to ban abortion, which has been legal since 1965.

The constitution does, however, contain perhaps the world's most progressive constitutional provision on women's representation in politics. Article 46 states that the state "seeks parity between men and women in elected assemblies." The article was agreed to in the consensus committee with backing from the Al-Nahda leadership, but the plenary debate revealed a rare discord within the Al-Nahda ranks. Monia Ibrahim, an Al-Nahda MP from Sousse, made an impassioned plea against the parity provision on the floor of the Assembly, arguing that it was against the principle of equality of all Tunisians. The article was adopted nevertheless, with Al-Nahda outpacing the rest of the Assembly in its vote in favor. Forty-six Al-Nahda MPs voted in favor and 57 against the article (80 percent), as compared with 70 in favor and 99 against (70 percent) among non-Al-Nahda Assembly members, according to data from Marsad. Habib Kheder said in explaining the article that the consensus committee agreed that, in practice, the parity article would only require parity on electoral lists, which was reflected in the electoral law that the Assembly adopted on May 1, 2014.

Conclusions

Post-revolution Tunisia represents the first time that an Islamic party has taken the lead in drafting a new democratic constitution after credible elections. Al-Nahda's performance suggests the work of a rational political actor operating under a calculus not unlike those of its secular counterparts: the party entered with a set of interests and constituencies to satisfy that it has done to the best of its ability. The Tunisian constitution does not even attempt to propose an alternative, Islamic governance model to that of the "Western democracy" that Ghannouchi identified in his early writings. The party has built on the institutions of democracy, such as elections, multipartyism, the balance of power. Al-Nahda has abandoned references to Islamic *sharia* and indeed only proposes that would be familiar to a Western audience. Al-Nahda does not advocate for the creation of Islamic courts, as in Pakistan, or of any legal reference beyond the framework of constitutional law. This is in contrast to the Islamist-driven constitution in Egypt that compelled legislators to factor in principles of Islamic law and created a role for clerics at Al-Azhar in lawmaking. Al-Nahda has achieved not so much a blend of Islam and democracy but rather a compromise between the two positions, leaving little room to call it Islamic at all.

Al-Nahda's principled stance can be called one of thoughtful self-interest, compromise, and party discipline. Al-Nahda's goals for the constitution have at all times advocated compromise. Al-Nahda at first proposed a parliamentary system, itself because it would require parliamentary negotiations among political parties. Parliamentary systems also encourage the dispersal of political parties, since even small parties can earn a seat at the negotiating table if they win just one seat in one constituency. Secular parties, which have a greater incentive to band together, prefer a presidential system. Presidential systems tend toward consolidation since parties find strength in numbers to win the biggest prize in the political game: the presidency. Secular parties, perhaps naively, believe that a secular president would defeat an Islamic one in a runoff election since Al-Nahda won only 40 percent of the votes in the last election. Electoral politics aside, Al-Nahda is aware of the divisive role that it plays in Tunisian politics and from the immediate aftermath of its win has sought to rule in coalition with secular partners.

Not all Al-Nahda parliamentarians supported a parliamentary system or the omission of Islamic *sharia,* but the party's unified stance in the

Assembly is a testament to members' loyalty and discipline. Indeed, Sahbi Atig, the president of the Al-Nahda parliamentary group, opposed both decisions. Al-Nahda is the best-organized and most strategic party in the assembly, putting forward well-coordinated policy positions respecting a hierarchy of decision-making at party headquarters. Al-Nahda members are keen political actors.

Al-Nahda policymakers applied sharply their skills at political analysis in order to maintain an at-times impossible balance between competing stakeholders: secular Tunisians, its own moderate base, and hardline members and spinoffs. Al-Nahda knows that its policies must cater to all Tunisians, including the secular opposition, and its leadership has stayed true to Ghannouchi's moderate Islam on which the party was founded. Leaders also have one eye turned westward, knowing that a friendly relationship with Europe and the Americas are essential to its good standing in the international community. Al-Nahda leaders are also aware, however, of the more Islamist track in its own party and elsewhere in Tunisia: those advocating for a role for Islamic *sharia* in lawmaking and in the constitution, and a further rejection of secularism. Ghannouchi throughout his career has balanced these two positions, juggling these multiple constituencies.

Why did Al-Nahda compromise and take a moderate position on key questions of constitutional design? Perhaps Al-Nahda were poor negotiators. Al-Nahda did not label the omission of Islamic *sharia* as a concession when the decision was made, effectively giving them no capital to bring into future debates about executive powers. Al-Nahda could have threatened to push for a reference to Islamic *sharia* or a repugnancy clause if the president was kept strong. Furthermore, Al-Nahda estimated that they would have been able to achieve enough support for a referendum on the constitution should it fail two votes in the assembly. The referendum only required a simple majority of Tunisians in favor, which is a number well within reach of Al-Nahda's public-outreach capacity.

Another explanation, favored among secularist critics of Al-Nahda, is that making early compromises up front and throughout the constitution-making process is a ploy to endear Al-Nahda to moderate secularists, devise a constitution favorable to their electoral picture (such as a strong parliament and prime minister), and enact conservative reforms after a new round of elections. According to this argument, Al-Nahda is hiding its true intentions while stacking the cards in their favor. A strong presidency, therefore, is a safeguard against Al-Nahda dominance in the short-term electoral picture.

It is likely that Al-Nahda's policies will become more conservative when the constitution is finished. This is due to increasing pressure from its base. But more importantly, it is due to the fact that Al-Nahda made exceptional compromises during the constitution-making phase. Constitutions take a longer-term view of governance questions and cannot be changed through periodic elections. Al-Nahda wanted a consensus-driven constitution-making process. If Al-Nahda's policies become more conservative, it is because the incentive to compromise is not as strong when short-term policies can be changed through periodic elections.

Ghannouchi's writings give some insight into his vision for Tunisia and the best way to get there. His work in the 1980s justified adjusting tenets of Islamic governance to particular contexts. Al-Nahda might wish that Tunisia were ready for governance by Islamic law, and the advocacy arm of the movement might push for Islamic governance in its teachings and even in statements by senior officials. There is a tension within Al-Nahda between realism (seen in the policies of moderation and compromise of the party) and idealism (represented by the preachers of the movement and their aspirations for Islamic governance in Tunisia). Al-Nahda has competing incentives to shape Tunisian society in the mold of an Islamic democracy and to strike a constitutional balance with secular parties to move toward the consolidation of democracy after autocracy. The expressions of these incentives, in speeches and policy positions, leads to accusations of doublespeak. A clearer picture of Al-Nahda's priorities in the constitution-making process can be gleaned by its actions—compromise and moderation—as opposed to posturing by Al-Nahda officials or speculation about future policy shifts. Al-Nahda's social project to support the empowerment of Tunisians through Islam will continue regardless of its politics.

Al-Nahda's motivations for accepting a stronger president and for omitting Islamic *sharia* from the constitution, whether wise or not, could be tactical or ideological. But either case points to a key ingredient to the success of the Tunisian constitution-making process so far: Al-Nahda's willingness to work in compromise and coalition. Al-Nahda has given concessions to ideological opponents and even shared power in the assembly and the government with secular partners. Contrast this with the Egyptian constitution-making process, exclusively led by an alliance of the Muslim Brotherhood and the Salafi Noor party. Islamists were so unwilling to soften their position on Islamic *sharia* as a source of legislation in the constitution, among other issues, that secular members of the constituent assembly boycotted the meetings. In their absence, the Islamists built in an oversight mechanism from Islamic clerics at Al-Azhar. Compromise by the Muslim Brotherhood on the constitution might not have saved Mohamed Morsi from his overthrow, but it would have softened the tone of the Brotherhood in an appeal to Egyptians beyond their base. Al-Nahda's stewardship of the constitution-making process, by contrast, has given a broader swath of Tunisians an opportunity to feel represented in the process via a range of political parties.

Ultimately, Al-Nahda leaders see their role as chief drafters of the Tunisian constitution as instituting a system that can guarantee the peaceful transfer of power between elected governments, elegantly called *alternance* in French. Al-Nahda does not read its success in the 2011 elections as license to impose an Islamic state on Tunisia. Al-Nahda is advocating for a political arrangement that it estimates will be in the party's best interests in the future—a parliamentary system that will keep secular parties divided. But Al-Nahda is not creating institutions that will change the democratic nature of the state or make it more Islamic. If Al-Nahda won no seats in the next elections and all seats went to secular parties, the constitution would not require that the new government adhere to remnants of an Islamic administration. The evolution of Islamic governance in Tunisia will come, if at all, through the policies adopted by an Al-Nahda government should Tunisian voters choose one in future elections.

References

Alexander, C., "Back from the Democratic Brink: Authoritarianism and Civil Society in Tunisia," *Middle East Report*, no. 205, Fall 1997.

Amara, T., "Tunisia's Ruling Islamist Party, Opposition Start Crisis Talks," *Reuters*, 25 October 2013.

Ben-Ismail, Y., *The Political Rise of Al-Nahda's Women in Tunisia*, M.A. thesis, Harvard University, 2014.

Carey, J., *Electoral Formula and the Tunisian Constituent Assembly*, 17 January 2013.

Choudhry, S., and Stacey, R., *Semi-Presidentialism as a Form of Government: Lessons for Tunisia*, New York University and International IDEA, June 2013.

El-Khawas, M.A., "Revolutionary Islam in North Africa: Challenges and Responses," *Africa Today*, vol. 43, no. 4, Fall 1996.

Elgie, R., "Varieties of Semi-Presidentialism and Their Impact on Nascent Democracies," *Taiwan Journal of Democracy*, vol. 3, no. 2, December 2007.

Esposito, J., and Piscatori, J., "Democratization and Islam," *Middle East Journal*, vol. 45, no. 3, Summer 1991.

Feldman, N., *Fall and Rise of the Islamic State* (Princeton: Princeton University Press, 2008).

Hostrup Haugbølle, R., and Cavatorta, F., "Beyond Ghannouchi: Islamism and Social Change in Tunisia," *Middle East Report*, no. 262, Spring 2012.

International Crisis Group, *Tunisia: Violence and the Salafi Challenge*, 13 February 2013.

Lombardi, C., and Brown, N., "Islam in Egypt's New Constitution," *Foreign Policy*, 13 December 2012.

Lynch, M., *The Arab Uprising* (New York: Public Affairs, 2013).

Marks, M., "Who are Tunisia's Salafis?," *Foreign Policy*, 28 September 2012.

Merone, F., "Tunisia and the divided Arab Spring," *Open Democracy*, 9 August 2013.

Merone, F., and Cavatorta, F., "Ennahda: A Party in Transition," *Jadaliyya*, 25 March 2013.

Owen, R., *The Rise and Fall of Arab Presidents for Life* (Cambridge, MA: Harvard University Press, 2012).

Pickard, D., "Prospects for Implementing Democracy in Tunisia," *Mediterranean Politics*, forthcoming 2014.

Skach, C., *Borrowing Constitutional Designs: Constitutional Law in Weimar Germany and the French Fifth Republic* (Princeton: Princeton University Press, 2005).

Tamimi, A., *Rachid Ghannouchi: A Democrat within Islamism* (Oxford: Oxford University Press, 2001).

Tunisia-Press, "Rached Ghannouchi à l'opposition: nous craignons que vous ne quittiez plus le pouvoir," 7 September 2013.

Waltz, S., *Human Rights and Reform: The Changing Face of North African Politics* (Berkeley: University of California Press, 1995).

Notes

1 A. Tamimi, *Rachid Ghannouchi: A Democrat within Islamism* (Oxford: Oxford University Press, 2001), pp. 33–36.
2 Ibid., p. 87.
3 Ibid., pp. 89–90.
4 See N. Feldman, *Fall and Rise of the Islamic State* (Princeton: Princeton University Press, 2008).
5 Tamimi, op. cit., p. 236.
6 Ibid, p. 59.
7 J. Esposito and J. Piscatori, "Democratization and Islam," *Middle East Journal*, vol. 45, no. 3, Summer 1991, p. 431.
8 Ibid., p. 432.
9 S. Waltz, *Human Rights and Reform: The Changing Face of North African Politics* (Berkeley: University of California Press, 1995), p. 72.
10 M.A. El-Khawas, "Revolutionary Islam in North Africa: Challenges and Responses," *Africa Today*, vol. 43, no. 4, Fall 1996, pp. 392–4.
11 Interview with Abdelfattah Mourou in *Le Quotidien de Paris*, 16 November 1987, quoted in Esposito and Piscatori, op. cit., p. 432.
12 C. Alexander, "Back from the Democratic Brink: Authoritarianism and Civil Society in Tunisia," *Middle East Report*, no. 205, Fall 1997, p. 35.
13 R. Owen, *The Rise and Fall of Arab Presidents for Life* (Cambridge: Harvard University Press, 2012), pp. 172–5.
14 Farida Labidi, interview with author (tape recording), Tunis, 6 March 2014.
15 J. Carey, "Electoral Formula and the Tunisian Constituent Assembly," 17 January 2013.
16 Farida Labidi, interview with author.
17 R. Hostrup Haugbølle and F. Cavatorta, "Beyond Ghannouchi: Islamism and Social Change in Tunisia," *Middle East Report*, no. 262, Spring 2012, p. 21.
18 M. Lynch, *The Arab Uprising* (New York: Public Affairs, 2013), pp. 147–9.
19 Hostrup Haugbølle and Cavatorta, op. cit., pp. 22–3.
20 Ibid., pp. 24–5.
21 M. Marks, "Who are Tunisia's Salafis?," *Foreign Policy*, 28 September 2012.
22 F. Merone and F. Cavatorta, "Ennahda: A Party in Transition," *Jadaliyya*, 25 March 2013.
23 International Crisis Group, *Tunisia: Violence and the Salafi Challenge*, 13 February 2013, p. 2.
24 Merone and Cavatorta, op. cit.
25 International Crisis Group, op. cit., pp. 28–9.
26 Farida Labidi, interview with author.
27 See Y. Ben-Ismail, *The Political Rise of Al-Nahda's Women in Tunisia*, M.A. thesis, Harvard University, 2014.
28 Merone and Cavatorta, op. cit.
29 C. Lombardi and N. Brown, "Islam in Egypt's New Constitution," *Foreign Policy*, 13 December 2012.
30 On the performance of semi-presidential systems in transitional contexts, see: C. Skach, *Borrowing Constitutional Designs: Constitutional Law in Weimar Germany and the French Fifth Republic* (Princeton: Princeton University Press, 2005), pp. 12–29; and R. Elgie, "Varieties of Semi-Presidentialism and Their Impact on Nascent Democracies," *Taiwan Journal of Democracy*, vol. 3, no. 2, December 2007.

31 Weak, directly elected presidents are rare, but democratic models can be found in Austria, Bulgaria, Finland, Iceland, Ireland, Portugal, Slovakia, and Slovenia.

32 For an analysis of semi-presidentialism in the Tunisian constitution, see S. Choudhry and R. Stacey, *Semi-Presidentialism as a Form of Government: Lessons for Tunisia*, New York University and International IDEA, June 2013; D. Pickard, "Prospects for Implementing Democracy in Tunisia," *Mediterranean Politics*, forthcoming 2014.

33 F. Merone, "Tunisia and the divided Arab Spring," *Open Democracy*, 9 August 2013.

34 Tunisia-Press, "Rached Ghannouchi à l'opposition: nous craignons que vous ne quittiez plus le pouvoir," 7 September 2013.

35 "Tunisia's ruling Islamist party, opposition start crisis talks," *Reuters*, 25 October 2013.

2 Egypt: A constitutional court in an unconstitutional setting

Nathan J. Brown

Introduction

On February 11, 2011, Egypt's Supreme Council of the Armed Forces (SCAF) suspended the constitution and assumed full authority in Egypt. From that point until August 12, 2012, the SCAF continued to assert an oversight role, essentially insisting that Egypt's governing constitutional framework was whatever the SCAF said it was. From August 15, 2012 until the proclamation of a new constitution on December 25, 2012, President Mohamed Morsi essentially claimed the same authority. And that new constitution had some articles that clearly took aim at the country's constitutional court. On July 3, 2013, the commander of the armed forces dismissed Morsi from office and suspended the constitution, ordering that it be amended before it be reinstated.

There is likely no similar revolutionary setting in which judges proved just as significant players as generals, politicians, or leaders of security forces. In Egypt after 2011 constitutional court judges in particular played a role that was especially remarkable given the extra-constitutional nature of the changes. Most dramatically, in June 2012, the SCC dissolved the first post-revolutionary parliament. In November 2012, anticipation of an unfavorable judgment from the SCC led President Morsi to take an extraordinary set of measures immunizing the process of writing a new constitution from judicial oversight—and to push ahead to get the constitution ratified the following month. In June 2013 the SCC issued a string of verdicts that effectively ended the debate over whether the December 2012 constitution was the document governing Egypt. Thus the constitution was suspended (pending amendment) on July 3, 2013—rather than cancelled. And it was the SCC's chief justice, Adly Mansour, who was installed as acting president to oversee that process. Indeed, it was not merely in an institutional sense that the SCC was an important actor. Justices from the court played a prominent role in political life and in the electoral process.

Revolutions are not friendly times for courts, constitutions, and the rule of law. Indeed, it is far from certain that Egypt's judicial framework will emerge from the revolutionary tumult unscathed. But it is still remarkable how much a judicial actor was able to play a pivotal role in such an unfriendly environment.

The emergence of Egypt's Supreme Constitutional Court

Egypt's Supreme Constitutional Court began in fairly modest circumstances. In 1969, in a series of steps remembered by Egyptians as the "massacre of the judiciary," then President Gamal Abdul Nasser dismissed a large number of sitting judges and established by decree a new "Supreme Court" at the apex of the Egyptian judicial system. The Supreme Court—staffed with presidential appointments—was assigned the task of the judicial review of the constitutionality of legislation in order to keep it in the hands of the new, politically reliable body.

The irony of establishing such a body by a simple presidential edict was not lost on Egypt's more punctilious legal minds, and when Anwar al-Sadat (who succeeded Abdul Nasser in 1970) began to reverse some of the most egregious moves of his predecessor, they managed to write a constitutional provision instituting a "Supreme Constitutional Court" in the 1971 constitution, with the details to be determined by legislation. The SCC law was finally passed in 1979 and it provided for the basis of a surprisingly autonomous court. Presidents were to select justices who had been a candidate nominated either by the court itself or by its chief justice (a post which remained a pure presidential appointment). In practice, al-Sadat—and, more notably, his successor—allowed the SCC to pick its own justices; the chief justice did not exercise his legal right to pick an alternative candidate. And the chief justice position went to the most senior sitting justice.

The combination of a favorable law with presidential deference resulted in a steadily more autonomous and bold court. By the 1990s, the SCC had attracted international attention for an assertive jurisprudence that pushed the vague liberal language and promises of the 1971 constitution to their limit. The chief justice of those years, 'Awad al-Murr, took enormous pride in developing an ambitious jurisprudence that departed from the narrow textualism characteristic of the Egyptian judiciary and based itself on an expansive reading of rights provisions, using developing international human-rights standards to anchor the SCC's rulings in as broad a reading of the liberal elements of the text as possible.[1]

In the 2000s, the SCC found that it had pushed past the limits of Egypt's presidential and authoritarian system. The president abandoned the practice of appointing the most senior justice and instead brought in a series of figures (of varying stature) who gradually tamed the court. Those new chief justices persuaded their colleagues to bring in colleagues who were more diverse but also less inclined to buck the system. The cascade of bold judgments came to a gradual end.[2] In the period after the revolution, it became common to refer to the SCC as composed only of "Mubarak-appointed judges." That was technically true but completely missed the subtlety of the way the system operated. Of course all judges were formally appointed by the president, but they had not been nominated by him. Instead, it was a key appointment (the chief justice), occasional hints that the SCC had gone too far, and workarounds of most of its major judgments that had the effect of taming the SCC's jurisprudence. When the revolution of 2011 came, the SCC showed no inclination to rally around the old regime. Instead, like many other Egyptian institutions, it saw an opportunity to realize its dream of fuller independence.

After the revolution

The SCC itself did not play a significant role as a body in the year after the revolution, although three potentially significant developments occurred that largely escaped notice.

First, the SCC, by avoiding issuing rulings based on any post-February 11, 2011, constitutional framework (the date on which the 1971 constitution was suspended), abstained from resolving ambiguity about the legitimacy of the constitutional moves taken by the SCAF. And ambiguity there was, since Egypt's interim rulers behaved in a constitutionally incoherent fashion. The SCAF first suspended the constitution, then submitted amendments to the 1971 constitution to a popular referendum, then inserted those amendments not into a fully revived 1971 constitution but instead into a March 2011 "constitutional declaration" that was based on large portions of that earlier document, and then made minor unilateral changes in that text. And there was sloppiness every step of the way. When inserting the approved amendments into the constitutional declaration, for instance, the SCAF made some minor modifications in the wording the people had just voted on, effectively overturning the popular will. When it issued subsequent constitutional declarations involving minor changes in the March 2011 text to make it compatible with a new electoral law, it left a significant gap that made the law incompatible with some past SCC rulings, effectively (and likely unintentionally, although suspicious minds suspected differently) inserting a time bomb into the transition process that exploded the following summer.

Second, in the summer of 2011, the SCAF issued a law by decree governing the SCC's formation. It was a remarkable set of provisions that, in combination, allowed the SCC to select its own chief justice (from among the three most senior members) and appoint members to its own bench. In the 1980s and 1990s, the SCC was self-perpetuating more by custom (the president deferred to the sitting justices on appointments) than by law; in the 2000s, the president had used his authority to appoint the chief justice to bring in a series of figures who reined the court in. The 2011 decree awarded the SCC a degree of autonomy unmatched by any such court in the world.

Third, and far more ominously for the court, its public position began to come under question. Its chief justice at the time, Faruq Sultan, was seen as a creature of the old regime and as close to the military.[3] As the SCAF lost some of its luster in popular eyes, the court itself was tarnished. The small committee drafting the constitutional amendments in March 2011 included three judges assigned to the SCC. The interim constitution made the chief justice head of the presidential election commission; the chief justice in turn selected another judge from the body to be the commission's chief administrator. The commission played a critical role, disqualifying several leading candidates on grounds that appeared to have some legal basis but still attracted considerable controversy. Finally, a small number of SCC justices began to speak out boldly on public issues. The most notable figure here was Tahani al-Gebali, the SCC's first and only female justice. Her outspoken words on behalf of continued military tutelage and in opposition to the rising Islamist trend was taken by many (quite inaccurately) to be an indication of the leanings of the entire SCC. Less noisily, some justices played an advisory political role when called—one, for instance, attended meetings where the country's new parliamentary election law was bargained out.

All of these features of the transitional period—the ambiguities, the newly won autonomy, the significant political role played by the SCC justices—combined not only to raise the prominence of the court but also to draw it into political struggles. Rising Islamist forces in particular began to mistrust the SCC, seeing it as a bastion of the old regime and as an obstacle to their legislative agenda. Some Salafis also viewed the SCC warily because its jurisprudence on the constitution's second article (carried over into the interim constitution, in which the "principles of the Islamic shari'a" are "the main source of legislation") seemed overly permissive to their narrow textualist outlook.

When the new parliament met for the first time in January 2012, some deputies in the Islamist camp moved to revise the law on which the SCC was based. This led to what began as a war of words between the SCC and the parliament—a conflict that soon escalated into a protracted constitutional crisis permanently changing the course of Egypt's transition.

Dissolving the parliament and the constitutional confrontation

In January 2012, the parliament elected under the provisions of the March 2011 constitutional declaration sat for the first time. It had a very crowded list of issues to deal with but the structure was untested and filled with inexperienced parliamentarians. Even diligent members or those with a role in past parliaments found that they had an impossibly long list of legislative proposals to work with. Oddly enough, one of the ideas drawing initial attention in the summer of 2012 was reforming the SCC.

It is unlikely that the parliament would have acted quickly on these proposals involving the SCC, but its members (especially in the Islamist majority) did not mind making a forceful point. The newly-elected parliament was quickly frustrated by its discovery that it had few certain tools under the interim constitutional order: it could not determine or even affect the composition of the cabinet nor could it effect any legislative change without SCAF approval. Islamist leaders did not mind launching a shot across the SCC's bow as a preemptive strike against a body they regarded as headed by an old-regime holdover. They had already seen an administrative court disband their only real achievement: a constituent assembly had been elected under the terms of the interim constitution but that election had been overturned a couple months later. The court had ruled that the body was insufficiently representative; it further claimed that the parliament had improperly elected some of its own members to the body. The ambitious sweep of this logic—and the way that non-Islamist forces greeted the decision—began to instill a feeling among Islamists that they had encountered a "deep state" allied with hostile elites, determined to thwart the will of the majority and their elected representatives.

If the attempt was to fire a warning shot, however, it missed the mark. To switch metaphors, the SCC reacted as if it was in a mortal duel in which the first party to draw its weapon would emerge. On June 14, 2012, the SCC issued a decision dissolving the parliament. Its ruling should not have come as a complete surprise, since it followed on some previous precedents. But it was still politically bold. The parliamentary election law had been negotiated by leading political forces and then promulgated by decree by the SCAF in the fall of 2011. It provided for a mixed system—two-thirds of the deputies would be elected by proportional representation and one third in individual races. The first ballot was open to party lists; the second to individual candidates. The SCC found that system constitutionally flawed, arguing that it allowed independents only access to some seats but allowed party members to compete on either ballot, therefore discriminating against the former.

The ruling's logic can seem strained; all other countries with party list systems of various kinds do not consider them an infringement on the rights of independents who lacked party affiliation. But the ruling in Egypt had a history behind it: on two occasions in the Mubarak era, the SCC had moved to strike down electoral laws on similar grounds. Those who knew the court well should not have been surprised by the decision.

But what was extremely startling in this case, even for such observers, was the rapidity of the ruling. On the two previous occasions, it had taken several years for a case to find its way to the SCC and for the SCC to decide. On this occasion, the SCC issued its ruling hours after hearing the arguments. (Suspicious Brotherhood members alleged that the SCC had even sent off its ruling to the Official Gazette before finishing hearing the case, but they could not produce any evidence of this.) Thus, as thoroughly as the ruling might have been grounded in legal precedent, its timing was inexplicable outside of the political context in which it was issued.

Islamists recovered in part by winning the presidency the same month that they had lost the parliament. And newly-elected President Morsi even tried to find a legal formula to bring the parliament back, but he found himself blocked by the SCC, which overturned the effort.

While first accepting legal defeat, Morsi simply bided his time. In August he wrested the very considerable residual authority the SCAF had retained even after the presidential inauguration away from the generals. He issued his own "constitutional declaration," not only retiring the most senior generals but also denying them their oversight role over the political process. The military was hardly subject to civilian oversight within its own (rather considerable) realm, but the president withdrew its directly political tasks and assigned them to himself.

And the focus then turned to writing a permanent constitution. Before its dissolution, the parliament had elected a second constituent assembly (to replace the one sent home by the administrative court) and that assembly began work on a new document. And that led to the next two crises centering in part on the SCC.

Crossing the Rubicon: Morsi's autogolpe

While the constituent assembly toiled away at its task, the various opponents of the Islamists began to sense that a Brotherhood juggernaut was beginning to overwhelm the Egyptian political system. The Islamists had gained the presidency and dominated the constituent assembly; they had been prevented from enjoying a strong parliamentary majority only by that body's dismissal; Morsi's August move had sidelined the military as a counterweight. Divided among themselves and without a strong organized constituency, the opposition (which increasingly came to see itself as such) had trouble developing a clear strategy or even focusing on a set of tactics to counter the Islamist rise. Non-Islamists gradually dropped out of the constituent assembly, and some of the activists of the 2011 uprising began to try to revive street mobilization. And a series of legal challenges were mounted, most notably to the second edition of the constituent assembly, with that dispute transferred to the SCC.

The outspoken Tahani al-Gebali of the SCC made no secret of her position favoring a political orientation that began to favor the term "civil" to distinguish it from the Islamist camp without adopting terms such as "secular" that had little resonance with the Egyptian public. She also favored a continuing role for the Egyptian military in what she saw as a more protracted transition process.

Watching these developments, the Islamist camp in general and the leaders of Brotherhood specifically began to sense a coordinated effort to bring them down. And indeed there was a legal path that would have dealt them a severe blow. If the SCC dissolved the constituent assembly—as some feared it would—that step alone would only have allowed President Morsi (under the terms of the interim constitution as he had amended it in August) to name a new one. But if the SCC also struck down his August amendment to the interim constitution, it would have restored the SCAF to political authority with ousted Field Marshal Tantawi (forced into retirement by President Morsi in August) at its head, allowed the SCAF to name a new constituent assembly, and given an oversight role to the SCC in writing the new constitution.

And the Brotherhood leadership was convinced that such a move was in the works. Their evidence was sketchy and seemed to be based on allegations that a group of civilian politicians had met with al-Gebali to discuss how this might be done. In fact, it seems doubtful that such a plan could have progressed far beyond the stage of idle speculation. The Brotherhood was mistaking al-Gebali for the entire SCC (my own strong impression is that she was an outlying voice)[4] and assuming that the relevant institutions (most particularly the military) could be brought on board. (As became clear in June 2013, the SCC's position was a bit more complex in its implications than either side anticipated in November).

Acting then perhaps out of a sense of panic, President Morsi issued a startling new amendment to the interim constitution in November 2012 that had the effect of immunizing the constitutional process from judicial review. That step (and some associated ones taken at the same time, such as dismissing the prosecutor general, a move that he had been legally barred from taking up to that point) had the effect of entrenching Egypt's polarized camps more deeply, profoundly alienating the judiciary, and setting off a round of street protests as severe as any since the January uprising. And the Brotherhood's actions were heavy-handed beyond the legal realm: Islamists launched a demonstration outside the Supreme Constitutional Court building, obstructing its work and provoking fear and outrage among a judiciary that saw itself as above politics but also without allies or protection.

However, in a strictly procedural sense, the Brotherhood's moves worked: the constitutional draft was completed, submitted to voters, and ratified in a December 2012 referendum.

Reconstituting Egypt

And what did the new constitution say regarding the SCC? The justices on the SCC had lobbied hard to write as much of their new autonomy into the document. They focused on both the structural (supporting the self-perpetuating nature of the court) and the symbolic (devoting a separate chapter to the SCC rather than including it within the chapter on the judiciary). The SCC was offered a seat in the assembly, but it declined to fill it, viewing that body as one that was a political in nature and therefore not suitable for the SCC to help fill. But the court did communicate its preferences to the assembly.

And it lost most of what it wanted. The November crisis augured a breakdown in trust, and the assembly moved by tailoring a constitutional clause to oust al-Gebali from the SCC. Under the existing constitution and law, the number of justices on the SCC had not been fixed. The new constitution provided for a chief justice to be joined by ten others. It allowed those positions to be filled at first by the ten most senior sitting SCC justices. Not coincidentally, al-Gebali was the eleventh most senior judge.

The 2012 constitution deferred most of the matters related to the SCC to normal legislation. Anticipating, perhaps, an Islamist parliamentary majority, this gave little comfort to the SCC justices. In the short term, they still had their 2011 SCAF-issued law, making the court self-perpetuating. But there were strong hints from the Islamist camp that suggested that it might want the parliament to revisit the legal framework governing the court's formation.

The SCC was assigned one novel task in the new document: it was to review the constitutionality of draft electoral legislation before it was promulgated. And such laws were specifically exempted from the SCC's exclusive jurisdiction over constitutional issues. The intent was clear: the SCC would review such laws before elections were held; if it upheld the law then it could not come back and strike it down later. There was to be no repeat of the experience of parliamentary dissolution by judicial decision.

If that was the intent, however, drafting was sloppy. When the upper house of the parliament (which had not been dissolved) drafted an electoral law (under the 2012 constitution, the upper house had emergency legislative authority if the lower house were not in session) and had President Morsi submit it to the SCC for review, the SCC found a number of constitutional flaws. The upper house tried to address those and then sent its amended version back to Morsi for promulgation. But in declining to send the revised draft back to the SCC, the upper house left the matter highly confused.[5] The matter was resolved by the courts themselves, which insisted that any draft law would have be reviewed over and over until the SCC found it devoid of any constitutional flaw. Egyptians found themselves watching a game of ping pong between the upper house and the SCC, one that delayed elections indefinitely. At the time that it was dispersed in the wake of the July 2013 coup, the upper house of the parliament had just approved one more draft of the parliamentary election law and the SCC was beginning to study it. Ironically, perhaps, when announcing the coup, the military laid out a transition plan that required the SCC to review that draft as quickly as possible, allowing the draft to outlive the body that produced it.

Seeking (but not quite succeeding) to return to normality

How would the SCC approach the new environment? Would it use its tremendous power to resist the newly elected Islamist leadership? Would it accept the 2012 constitution as a governing document? Would it continue its pattern of bold rulings? And how would other actors respond? Would opponents of its past rulings continue to surround the building with demonstrators, enhancing a sense among the justices that they were besieged?

In an almost unnoticed ruling at the end of 2012, the court gave a strong indication that it was backing away from confrontation. In November—just as the showdown between the Islamist president and the opposition was taking place on the streets—the SCC issued a decision upholding a ban on diplomats marrying foreign citizens that marked a dramatic departure from its past jurisprudence. To understand the significance of the decision, it helps to review the court's history, real and imagined.

Navigating the right to marry before and after the revolution[6]

The SCC has found itself caricatured in a number of contradictory ways over its relatively short lifespan. From 1969 (when it was founded as the Supreme

Court) it was seen as a political court subservient to the executive with jurisprudence that largely escaped notice even inside the country; in the 1990s under the leadership of 'Awad al-Murr, it achieved an international reputation for bold activism. In the 2000, it suddenly became seen as subservient again, and after 2011 was been routinely described by journalists as "Mubarak appointed" and by some political activists as dominated by old regime elements.

All of these portraits had some basis but also very significant degree of exaggeration. The series of caricatures is most accurate for the al-Murr years (as well as short periods and after) when the SCC really was a formidable body. Al-Murr himself was a powerful presence, and he will likely be remembered as one of the most powerful judicial figures in a country where judges are acutely aware of their own stature.

While it was at the center of political struggles in the two years after Egypt's January 25 uprising—and was an active participant and not merely a victim in those struggles—Egypt's SCC also continued in its more prosaic work of adjudicating less portentous constitutional disputes.

The first time I met 'Awad al-Murr, the legendary chief justice of the 1990s, he launched a conversation by quizzing me on what the word "penumbra" meant. I was barely able to explain, but at least I knew why he was asking: he was referring to the US Supreme Court's 1965 decision that found a right to contraception not directly in the constitutional text but "within the penumbra of specific guarantees of the Bill of Rights." And the question was not merely a theoretical one. Al-Murr was leading the SCC to plunge into penumbra in a manner that few constitutional courts in the world would have the nerve to explore. In some years the SCC overturned more laws than it affirmed, but it was the nature of those laws and the reasoning of the decisions that attracted so much attention. Al-Murr's SCC forced the dissolution of parliament, struck down authoritarian measures, and did so by speaking a language of human rights that was grounded in international norms and documents.

Oddly, however, the ruling that he spoke most proudly of was one that drew little attention—what he liked to call the "right to marry" case—and it drew directly from his interest in penumbra. Egyptian judges were barred from marrying foreign citizens. One ignored the rule and, judicially oriented as he was, brought the case to court. When the SCC reviewed the law, its justices struck it down. They did so not by mechanically applying a specific text, since there was nothing about whom judges could marry in the constitution. Instead they looked at the practices of other countries, jurisprudence of other courts, and international human rights instruments. They used these to construct a broad reading of the country's vague constitutional guarantees.

The approach did turn the court into a political nuisance and, over its last decade, the Mubarak regime used a variety of techniques to tame the body, and the court retreated to a more timid jurisprudence. When he fell, the justices of the court had managed to persuade the interim military leaders to give them total control of the SCC appointment process, with the result, as we have seen, of making it a self-perpetuating body.

Selectively reading the court's history, many assumed the justices were acting boldly in defense of the old order rather than in narrow interpretation of the law. The attention given to the major political battles convinced observers (and the Brotherhood) that the SCC was wielding its new autonomy to hem in the country's elected Islamist leaders. In fact, something more complex was occurring.

Much of the attention given the court in the post-revolutionary period focused on major political battles—the dissolution of parliament, popular demonstrations at the SCC building, the challenge to the constituent assembly. But those noisy clashes may have distracted attention from a quiet shift in the court's jurisprudence. When it disbanded the parliament over the summer in June 2012, its decision hearkened back to the 'Awad al-Murr years in both style of reasoning and substance. It anchored its decision not in any specific constitutional provision—nor even in the interim constitution—but instead in an Egyptian constitutional tradition, interpreted, it said, in light of international understandings.

But when the court finally ruled on a long-slumbering case brought by a diplomat seeking to win the same right to marry foreigners that judges had achieved through the earlier ruling, it showed its new face. The ruling was solidly reasoned and argued—but also narrowly textual and cautious. The constitutional declaration then in force said nothing about any right to marry, so the diplomat could not claim his constitutional rights were being infringed.

What explained the caution? Why is this narrow textualism now likely to prevail? The moments of the court's boldness in decisions or rhetoric in 2012 after 2011 came when the institution itself felt threatened—by parliamentary legislation in the summer of 2012 or by demonstrators outside the building in the past couple months. Fundamentally, however, it is a body that is politically exposed (and perhaps legally as well, since any moves the newly elected parliament can make great changes in the SCC statute). And it is about to experience significant turnover as many of its most senior members reach the retirement age.

Egyptian judges pride themselves on their independence, but many are extremely cautious as well. The SCC in the 1990s showed much independence and little caution, but the SCC after 2012 seemed inclined to reverse those characteristics.

Getting dragged (and being tempted) into more activism: the implications of prior review

But if the SCC wished to take a less active role, it found itself forced to behave otherwise. Part of the problem was the constitution itself—by introducing prior review for electoral laws, the SCC was compelled to play ping pong, as described above. While Egyptians had debated the correct sequence of the country's transition process endlessly, the 2012 constitution had come to require that the process could not be completed until a court has ruled that there is no flaw whatsoever in Egypt's electoral framework. And given the way that Egyptian elections have been run in the past—and the vagueness of much constitutional language the SCC has been asked to apply—that took some time.

None of this is due to any proactive attitude on the part of the SCC. The justices did not request the right of prior review and indeed resisted proposals in the past to give it to them. In a sense, the court's boldness came in large part because prior review forced its justices into a corner, required to find any possible constitutional flaw now for fear that if they let it pass it would prevent them from examining the law after it is implemented. In the past, the SCC had found that a mixed system—in which members of parties could run either according to lists or, in separate races, for those seats open to all—discriminated against those who were not members of parties (who could run only for the second kind race). And SCC justices in the 'Awad al-Murr years confessed to having been influenced by the US Supreme Court's ruling in *Baker vs. Carr* regarding the size of electoral districts. In these respects, the SCC was marching down well-trodden paths when it found flaws in the electoral law passed by the country's upper house.

But if the bottom line was no surprise, some aspects of the many pages of constitutional flaws found by the SCC merit attention. Most notable in domestic debates, for instance, was the SCC's insistence that soldiers and security personnel had the right to vote—a requirement that seemed based on a justifiable application of the constitution's principles, but one that made some Egyptians nervous that such ballots will not be fully freely and autonomously cast. (Indeed, when the 2012 constitution was systematically rewritten after Morsi's fall, such an exclusion was specifically allowed).

And in this regard, the SCC's approach was bold. One of the flaws found by the court was the electoral law's failure to bar religious slogans and propaganda in campaigns. Why was this remarkable? Because the SCC went beyond faulting the law for what it did say but struck it down for what it omitted. Put differently, the SCC was directing legislators to ban certain electoral practices, based on an expansive and detailed reading of what references to "citizenship" in the constitution required. If the parliament passed a law that did not specifically name religious campaigning as a violation of the concept of equal citizenship, the law would be invalid. The legislature was not free to be silent on the issue. No other kind of electoral propaganda must be banned, only religious campaigning.

The issue itself was largely symbolic. It would, of course, be very difficult for a legislative body overwhelmingly populated by Islamists to pass a law that bars religious campaigning. But even with Islamists losing control of the parliament, they would likely find the bar easy to circumvent in all sorts of creative ways. The SCC's boldness will therefore not likely deeply affect the nature of Egypt's parliamentary campaigns whenever they occur. But it did deepen the suspicion between judiciary and Islamists.

The final voice settling Egypt's constitution

But it was not only the electoral framework that was at issue. Because the SCC adjudicated constitutional disputes, it had no choice but to rule on what the constitution actually was. And that was an intensely political task because many within the opposition regarded the constitution as illegitimate. And the SCC also had the legacy of the al-Murr years to carry as well—a series of clear precedents on political matters that had become a core part of the court's self-image and therefore difficult both jurisprudentially and institutionally to repudiate.

The end result was largely in the interest of the country's rulers. They had their constitution acknowledged, the upper house of the parliament retained (despite the fact that the electoral law for that house had features deemed unconstitutional for the lower house), and some of their constitutional arguments vindicated. But occasionally the SCC showed a far bolder streak and sometimes spoke in a tone that might best be described as deeply annoyed.

The most significant set of rulings came on June 2, 2013 when the SCC released three judgments—one overturning the electoral law for the upper house (but allowing that body to continue in operation until the lower house was seated); one overturning the law governing the constituent assembly, and one overturning a provision of the country's emergency law.

On the constituent assembly, the SCC was faced with a knotty problem indeed. The question before the court was whether the law by which the assembly had been elected was constitutional. While that seemed straightforward, in fact that law had been written after the assembly itself had been elected, so it was not clear what a ruling against the law would do—especially since the constitution produced by the assembly had been approved in a popular referendum. And indeed the SCC struck down the law, and in the process implied the matter should never have been before the courts in the first place.

To untangle the knot, it is useful to start with the history of the law in question. In March 2011, the SCAF issued its constitutional declaration that provided for parliamentary elections. The elected members of both chambers of parliament were supposed to elect a constituent assembly. This they did. But the administrative courts dissolved the assembly because they claimed it was not representative and because parliament had named some of its own members to the body. The administrative courts claimed jurisdiction by saying that the parliament was acting in an administrative capacity when it elected the constituent assembly. To comply with the ruling, the parliament elected a second constituent assembly. But they still named a few of their own members to the body. Worried that the administrative courts would dissolve the second constituent assembly, the parliament then passed a law justifying what it had done. The purpose of the law was to keep the matter out of the administrative courts because now the parliament was acting in a legislative rather than administrative capacity (a distinction that only years of Egyptian legal training could help one make). It might perhaps be up to the SCC to rule on the constitutionality of the law, but that would take time while the assembly carried out its task.

That draft law was passed by the parliament sent to the SCAF for approval, but the SCAF did not act. In June 2012, shortly after passing the law, the parliament was dissolved. And Mohamed Morsi of the Muslim Brotherhood was elected president. After taking office, Morsi approved the law.

When a lawsuit was filed against the second constituent assembly in an administrative court, the judges there decided to send the matter of the law over to the SCC. The question before the court centered then on the law passed by the parliament to justify what it had done. In its ruling, it was up to the court to decide whether this was an administrative or a legal matter—or perhaps something different, a "political act."

The idea of "political acts" is the SCC's preferred term for what had been called "acts of sovereignty." These are acts that are not ones subject to judicial oversight. While accepting that there are such acts, the SCC insists that it alone has the authority to decide what is a political action. In this case, the SCC reasoned that the constitutional declaration meant to make the entire procedure of electing the constituent assembly something special, outside of regular channels. It was not a normal administrative act. Nor should the parliament be passing laws, restricting or defining the process because the body that elected the constituent assembly (that body was not the parliament acting normally but a special assembly of all elected members of the two chambers) was not subject to parliamentary laws; it had been called into being by constitutional text and the voters' will. So the law on the subject was unconstitutional. But that did not remove the legitimacy of the constituent assembly, it affirmed it.

The SCC did not specifically declare that the election of the constituent assembly was an act of sovereignty, but the court seemed to be drawing on that mode of thinking. And if that was the case, then it means that no court should be reviewing what the parliamentary deputies did when they elected the second constituent assembly. Rather than throwing the second constituent assembly under a cloud, it implies that the first one never should have been dissolved. On this issue there could be no clearer vindication of the Islamist majority's actions.

But not on all issues. In the ruling, the SCC explicitly defined the "revolutionary period" as one that ended with the elections of the upper and lower houses of parliament and the president. That meant Morsi had no authority to issue constitutional declarations—ever. And the implications of that would be potentially far-reaching if the SCC at the same time were not making crystal clear at the same time that the 2012 constitution was an accomplished fact.

And there were other ways in which the SCC showed discomfort and resentment at the emerging Islamist leadership and its legal actions. In the earlier rulings, it had simply applied the 2012 text without comment. This time it was not silent. It did respect the 2012 constitution as the one in effect. But the tone of some rulings made clear that justices were unhappy. Their attitude sometimes came off as institutional modesty (judges have to respect the clear will of the voters), sometimes as resignation (the 2012 constitution was a *fait accompli*), and sometimes as barely muffled outrage.

As an example of this attitude, the SCC found the electoral law by which the upper house of parliament is elected unconstitutional. But because the current body was specifically named by the 2012 constitution as having legislative authority in the absence of the lower house of parliament, the SCC had no choice but to allow that body to continue operating—but only until the moment when the new lower house was elected and met for the first time.

And in a final ruling, the SCC took a swipe at the country's emergency law with little short-term effect but potential significance in the future. Indeed, when it issued the ruling, the law was in abeyance since there was no state of emergency in effect. (There were admittedly some lingering effects of Egypt's past state of emergency, which lapsed in 2012, still in effect, such as trials and imprisonment of individuals charged at that time.) The provision struck down was minor. But this is an area the SCC had not dared to tread in the Mubarak years. It was clear that some judges were resentful of Egypt's emergency regime, but they thought it would be the end of the SCC if they questioned it. But in 2013, the emergency law became fair game for the SCC.

The post-Morsi SCC

Just as the SCC had apparently made its limited peace with the Morsi presidency and its full peace with the 2012 constitution, that presidency collapsed and the 2012 constitution was suspended. The constitutional battles of the preceding two-and-a-half years had been a major part of the battles that led to Egypt's second popular uprising and military takeover. But constitutional upheavals had led not to the marginalization of the SCC but to its increasingly central role. Even when the court seemed to wish to withdraw into a narrow, more traditional jurisprudence, it found itself summoned forward to play a more ambitious role.

And the fall of Morsi seemed at first to further enhance the SCC's role. The military installed the SCC chief justice, Adly Mansour, as acting president. It did so not on the basis of the 2012 constitution (which it suspended) but on the 1971 constitution which placed the chief justice in the line of succession. Mansour himself, reputedly among the more cautious of the SCC's justices, lived up to that reputation (or lack thereof) but keeping public speeches extremely short and acting as a very modest caretaker indeed. But he brought with him to the interim presidency a group of constitutional figures (some from the SCC itself) who were punctilious in their legalism, mindful as they were of all the missteps of the preceding two years. The effect was not only to iron out legal kinks from Egypt's transition but also to slow the process down considerably as Mansour seemed to insist that no step could be legally or constitutionally questioned afterwards. The political process was characterized by deep bitterness and unprecedented violence, but everything was duly written up in legal form.

And the SCC protected its interests even as it saw one of its more modest members at Egypt's helm. The 2014 constitution—drafted by two committees appointed by Mansour and then approved by Egyptian voters—seemed to give the SCC what it wished (although many of its critical protections were enshrined in legislation that could be amended rather than in the constitutional text). The SCC also moved to insulate one of its decisions from other jealous judicial actors in a seemingly technical dispute. The presidential election law drafted by Mansour insisted that decisions by the presidential electoral commission—itself staffed in part by SCC personnel—could not be appealed to a court. The administrative courts attacked the provision, claiming that the 2014 constitution prevented such matters from judicial review. But the SCC, consulted on the matter, cited an earlier decision that the presidential election commission formed in 2012 was itself a judicial body and thus there was no need for review by any other court. The argument—since it applied only to the presidential elections held in 2014—was a minor one, but Mansour not merely adopted his colleagues' views when he promulgated the presidential election law but vigorously defended it. The ostensible argument was that it was necessary to avoid protracted litigation in such matters, but there was a hidden agenda as well: the SCC was resentful of the way the administrative courts seemed to be treading on constitutional ground and wished to turn back any attempt by those courts to share the SCC's jurisdiction on fundamental constitutional matters.

Over the short term, Egypt's SCC seems to have weathered a wave of revolutionary change institutionally intact. But with its formation and jurisdiction determined as much by legislation as by constitutional text, its continued role and viability is now subject to the political process. It seems unlikely that the current law issued by the SCAF will stand indefinitely; the main question is when a parliamentary supermajority (since the 2014 constitution likely requires one for the SCC law) will come to exist that will take on the task of rewriting the statute. Given the tremendous press of other business and the chaotic nature of Egypt's political system, it is possible (although hardly inevitable) that such a step will take some time.

In the meantime, and likely afterwards, the SCC will likely find itself forced to tread more carefully than it did during the tumultuous year of 2012. The underlying anomaly of Egypt's revolution will be sealed: the country's constitutional court reached the zenith of its influence at a time when nobody seemed to know precisely what the constitution was.

References

Bernard-Maugiron, N. (ed.), *Judges and Political Reform in Egypt* (Cairo: American University in Cairo Press, 2009).

Boyle, K. (ed.), *Human Rights and Democracy: The Role of the Supreme Constitutional Court of Egypt* (Heidelberg: Springer, 1996).

Brown, N.J., *Constitutions in a Nonconstitutional World: Arab Basic Laws and the Prospects for Accountable Government* (Albany: SUNY Press, 2001).

——, *The Rule of Law in the Arab World* (Cambridge: Cambridge University Press, 1997).

——, "*The Supreme Constitutional Court in Post-Revolution Egypt*," 25 January 2013, http://tahrirsquared.com/node/110.

——, "Why Did the Egyptian Regime Appoint a New Chief Justice?," *Foreign Policy*, 21 July 2009, http://lynch.foreignpolicy.com/posts/2009/07/21/why_did_the_egyptian_regime_appoint_a_new_chief_justice.

Cotran, E. and Sherif, A.O. (eds.), *The Role of the Judiciary in the Protection of Human Rights* (Leiden: Brill, 1997).

El-Ghobashy, M., *Taming the Leviathan: Constitutionalist Contention in Contemporary Egypt*, Ph.D. dissertation, Columbia University, 2006.

Moustafa, T., *The Struggle for Constitutional Power in Egypt* (Cambridge: Cambridge University Press, 2009).

Rutherford, B., *Egypt after Mubarak: Liberalism, Islam, and Democracy in the Arab World* (Princeton: Princeton University Press, 2008).

Notes

1 Some of the SCC's jurisprudence during the al-Murr years are examined in two volumes that emerged from conferences sponsored by the court. See E. Cotran and A.O. Sherif (eds.), *The Role of the Judiciary in the Protection of Human Rights* (Leiden: Brill, 1997); and K. Boyle (ed.), *Human Rights and Democracy: The Role of the Supreme Constitutional Court of Egypt* (Heidelberg: Springer, 1996).

2 I have written of the court's history and development in *The Rule of Law in the Arab World* (Cambridge: Cambridge University Press, 1997); and *Constitutions in a Nonconstitutional World: Arab Basic Laws and the Prospects for Accountable Government* (Albany: SUNY Press, 2001). See also T. Moustafa, *The Struggle for Constitutional Power in Egypt* (Cambridge: Cambridge University Press, 2009); B. Rutherford, *Egypt after Mubarak: Liberalism, Islam, and Democracy in the Arab World* (Princeton: Princeton University Press, 2008); M. El-Ghobashy, *Taming the Leviathan: Constitutionalist Contention in Contemporary Egypt*, Ph.D. dissertation, Columbia University, 2006; and N. Bernard-Maugiron (ed.), *Judges and Political Reform in Egypt* (Cairo: American University in Cairo Press, 2009).

3 I explained these suspicions in a short article entitled "Why Did the Egyptian Regime Appoint a New Chief Justice?," *Foreign Policy*, 21 July 2009, http://lynch.foreignpolicy.com/posts/2009/07/21/why_did_the_egyptian_regime_appoint_a_new_chief_justice (accessed 20 May 2014).

4 Since the SCC issues opinions as a court without publishing dissents, it is hard to say where individual justices' inclinations lie. My own sense comes from observing the SCC over time and interviewing some of its justices on numerous occasions. The justices are very careful not to give their opinions in specific cases but one can discern general orientations at times.

5 There was some precedent for the upper house's actions here. Egypt's only other experience with prior review came in early 2012 when the SCAF issued a presidential law by decree. Under the interim constitution, the SCC was required to review that law (but not the parliamentary election law, a gap that turned out to be fatal to the new parliament). The SCC found a large number of flaws, mostly minor, in the presidential election law. The SCAF made amendments and then issued it without submitting the revised draft to the SCC. At the time, nobody complained.

6 An earlier version of this section appeared in the Tahrir Squared website as "The Supreme Constitutional Court in Post-Revolution Egypt," 25 January 2013, http://tahrirsquared.com/node/110 (accessed 20 May 2014).

3 The pilot of *limited* change: Mohammed VI and the transition in Morocco*

Francesco Biagi

Introduction

Out of the North African countries involved in the Arab uprisings, Morocco has at least two distinguishing features. First of all, together with Algeria,[1] it is the only country in which the head of state has remained unchanged: in fact, in contrast to Presidents Ben Ali in Tunisia, Qaddafi in Libya and Mubarak in Egypt, King Mohammed VI has been able to retain his role in spite of the protests that broke out across the country after February 20, 2011. Second, Morocco was the first country to adopt a new constitution following the Arab upheavals. Indeed, in order to keep the protests under control, the king decided to "grant" a new constitution to the people, replacing the one promulgated in 1996. It should be pointed out that the new constitution is not only the result of the protests, but also represents the last (and undoubtedly most important) link in the chain of a broader process of reform that has been pursued by the Moroccan sovereign since the start of his reign.

In this chapter I analyze the role played by Mohammed VI in the process of transition from the autocratic regime of Hassan II. In particular, I argue that Mohammed VI has guaranteed his country only a *limited* transition: in fact, although the adoption of the 2011 constitution is effectively a sign of greater democratization of the country, for the time being Morocco continues to be a hybrid regime, in which the king remains the fulcrum of the political and institutional system.

Accordingly, this chapter proceeds as follows. In the first part I examine the move from the autocratic regime of Hassan II to the hybrid regime of Mohammed VI. I then indicate the reasons that led part of the Moroccan people to demonstrate against the regime in February 2011, and the measures by which the king managed to calm the protest demonstrations. Afterwards, I show that the constituent process was driven by Mohammed VI and was characterized by some major democratic deficits. I then examine the new arrangements introduced by the 2011 constitution to regulate the form of government including, in particular, the rules on the division of powers between the sovereign and the head of government. I show that, despite what is formally stated in the constitution, Morocco has not become a parliamentary monarchy. Subsequently, I underline that for the moment the head of government, Abdelilah Benkirane, has not established himself as a serious "counterweight" to the king, and that the process of constitutional implementation is proceeding quite slowly. Finally, I draw some conclusions.

The autocratic regime of Hassan II

After the long years of the French and Spanish protectorates, in 1956 Morocco became an independent state. In the following year Sultan Mohammed V, who had been one of the principal architects of independence, assumed the title of king and, over the course of his four-year reign,[2] attempted—albeit unsuccessfully—to provide the country with its first constitution.

Mohammed V was succeeded in 1961 by his son Hassan II, who led the country without interruption for 38 years until his death in 1999. His reign may be divided into two distinct phases. The first lasted from 1961 until 1989: these years "were a period of turmoil and crisis within the representative system, and without doubt the darkest years of post-independence Moroccan history."[3] These are referred to as the "Years of Lead," an expression that is used in order to stress the serious and systematic violation of human rights, in particular of opponents and dissidents, who were imprisoned, killed, or exiled.

The king used several instruments in order to exercise his autocratic power over the country. One of the most important undoubtedly consisted of the "*makhzen*" (which literally means "warehouse"), that represents "the fulcrum of Morocco's formal and informal power structures, composed of the King's family and patronage network."[4]

Another very relevant tool was given by the legal system. Indeed, the five constitutions issued under Hassan II (in 1962, 1970, 1972, 1992, and 1996) granted him practically unlimited powers. In particular, Article 19 of the constitution was defined within the literature as the "Supra-Constitution,"[5] or "a Constitution within the Constitution"[6] on which the "hard core"[7] of the sovereign's power was based. This granted the king the role of "*Amir Al Mouminine*," that is the "Commander of the Faithful": as such, he was the supreme representative of the nation, the symbol of its unity, guarantor of the continuity of the state, custodian of respect for Islam and the constitution, protector of the rights and liberties of citizens, social groupings and society at large, and the guardian of the independence of the nation and the territorial integrity of the realm.

The king also had an almost complete control over the political system. Although a multiparty system was granted by the sovereign, in practice Hassan II managed to strongly weaken divergence and opposition[8] through cooptation, patronage, and repression. In particular, the king used the "*divide et impera*" strategy: "He co-opted party leaders, pitted parties against each other so that no group could become strong enough to challenge his power, and encouraged the rise of new political organizations to divide and check old ones he saw as threatening."[9] The fragmentation of the political parties reinforced the role of the king as the ultimate arbiter of the political system.

The second phase of the reign of Hassan II covered the years between 1989 and 1999. During this period the sovereign initiated a slow and cautious process of reform. Among the reasons that explain this change, the new international context has to be mentioned. Indeed, the Berlin Wall had just fallen and the Soviet Union was collapsing. The international community, and in particular the United States and France, urged Hassan II to start a process of democratic transition.[10] Moreover, one should not underestimate the effects of the book *Notre ami le Roi* (1990) by the French writer Gilles Perrault, in which the harsh repressions perpetrated during the "Years of Lead" were denounced.[11]

In 1990, the king decided to create the Advisory Council on Human Rights, a body intended to provide protection to individual rights, which was vested with the specific task of investigating violations of human rights that had occurred in the past; several—albeit extremely limited—changes were then introduced in 1993 to the Code of Personal Status (the *Moudawana*) in order to improve conditions for women; subsequently in 1998 the policy of "*alternance*" was implemented for the first time, according to which members of the opposition parties could be appointed to government office.[12]

However, it should be pointed out that as a whole the reforms pursued by Hassan II over the last ten years of his reign were rather limited and did not significantly change the authoritative nature of the state. In fact, rather than constituting the expression of a genuine desire to democratize the country, the changes introduced by the Moroccan sovereign appear to have had the aim of maintaining his autocratic power. In other words therefore, the strategy pursued by Hassan II appears to have been "to liberalize in order *not* to democratize."[13]

Mohammed VI and the birth of a hybrid regime

Mohammed VI came to the throne in 1999, following the death of his father Hassan II. In a certain sense this event marked a significant departure from the authoritarian past. Indeed, the young king presented himself as a reformer, who intended to improve living conditions for the poor and downtrodden, and in particular those of women and children. As soon as he came to power Mohammed VI replaced some of his father's officials, such as Driss Basri, the interior minister regarded as the personification of political repression under Hassan II. The new sovereign then authorized the return of various political exiles, launched a campaign against poverty and unemployment, and lent his support to a process of economic structural adjustment previously initiated by Hassan II.

The fundamental pillars of the reform process included first and foremost the amendment of the Code of Personal Status. In contrast to the changes made to the *Moudawana* in 1993 under Hassan II, the amendments introduced by the Commission appointed by Mohammed VI entailed a tangible improvement to the conditions of women.[14] The entry into force of the new Family Code on March 8, 2004, thus represented an event of significant importance for Moroccan society as a whole: in fact, there is no doubt that there is a close link between the reform of the *Moudawana* (with the resulting improvement—at least in formal terms—of the conditions of women) and the democratization process within the country.[15] However, these changes came up against resistance and perplexity, due to the fact that the new provisions had to engage with a patriarchal society strongly rooted in male chauvinist values that are undoubtedly very difficult to uproot.[16]

On January 7, 2004, Mohammed VI announced the creation of the Equity and Reconciliation Commission, the first Truth Commission to be created in the Arab world. This body was then requested to investigate cases of "disappearances" and arbitrary imprisonment between 1956 (the year in which the country gained independence) and 1999 (the year in which Hassan II died), to pay compensation to victims, and to present a report containing an analysis of human rights violations, providing also recommendations and proposals on how to preserve the memory and ensure a definitive break with the practices of the past.

Despite the various limits,[17] the establishment of the Truth Commission was an important event for the country. Indeed, it was now possible for the victims of past abuse to make public statements even on television and radio. Moreover, the work of the commission "gave visibility and legitimacy to a part of the country's history that had been obscured by official history."[18]

However, alongside this democratic progress, various elements of continuity with the previous regime remained. First and foremost, it must be recalled that the constitution was not reformed, thus leaving the institutional architecture of the state unchanged. In fact, since the 1996 constitution granted unlimited power to the king, he was able to continue to exercise his command over the country without any effective or efficacious limitations on his freedom of action. In other words, "the Moroccan political system lack[ed] any meaningful framework of checks and balances."[19]

Moreover, the moves towards the creation of a democratic regime referred to above must be read in the light of a very special context. On May 16, 2003, Morocco was forced to confront terrorist attacks by Islamic fundamentalists in Casablanca. It is beyond doubt that this event significantly undermined the progress that had been made towards the creation of a state based on the rule of law. In fact, within one week of those attacks Parliament adopted an anti-terrorism law (no. 3 of 2003) that imposed significant limits on fundamental rights. The implementation of that legislation resulted in strong repression by the Moroccan authorities.[20]

Fundamental rights were significantly limited between 1999 and 2011 also in other areas: freedom of association, assembly, expression, and religion were in fact permitted only within certain bounds, and violence against women continued to be very frequent.[21] Another serious problem affecting the country was the lack of independence of the judiciary, especially in politically sensitive cases.[22]

Overall therefore, it may be asserted that the period between 1999 and 2011 was characterized by two conflicting tendencies: democratic reforms on the one hand and repression and limitation of fundamental rights on the other. These characteristics had the effect of locating Morocco—along with many other Arab countries—within the "political gray zone"[23] of "hybrid" or "mixed" regimes.[24]

The "Arab Spring" in Morocco: the 20 February Movement and the regime's response

The protests that started to break out in Morocco after February 20, 2011 (the date from which the eponymous movement "*Mouvement du 20 Février*" took its name) occurred against the backdrop of the Arab Spring. The 20 February Movement, largely comprised of young people, denounced in particular the systematic and endemic corruption, the high cost of basic products, low wages and increasing poverty; it also called for greater social justice, free access to healthcare, greater employment opportunities and the right to housing. Young Moroccans also hoped for the achievement of profound and radical constitutional and political reforms, the construction of a state based on the rule of law and a free and independent legal system in order to enable the country to turn into a parliamentary monarchy.[25] Therefore, the 20 February Movement did not call into question the sovereign, but called for change in the form of government: what was requested was in fact the move to a parliamentary monarchy based on the Spanish or British model, where the king "reigns but does not govern."

The movement was supported by numerous non-governmental organizations, human rights associations, political parties from the left and the extreme left, the Islamic movement Al Adl Wa Al Ihssane, trade unions, associations of emigrant communities resident abroad, intellectuals, and businessmen. These actors, who had participated in the past in other protest movements against the regime, subsequently founded the National Council of Support for the 20 February Movement.

With a view to calming the protests and growing dissent as quickly as possible, the king—who was concerned by the revolts and revolutions breaking out in neighboring countries—decided to adopt certain "preventive measures,"[26] such as a wage increase for public sector employees, the creation of new jobs, the guarantee of unemployment benefit, provision for mandatory medical insurance, and free access to the health service for a greater number of citizens. The Economic and Social Council was also established, a body provided for under the 1992 constitution but that had remained on paper until that moment.

Another important novelty regarded the transformation of the Advisory Council on Human Rights (created in 1990 by Hassan II) into the National

Council on Human Rights. Chaired by the renowned human rights activist Driss el-Yazami, this body had the purpose of addressing all questions relating to the protection of human rights, the guarantee of their full exercise and promotion, and the preservation of the individual and collective dignity, rights, and freedoms of citizens. Alongside the power to pursue investigations and inquiries, and to submit the relative reports to the competent authorities, the council was requested to verify how legislation could be brought into line with the international conventions on human rights that had been ratified by Morocco.

Moreover, again with the goal of calming the growing dissent within the country, the regime significantly stepped up contacts with the major political and social players: the prime minister and the interior minister met with representatives of the principal political parties, various trade unions, several associations of unemployed graduates, the Moroccan Human Rights Association, and the Forum for Truth and Justice.

Finally, as will be noted in the following section, on March 9, 2011, Mohammed VI announced to the country his decision to complete a "global constitutional reform."

However, alongside the carrot, the regime did not hesitate to use its stick. Members of the 20 February Movement, who were depicted as enemies of the state and accused of jeopardizing its territorial integrity, were subjected to various forms of intimidation and harassment. In addition, the terrorist attack in Marrakesh on April 28, 2011, was used in some cases as a pretext for prohibiting anti-regime demonstrations.

It is important to stress that, compared with other neighboring Arab countries, the protests that took place in Morocco involved decidedly fewer demonstrators[27] and made more moderate requests: in particular, it is sufficient to consider the fact that the position of Mohammed VI was not called into question.[28] One should not be taken by surprise, since the king continues to be "genuinely popular."[29] According to a survey carried out in 2009, 91 percent of Moroccans considered "positive" or "very positive" the first ten years of Mohammed VI's reign.[30] His popularity appears to be due essentially to three reasons.

The first lies in the fact that the Moroccan sovereign, as a member of the Alaoui dynasty, claims direct descent from the Prophet Mohammed, and this gives him a very strong legitimacy. Second, in contrast to other countries such as Tunisia, Egypt, or Libya, Morocco had initiated an important process of democratic reform in 1999 (and in some senses even in 1989).[31] Third, the idea according to which without the king and his "unifying role" the country would be ungovernable, is very strong among the population.[32]

Finally, it should be pointed out that if the regime has been able to keep protest movements under control, this was also due to the fact that it responded quickly to the requests being made. In particular, it must be noted that the king's announcement of a far-reaching constitutional reform on March 9, 2011, occurred less than three weeks after the first protest demonstrations, which broke out on 20 February of the same year. Thus, Mohammed VI managed to turn the time factor to his advantage, catching the demonstrators off balance.[33]

The constituent process: another "*octroyée*" constitution

The need to adopt a new constitution had been apparent since Mohammed VI came to the throne in 1999. It was in particular the *Mouvement de Revendication d'une Constitution démocratique*, made up principally of members of left-wing parties, which pushed for the adoption of a new constitution providing for greater protection for fundamental rights, a more robust recognition of the pluralist nature of Moroccan identity, and a far-reaching reform of the system for distributing political power.

There appear to be two principal reasons why, despite a rather intense debate on this issue, a new constitution was adopted only following the king's March 2011 speech. The first reason results from the fact that the adoption of a new constitution did not represent a priority for the major parties represented in parliament: in fact, these parties considered the 1996 constitution to be satisfactory, "and that what needed to be changed was not the Constitution, but practices; compliance with the [then] Constitution was all that was needed."[34]

The second—and more important—reason resulted from the fact that the sovereign did not have any interest in making any amendments to the 1996 constitution, and even less in adopting a new one when he was not under any political pressure to do so.[35] It was not therefore particularly surprising that Mohammed VI had no intention of debating constitutional reform. Besides, history has demonstrated that democratic reforms are only implemented in Morocco when the monarchy is put under significant pressure (from the army, the parties, the population, or the international community), and it is for this reason that the literature uses the expression "top-down democratization."[36] The sovereign's decision on March 9, 2011, to announce a far-reaching reform to the constitution undoubtedly provides further confirmation of this tendency.

On that date, under the pretext of pursuing the process of an "advanced regionalization system,"[37] and without mentioning the 20 February Movement, Mohammed VI gave a genuine "constituent speech," in which he asserted the "seven key elements" on which the constitutional reform was to be based: 1) a guarantee of the pluralist nature of Moroccan identity, including the *Amazigh* component; 2) consolidation of the rule of law, the promotion and expansion of the scope of fundamental rights and guarantee of their exercise; 3) guarantee of the independence of the judiciary and reinforcement of the powers of the Constitutional Council; 4) consolidation of the principle of the separation of powers through the transfer of new powers to parliament and the appointment as prime minister of a member of the party obtaining the largest number of votes in elections, and the reinforcement of the prime minister's status as the head of the executive branch; 5) consolidation of the role of political parties within a pluralist system, reinforcement of the role of the parliamentary opposition and civil society; 6) bolstering of mechanisms intended to guarantee moral integrity within public life and to favor responsible conduct within public office; and 7) guarantee of the institutions addressing the issues of good government, human rights and protection of freedoms.[38]

On March 10, the day after the speech was delivered, the king appointed an *ad hoc* body, the Consultative Commission on Constitutional Reform, which was charged with the task of preparing a new draft Constitution. The commission was chaired by Abdellatif Menouni—a renowned constitutionalist and former member of the Constitutional Council—and was comprised of 18 members, all appointed by the king and most of whom were university professors and activists from human rights associations. It should be stressed that, with the exception of Rajae Mekkaoui,[39] the commission lacked religious members or *oulema*, thereby stressing the path towards secularization that the new constitution was intended to pursue.

In parallel with the appointment of the commission, Mohammed VI ordered the establishment of a "Political Mechanism Accompanying the Constitutional Reform," a body directed by his advisor Mohamed Moatassim, a university professor and expert in constitutional law, which was comprised of representatives of political parties and the trade unions. This mechanism was expected to facilitate dialogue and concerted action between the various political actors, and was intended to operate as a channel for communication between the commission and the political forces and trade unions.[40]

All of the political and social organizations within the country—including the 20 February Movement—were invited to submit proposed constitutional amendments to the commission, which also organized around a hundred meetings in order to enable the representatives of the organizations to present their requests orally. Only a small number of minority left-wing parties failed to reply to the commission's invitation, along with the 20 February Movement, complaining that the commission lacked democratic legitimacy and that the constitution was being granted as an act of "largesse."

It should be pointed out that the requests presented by the political and social organizations were largely of the same tone as the "constituent speech" delivered on March 9, 2011. Indeed, most of the proposals were already stated in the king's speech, and therefore they did not introduce any significant novelty in the debate.[41] Therefore, the practical consequence was that the commission merely wrote the text of a constitution whose content had been "dictated" directly by Mohammed VI. Driss Maghraoui has rightly stressed the fact that this passive position of the political parties was an excellent example of their "domestication"[42] by the king, thus confirming the "politics of consensus" that has been characterizing Morocco for many years. According to this notion, the role and the absolute powers of the king are not the object of discussions and divergence among the parties. The latter, regardless of their ideological orientations, "seem comfortable with not taking the initiative and leaving the palace full control of the political game and orientations of the country."[43]

The work of the commission, the meetings of which were not open to the public, was completed with particular speed, given that in his speech the king had stated that he expected an initial report to be presented to him before the end of June. The commission met with the political parties and trade unions on June 7, 2011: on that occasion, commission president Menouni made an oral presentation of the key features of the reform, although he did not distribute a written version of the new text of the constitution. This resulted in the decision by several political parties and trade unions to walk out of the meeting in a sign of protest. Subsequently, on June 10, Menouni presented the plan for constitutional reform to Mohammed VI, while Moatassim informed the sovereign of the decisions adopted by the Political Mechanism Accompanying the Constitutional Reform. Most political parties and trade unions were strongly critical of the fact that they had only received a written draft of the constitution on the day before the king's speech to the nation (June 17), when the latter set out the key planks of the reform, inviting the population to participate in a constitutional referendum to be held on July 1, and to approve the new text.[44]

The referendum result was a success for Mohammed VI, given the approval of the new constitution by 98 percent of the population. With some rare exceptions (consider the 20 February Movement), political parties, trade unions and social organizations invited the population to vote "yes" in that consultation. The turnout of 73.5 percent may be read in diametrically opposed terms depending upon one's point of view: while on the one hand it is double the rate registered at the 2007 parliamentary elections (which was a meagre 37 percent), it did however represent the lowest rate in the history of the constitutional referendums held in the country, being more than 11 percentage points lower than the 1996 constitution.[45]

The constituent process was strongly criticized both by certain political parties and social organizations as well as within the literature. The principal objection, as had already been asserted, regarded the lack of democratic legitimacy of the Commission on Constitutional Reform, since it had been appointed entirely by the sovereign. Once again in fact, the requests made by parties and associations that had been calling for the election of a Constituent Assembly by the people since as early as the 1962 Constitution were disregarded. The difficulties—which were practically insurmountable—in electing a body of that type may be summarized particularly succinctly by a commentator writing in 1963: "The Constituent Assembly is vested with supreme power and, in Morocco, *such supreme power lies with the King alone*. This power of His Majesty was not challenged even prior to the Protectorate" (emphasis added).[46] Mohammed VI continued to pursue this tradition of a "constituent King":[47] in fact, it was he who decided to engage in far-reaching constitutional reform, to identify the "key elements" on which that reform was to be based, to appoint the Commission on Constitutional Reform, and finally to grant his approval to the draft presented to him by Menouni. The king had the first and the last word.

Therefore, down to the present day, "*octroyées*" constitutions have been a constant feature of Moroccan history.

An argument that may be proposed in support of the position that the 2011 constitution did not result from an act of "largesse" flows from the fact that it was ratified by popular referendum.[48] However, this argument is decidedly weak, above all in the light of the fact that, during the two weeks running up to the consultation, the monarchy took every effort to promote the reform as much as possible, and strongly restricted the space available to those (such as the representatives of the 20 February Movement) who by contrast promoted a boycott of the vote. Moreover, on election day, reports of fraud came from all over the country. Thus, there was never going to be any doubt over the referendum result. It is evident, then, that this consultation was much more similar to an authoritarian plebiscite than to a democratic referendum. Indeed, "[autocratic] referenda [are] motivated more by a desire to legitimize the autocrat's control of a polity than to allow the citizens to render a considered verdict on the constitution."[49]

Another criticism that has been made is that the constitutional process was too short. Indeed, it took just three months to prepare the draft constitution and to consult with the representatives of political parties and trade unions. Therefore, Morocco seems to confirm that very rapid constitution-making periods are one of the distinguishing features of "non-democracies."[50]

A further objection addressed the lack of transparency within the work of the commission, since its meetings were not open to the public. It should be specified that secrecy in itself is not an absolute evil, while on the contrary

> debates in front of an audience tend to generate rhetorical overbidding and heated passions that are incompatible with the kind of close and calm scrutiny that ought to be the rule when one is adopting provisions for the indefinite future. By denying the public admission to the proceedings and by keeping the debates secret until the final document has been adopted, one creates conditions for rational discussion that are less likely to prevail in the presence of an audience.[51]

However, initial secrecy should be offset by subsequent publicity, for example in the form of discussions in a plenary assembly: in fact, with total secrecy, "partisan interests and logrolling come to the forefront."[52] In this sense, the Spanish constituent process was considered by Jon Elster as one which came closest to striking an "optimal balance"[53] between secrecy and publicity.[54] In Morocco, on the contrary, as noted above, the second—public—stage was entirely lacking.

A positive aspect is given by the fact that the level of participation by political parties, trade unions, and social organizations in the drafting of the constitution was undoubtedly higher compared to the past. In fact, for a very long period of time, the principal—if not only—instrument available to the parties in order to submit proposed constitutional amendments to the king was to send him "*memoranda*." This practice "affirmed the domination and authority of the King in the process of drafting the constitutional text, but at the same time it allowed other parties to get involved in the process and add their remarks and demands to the reform agenda."[55] On the contrary, during the process leading to the adoption of the 2011 constitution, parties and associations also had the opportunity to meet with the members of the Commission on Constitutional Reform and to present their requests orally, while dialogue and concerted action were also promoted by the presence of the Political Mechanism Accompanying the Constitutional Reform.

Considered overall, the 2011 constituent process was characterized by a greater degree of democracy compared to the past, in particular regarding participation of political parties and social organizations in the process. However, some major democratic deficits remain: the constitution continues to be a "concession" made by the sovereign,[56] the constitutional referendum was in reality much more similar to an authoritarian plebiscite, and the work of the Commission was too rapid and characterized by a lack of transparency.

The 2011 constitution: the introduction of relevant democratic novelties

The new constitution promulgated by Mohammed VI by *dahir* (royal decree) no. 1-11-91 of July 29, 2011, introduces significant changes. compared to the 1996 constitution.[57] As regards the recognition and protection of fundamental rights, it should be pointed out first and foremost that the preamble stipulates that the international conventions ratified by Morocco shall take precedence over domestic law, and that national legislation must consequently be brought into line with the former. Particular emphasis is also given to equality between men and women, thus pursuing the spirit of the 2004 *Moudawana* reform.[58] Moreover, Article 5 of the Constitution is of major significance in recognizing Amazigh as an official state language alongside Arabic, thus accepting a longstanding claim of the Berber peoples. It would not be rash to define this provision as historic, in that through its enactment Morocco has become the first Maghreb country to grant constitutional standing to its Berber identity.[59] As regards the instruments for the protection of fundamental rights, it is important to note in particular the introduction of concrete constitutional review: Article 133 provides that "the Constitutional Court shall have competence to look into an exception of unconstitutionality raised in the course of a trial, when one of the parties argues that the law on which depends the outcome of a trial undermines the rights and freedoms guaranteed by the Constitution." The introduction of such *ex post* review (which exists alongside *ex ante* review, already provided for under the previous constitution) thus appears to be extremely important in order to enable the Constitutional Court to reinforce its position as a counter-majoritarian body, and may thus contribute to the process of democratization in a more effective manner compared to the past.[60]

The new constitution introduces significant novelties also in relation to the horizontal separation of powers. Indeed, alongside the measures discussed below, the 2011 constitution reinforces the powers of the executive, the legislature, and the judiciary and guarantees greater independence and autonomy to each of them. As far as the legislature is concerned, the number of areas falling within the exclusive remit of the legislature increased significantly, while the role of the opposition was also reinforced, which "following a long period of marginalisation and neutralisation, has [now] emerged as a counterweight to the power of the Government and its majority."[61] As regards the judiciary, it should be recalled that justice has been elevated from a mere "authority" (as defined under the 1996 constitution) to the status of a full-blown branch of state, independent of the legislature and the executive. This independence is guaranteed principally through the Higher Council of the Judicial Power, the functions of which have been expanded.

The vertical separation of powers within the state has also undergone profound changes. Given that it is largely based on the principles and guidelines contained in the Final Report drawn up by the Advisory Commission on Regionalization (the body appointed by Mohammed VI in 2010), the new constitution provides for a territorial organization that is defined as "decentralized" and "based on an advanced regionalization system" (Article 1). It is important to point out that the issue of Western Sahara is still an open question. It is certain that the "Moroccan Initiative proposing the negotiation of a self-government statute for the Sahara region" envisages an autonomous statute for Western Sahara that would be at odds in various ways with the "ordinary regional arrangements" provided for under Title IX of the new constitution. Were it to be granted constitutional standing (as stipulated in Article 29 of the "Initiative"), the autonomous status granted to the region of Western Sahara would therefore constitute an exception to the homogeneous regionalism provided for under the 2011 constitution.[62]

Particular emphasis is also given to the fight against corruption, which is undoubtedly one of the scourges of Moroccan society.[63] In this regard, particular note should be afforded to the provision for institutions in charge of good governance and regulatory matters, such as the High Authority for Audiovisual Communication, the Competition Council, and the National Authority for probity and the prevention and combat of corruption.

The form of government: the failure to establish a parliamentary monarchy

At this stage it is appropriate to analyze in greater detail the arrangements introduced by the new constitution in relation to the form of government, in particular as regards the division of powers between the sovereign and the head of government.

The strengthening of the government's powers

While under the 1996 constitution the king was the effective holder of executive power (and the government often limited its action to the mere execution of the king's wishes), under the new constitution this power is shared between the sovereign and the government.

Title V of the constitution guarantees a central position to the government within the state apparatus and enhances its functions. Comprised of the head of government (which thus replaces the term "prime minister") and the ministers, the government "shall exercise executive power," and "under the authority of the Head of Government, carry out its program and ensure the execution of laws" (Article 89). Moreover, the government is no longer responsible to the king and to parliament (as provided for under the 1996 constitution), but exclusively towards parliament: in fact, the new Article 88 provides that the government "shall be inaugurated after its program has been endorsed by an absolute majority vote of the members of the House of Representatives."

Moreover, while under the 1996 constitution the Council of Government, chaired by the prime minister, had no official recognition under constitutional law and was limited to the exercise of "a function involving the preparation of decisions adopted by the Council of Ministers,"[64] the new constitution by contrast expressly recognizes its status and vests it with important functions. It is chaired by the head of government, and now decides in areas previously under the exclusive competence of the Council of Ministers, such as the state's general policy before its presentation to the Council of Ministers; public and sectorial policies; motion of confidence at the House of Representatives to enable the government to carry on with its mission; topical issues related to human rights and to public order; draft bills; decree-laws; draft regulatory decrees; international conventions before their submission to the Council of Ministers; along with appointments to high public office (Article 92).

One of the principal novelties regards the appointment of the head of the executive. While under the 1996 constitution the prime minister was appointed at the discretion of the king, the 2011 constitution stipulates by contrast that the sovereign shall appoint the head of government from the party that wins the most seats in the elections to the House of Representatives and "with a view to their results" (Article 47). This practice had already been followed on two occasions (following the 1997 and 2007 elections), although since it had no constitutional status it could be disregarded at any time, as occurred following the 2002 elections. This will evidently amount to a significant limit on the king's powers, who will now be unable to appoint a head of government without reference to the results of elections: it will therefore *de facto* be the people who choose the head of the executive.

Article 47 goes on to specify that the members of the government shall be appointed by the king acting upon a proposal by the head of government;[65] the latter may in turn request the king to remove one or more members of the government from office, either on his own initiative, or following their individual or collective resignation.

The principal powers that the new constitution vests in the head of government include the power to dissolve the Chamber of Representatives by decree adopted in the Council of Ministers, after consultation with the king, the president of the Chamber and the president of the Constitutional Court (Article 104). Under the 1996 constitution, on the other hand, this prerogative was vested exclusively in the sovereign. Moreover, the head of government is required to exercise regulatory power (Article 90) and to make appointments to civil public offices and high-ranking positions in the state corporations and companies (Article 91).

"Le Roi règne et gouverne"

Although—as demonstrated above—the new constitution significantly strengthened the head of government's powers, the sovereign nonetheless still remains the cornerstone of the system. In fact, the 2011 constitution makes provision for a range of prerogatives that enable the king to continue to operate as the central figure in the country's most important decisions. First and foremost, the sovereign continues to chair the Council of Ministers, the body that resolves upon matters of decisive interest for the state, such as strategic orientations of state policy; proposed revisions of the constitution; draft organic laws and draft framework laws; general guidelines of the finance bill; draft amnesty law; draft texts relating to military domain; declaration of state of siege and of war; along with appointments to high public office (Article 49).

Moreover, after consultation with the head of government, the king may dismiss one or more ministers (Article 47), and has the power to dissolve the houses of parliament (after consultation with the president of the Constitutional Court and after informing the presidents of the two houses of parliament and the head of government) (Article 96); he also makes appointments to military positions (Article 53) and appoints half of the members of the Constitutional Court (Article 130).

The sovereign also continues in his role as president of the Higher Council of the Judicial Power (Article 56),[66] supreme commander of the Royal Armed Forces (Article 53), and is also required to chair a new national security body, namely the Supreme Security Council, defined under Article 54 as the "forum for consultation on strategies regarding the internal and external security of the country, and for the management of crisis situations."

The person of the king ceases to be "inviolable and sacred" (as it was in the 1996 constitution), and is only defined as "inviolable, and respect shall be due to him" (Article 46). If at first sight this provision represents an important novelty (the king is not considered "sacred" any longer), a deeper analysis, however, reveals that this clause is not free from criticisms, since it states two different things depending on the language used. In fact, in Arabic

Article 46 reads: "The King's person is inviolable and *ihtiram* [respect] and *tawqeer* are owed to him". Ahmed Benchemsi underlines that

> *ihtiram wa tawqeer* is an ancient expression used to signify the privileged status of those who claim descent from Muhammad himself – a group that includes the members of Morocco's 350 years old Alaouite dynasty. Though dictionary definitions of *tawqeer* vary, the most commonly found are "reverence," "veneration," "adoration," and "obeisance." Some thesauruses also propose "augustness," "exaltation," and "glorification." To be fair, "respect" can be found among the alternate translations, but if *tawqeer* is simply meant as another word for *ihtiram*, one wonders what they are doing in the same sentence. More important, why would one of them – the bolder and more dramatic – be quietly left out when the Western public is watching? Has Morocco's King really renounced his "sacred" character ... or has he merely rephrased it, resorting to an ancient formula that stems from deeply archaic roots?[67]

There is no doubt that the "capital innovation"[68] (at the very least in formal terms) introduced by the new constitution results from the fact that Article 19 of the previous constitutions (which granted to the king practically unlimited powers)[69] has been "split" into Articles 41 and 42. The intention was to separate spiritual power from temporal power in order to remedy the "confusion of powers" resulting from the provisions of the previous constitutions. Article 41 in particular sets forth the king's prerogatives in the religious sphere, stipulating that as the "Commander of the Faithful" he shall ensure respect for Islam, shall be guarantor of freedom of worship and shall preside over the Higher Ulema Council, which is the only body empowered to issue officially approved religious opinions (*fatwas*). The purpose of this body appears to be to constitute "a bulwark against the flow of *fatwas* inspired by non-Malikite traditions originating from the Mashrek, and above all against the national promoters of Wahhabi or Shiite influence."[70] Moreover, the king "shall exercise, by royal decree, the religious prerogatives inherent in the institution of the Commandership of the Faithful, which are exclusively assigned to him under this article."[71]

Article 42 provides that the king, as

> Head of State, Supreme Representative, symbol of the unity of the nation, guarantor of the permanence and continuity of the State and supreme arbitrator between institutions, shall ensure compliance with the Constitution, proper functioning of constitutional institutions, protection of the nation's democratic options and of the rights and freedoms of citizens and communities, as well as compliance with the international commitments of the Kingdom. He shall be guarantor of the independence of the country and of the territorial integrity of the Kingdom, within its authentic borders.

From a symbolic point of view, the reform of the old Article 19 is a true revolution. For the first time after 50 years the most important provision of the Moroccan constitution has been changed, thus losing its "sacredness." On the contrary, from a practical point of view the novelties are not as evident. According to David Melloni, one of the most important consequences resulting from this division consists in the fact that the legislative power reserved to the sovereign under the terms of the old Article 19 of the previous constitution no longer exists.[72] In fact, in his capacity as commander of the faithful, the king had a monopoly on legislation pertaining to religious matters, family law, and the protection of rights and freedoms. However, according to Melloni, the division of Article 19 does not mean that it will be impossible for the sovereign to legislate, but rather heralds the start of legislative power shared with Parliament, in which the new constitution vests—*inter alia*—with competence over family status and marital status, citizenship and the status of foreigners, fundamental rights and freedoms (Article 71).[73] However, it should be recalled that in actual fact Mohammed VI had consented to parliament's intervention in these areas some years ago: in fact, both the new Family Code (from 2004) and the new Nationality Code (from 2006) were adopted by parliament, in spite of the fact that they related to areas in which, in his capacity as commander of the faithful, the king had always been the sole body with competence.[74]

Article 42 goes on to specify that the sovereign shall exercise his powers through royal decrees, which must be countersigned by the head of government. In this regard it is appropriate to stress that while the *dahirs* which do not require countersignature by the head of government are now the exception, they do relate to matters of particular importance: in addition to the appointment of the head of government (Article 47), consider the religious prerogatives inherent in the institution of the commandership of the faithful (Article 41), the appointment of the ten members of the Regency Council (Article 44), the dissolution of parliament (Article 51), the approval of appointments of magistrates by the Higher Council of the Judicial Power (Article 57), the proclamation of a state of emergency (Article 59), the appointment of half of the members of the Constitutional Court (Article 130), and the presentation of proposed constitutional amendments for referendum (Article 174).

The literature has highlighted that the proclamation of a state of emergency and the presentation of proposed constitutional amendments for referendum are the two powers that demonstrate with the greatest clarity the "constitutional supremacy"[75] of the king.

The first of the two is a very sensitive power, especially in a country—such as Morocco—that has already experienced a state of emergency in the past.[76] First of all, it must be acknowledged that this condition is now subject to various provisions regulating its use. In fact, before a state of emergency is declared, the sovereign is required to consult with the head of government, the presidents of the two houses of parliament and the president of the

Constitutional Court; a state of emergency may only be declared in cases in which "the territorial integrity" of the state is under threat or following the occurrence of "events … which hinder the normal functioning of constitutional institutions"; parliament cannot be dissolved during any period in which emergency powers are being exercised, and fundamental rights and freedoms must be guaranteed; the king is required to guarantee the return to the ordinary operation of democratic institutions as quickly as possible (Article 59). Nevertheless, it is essential to stress that the king remains

> the only body with authority to verify whether the aforementioned conditions are met and his powers, which are exercised without any requirement for countersignature, are not in any way circumscribed by a Parliament which, in contrast to the French example, is not automatically convened during a state of emergency and does not evidently dispose of the last resort – where such powers are abused – of the impeachment procedure.[77]

As regards the second power constituting an expression of the "constitutional supremacy" of the king, it should be pointed out that the constitution provides that the sovereign shall be the only power which is able to present *directly* a draft constitutional amendment for referendum, irrespective of whether any proposal has been made by the government or of a preliminary assessment by parliament (Article 172).[78] Moreover, the new constitution grants the king the power to submit draft constitutional amendments to parliament (and not to the people), thereby avoiding the requirement for a referendum (Article 174). For the first time in Moroccan history, the sovereign is therefore able to amend the constitution without any requirement for a referendum, simply by securing approval by parliament. It must also be added that the king retains a "veto right"[79] over proposed amendments originating from parliament and the head of government, since these must be subject to a referendum, which may only occur according to a *dahir* (Article 174). As highlighted above, this *dahir* is a royal decree that does not require countersignature by the head of government, and that is therefore classed as an act over which the sovereign enjoys full discretion. This means that the king will not be obliged to present these amendment proposals to the people whenever he considers them to be inappropriate.[80] This interpretation appears to be confirmed by the fact that, in contrast to the situation for the promulgation of legislation, which Article 50 stipulates must occur within 30 days, the constitution does not stipulate any time limit in relation to cases involving the presentation of proposed amendments for referendum.

Article 1 of the new constitution defines the monarchy not only as "constitutional," "democratic," and "social," but also as "parliamentary." In the light of the above, it is evident that whilst the 2011 constitution attributes significant new powers to the head of government and limits the sovereign's prerogatives in some areas, it does not by any measure establish a parliamentary monarchy analogous to the British or Spanish monarchies, in which the king's role is limited largely to the performance of a symbolic and representative function. Thus, the role of the Moroccan sovereign is not limited to "reigning," but to all intents and purposes continues to involve the "government" of the country: indeed, albeit in some ways on a more limited scale compared to the past, Morocco continues to be an "executive monarchy."[81]

The failure to move towards a parliamentary monarchy cannot be dismissed without comment. In fact, the establishment of that form of government has for some time "indisputably established itself as the ultimate objective of a successful constitutional transition,"[82] without forgetting that it was one of the core requests made by the 20 February Movement. It must nonetheless be acknowledged that the expectations of the Moroccan people cannot be said to have been betrayed, since Mohammed VI has not at any time hinted at the possibility of any such change in the political regime; on the contrary, in his speeches he has repeatedly referred to the need to pursue the reformist path embarked upon at the start of the 1990s, thus establishing a strong sense of continuity with the past.

The political challenge

It is clear that the real meaning and scope of the provisions of the new constitution with regard to the powers allocated to the sovereign and to the head of government, as well as the relations between them, will only become apparent through practice. It is two and a half years since the victory of the moderate Islamic party Parti de la justice et du développement (PJD) in the elections held on November 25, 2011.[83] These elections were undoubtedly of major importance, not only because the Parti authenticité et modernité (PAM), considered by Moroccans as the party of the monarch, did not win the elections (as several observers had predicted),[84] but also because the winner was an Islamic party that was vested with the task—for the first time in Morocco's history—of forming a government.

For the moment, the government and the head of government, Abdelilah Benkirane, have adopted very few measures to halt Morocco's economic slide or even to implement the provisions of the new constitution.[85] Moreover, they have encountered difficulties, especially during the first few months in office, also in exercising the powers expressly allocated to them under the constitution in full autonomy and in an effective manner. Consider, for example, the fact that

> the PJD still apparently consults with the palace even on the appointments the prime minister is entitled to make. In part, this is simply because the PJD does not have its own networks of expertise and contacts that would allow it to make independent choices. But in part it is

> also because the party does not want a confrontation with the king, as its leaders never tire of stressing.[86]

This deference of the PJD towards the monarchy may be explained in part as a psychological stance ("for the PJD government, as for so many Moroccans, the problem is not only the King but the King-inside-themselves"[87]), and in part by the desire to be accepted as a legitimate political player and to become fully integrated into the political-institutional system.[88] The weakness of the government has often permitted to the king to continue to exercise his powers and to make decisions in a discretionary manner, without any real political limitations (as occurred in the past).[89]

On the other hand, it is important to acknowledge that Benkirane—unlike the previous prime ministers—has managed to establish a direct contact with the Moroccans, especially through a strong and effective media presence. Mohammed VI, who is not a charismatic leader, may suffer of this: therefore, "this media breaking has opened a space for the political presence of the Head of Government who is potentially able to compete with the King."[90]

Thus, only time will tell whether the head of government will have the courage and political will to establish himself as a serious "counterweight" to Mohammed VI, or whether he will remain a weak actor incapable of bringing about significant changes.

The implementation of the constitution: a real priority in the king's agenda?

One of the principal challenges for Morocco now will concern the process—which will undoubtedly be very delicate—of effective implementation of the provisions of the constitution, a process that will imply the adoption of numerous ordinary and organic laws, depending on the circumstances of each case. In order to speed up the process of implementation, Article 86 stipulates that the organic laws provided for under the new constitution must be presented to parliament for approval before the end of the first legislature. While it is significant, this provision does not appear to be conclusive, and it has certainly not been drafted in exceptionally precise terms. In fact—as stressed by Cesare Pinelli—Article 86 does not require parliament to *approve* organic laws during the first legislature, but is limited to stipulating the duty to *submit* such laws to parliament before the deadline specified. Moreover, the provision does not assert the consequences of the failure to comply with that time limit.[91] It is certain that the implementation of the constitutional provisions is "one of the decisive factors in measuring the sincerity of the ambitious innovations introduced by the 2011 Constitution."[92]

In the speeches given to both houses of parliament on October 12, 2012, and October 11, 2013, during the first parliamentary sessions Mohammed VI urged parliament to speed up the process of implementing the constitution.[93] In fact, on those occasions the sovereign invited parliament to give full effect to the constitution, in particular in the following areas: advancing Morocco's regionalization, ensuring the independence of the judiciary, recognizing the official character of the Amazigh language, and promoting the practice and institutions in charge of good governance.

Almost three years after the promulgation of the constitution, one cannot fail to notice that the process of implementation is proceeding at a rather slow pace. Organic laws implementing the constitution have only been enacted up to this point in relation to the Chamber of Representatives (no. 27/11), the Chamber of Councilors (no. 28/11), political parties (no. 29/11), the election of the members of local government bodies (no. 59/11)[94] and appointment to high office within the public administration in accordance with Articles 49 and 92 of the constitution (no. 02/12).[95] It is worth noting that four laws were adopted in 2011, one in 2012, but none in 2013 and in the first half of 2014.

Moreover, it must be pointed out that the most "delicate" constitutional provisions representing the real novelty compared to the previous constitution have not yet been implemented: consider the provision recognizing Amazigh as an official language, the provisions on the independence and autonomy of the judiciary, the provisions on the process of "advanced regionalization," the provisions in the field of good governance, or again the provisions on the organization and functioning of the Constitutional Court, as well as the regulation of concrete constitutional review.

The issue of the constitutional implementation has been stressed also by the Human Rights Watch 2013 World Report, according to which the "human rights conditions were decidedly mixed in Morocco, as a 2011 constitution containing strong human rights provisions did not translate into improved practices."[96] The situation is such that constitutional provisions that grant rights and freedoms are often not implemented or are even denied by ordinary legislation. The Code of Criminal Procedure and the Criminal Code contain several provisions at odds with the 2011 constitution, as well as with international human rights treaties.[97]

As shown above, the king's powers are such that he could easily drive the process of constitutional implementation—if he wished so. In reality, the slowness of this process leads to the conclusion that for the moment—despite the speeches given to the parliament—this is not a real priority in Mohammed VI's agenda, and therefore several provisions will likely remain "virtual" for some time to come.[98]

Conclusions

To deny the fact that, since Mohammed VI came to the throne in 1999, Morocco has made extremely important steps towards greater democratization would not be to provide an objective account of the facts. Indeed, it is thanks to reforms such as the *Moudawana*, the establishment of the Equity and Reconciliation Commission, and above all the adoption of the 2011 constitution, that the country has made a clear break with the dark years of the autocratic regime of Hassan II.

However, these changes do not appear to be sufficient in order to guarantee a genuine move by the country in favor of democracy. In order for a democratic transition to occur, it is necessary that there be a change in the form of state, i.e., the passage from an autocratic regime to a democratic regime. This change has not yet occurred in Morocco. In fact, the most innovative parts of the new constitution (which was "granted" by Mohammed VI, and did not result from a democratically elected Constituent Assembly) have still to be implemented, and in some cases ordinary legislation is in contrast with the constitution and with international human rights treaties. Moreover, the constitution continues to vest the king with prerogatives that are such as to ensure that he remains "the cornerstone of Morocco's institutional architecture and … the master of the political game":[99] the sovereign continues to be the key figure in determining political direction and adopting decisions of strategic importance for the country, not to speak of the fact that he is still the commander of the faithful, the president of the Higher Council of the Judicial Power, supreme commander of the Royal Armed Forces, and president of the Supreme Security Council. Thus in many ways the separation of powers appears to be more theoretical than substantive.[100] In addition to all this, one must underline the fact that the head of government is encountering various difficulties in establishing himself as a serious "counterweight" to the sovereign. Probably the proof that Mohammed VI still holds the country in his power is given by the fact that on July 31, 2011, just one month after the constitutional consultation, government officials and dignitaries were once again lined up to bow to the monarch in the classic ritual of the "*bay'a*" (allegiance) that "has turned out to be one of the most symbolic acts of obedience and servitude."[101]

In one of his most renowned works, Charles T. Powell defined King Juan Carlos of Spain as "*el piloto del cambio*" ("the pilot of change"),[102] due to the fact that he played a decisive role in conveying Spain from the authoritarian regime of Franco towards a genuine form of democracy.[103] Mohammed VI may be considered as a "pilot of *limited* change," since the reforms initiated by him—which are undoubtedly of major importance—have not, however, affected the hegemony and central role of the monarchy. Therefore, it may be concluded that, to date, the sovereign has taken his country only halfway along the route of democratic transition: in fact, under Mohammed VI, Morocco has ceased to be an autocratic regime and turned into a hybrid regime, although not a democracy. The protests that occurred after February 20 and the subsequent process of drafting the new constitution could have represented a key moment for ensuring that the country did not remain "a halfway house." Despite the significant process made thanks to the 2011 constitution, Morocco still needs to take the decisive step towards becoming a fully democratic country.

References

Abdelaziz Lamghari, M., *Développements constitutionnels récents au Maroc (juillet – décembre 2011)*, 2 February 2012, www.venice.coe.int/webforms/documents/?pdf=CDL(2012)002-f.

Abdelmoumni, F., "Le Maroc et le printemps arabe," *Pouvoirs*, no. 145, 2013.

Abouchi, E.H., "La pratique référendaire dans le régime constitutionnel marocaine, 1962–2011: une analyse du contenu," in *Cinquante ans de vie constitutionnelle au Maroc. Quel bilan?*, Publications de l'Association marocaine de droit constitutionnel, 2013.

Azzouzi, A. and Cabanis, A., *Le néo-constitutionnalisme marocaine à l'épreuve du printemps arabe* (Paris: l'Harmattan, 2011).

Ba Mohammed, N., "Le Parlement dans la Constitution de 2011," in A. Bouachik, M. Degoffe and C. Saint-Prot (eds.), *La Constitution marocaine de 2011. Lectures croisées*, Publications de la Revue marocaine d'administration locale et de développement, Série "Thèmes actuels", no. 77, 2012.

Belal, Y., "L'Islam politique au Maroc," *Pouvoirs*, no. 145, 2013.

Benchemsi, A., "Mohammed VI, despote malgré lui," *Pouvoirs*, no. 145, 2013.

——, "Morocco: Outfoxing the Opposition," *Journal of Democracy*, vol. 23, no. 1, 2012.

——, "Presse: le printemps perdu," *Pouvoirs*, no. 145, 2013.

Biagi, F., "Il nuovo diritto di famiglia in Marocco," *Liberal Risk*, no. 7, October 2005 (supplement of *Liberal*, no. 32, October–November 2005).

——, "La Monarchia nella Costituzione del Marocco del 2011," *Percorsi costituzionali*, no. 3, 2012.

——, "The 2011 Constitutional Reform in Morocco: More Flaws than Merits," *Jean Monnet Occasional Papers*, Institute for European Studies (Malta), no. 7/2014, www.um.edu.mt/–data/assets/pdf_file/0020/208307/JM_Occasional_Paper_no._7_final,_5th_March_update.pdf.

Blanc, F.-P., "La régionalisation et la Constitution de 2011: genèse et prospective," in Centre d'Études Internationales (ed.), *La Constitution marocaine de 2011. Analyses et commentaires* (Paris: LGDJ, 2012).

Blount, J., "Participation in Constitutional Design," in T. Ginsburg and R. Dixon (eds.), *Comparative Constitutional Law* (Cheltenham: Edward Elgar, 2011).

Blount, J., Elkins, Z., and Ginsburg, T., "Does the Process of Constitution-making Matter?," in T. Ginsburg (ed.), *Comparative Constitutional Design* (Cambridge: Cambridge University Press, 2012).

Bouachik, A., Degoffe, M., and Saint-Prot, C. (eds.), *La Constitution marocaine de 2011. Lectures croisées*, Publications de la Revue marocaine d'administration locale et de développement, Série "Thèmes actuels", no. 77, 2012.

Bouchkars, A., *Politics in Morocco: Executive Monarchy and Enlightened Authoritarianism* (London: Routledge, 2011).

Bunce, V. and Wolchik, S., *Mixed Regimes in Postcommunist Eurasia: Tipping Democratic and Tipping Authoritarian*, Società per lo studio della diffusione della democrazia, Working paper no. 1/2008, www.sumitalia.it/ITA/link/documenti/wp_bunce_wolchik.pdf.

Buskens, L., "Sharia and National Law in Morocco," in J.M. Otto (ed.), *Sharia Incorporated: A Comparative Overview of the Legal Systems of Twelve Muslim Countries in Past and Present* (Leiden: Leiden University Press, 2010).

Carothers, T., "The End of the Transition Paradigm," *Journal of Democracy*, vol. 13, no. 1, 2002.

Centre d'Études Internationales (ed.), *La Constitution marocaine de 2011. Analyses et commentaires* (Paris: LGDJ, 2012).

——, *Une décennie de réformes au Maroc (1999–2009)* (Paris: Karthala, 2010).

Colombo, S., "Il Marocco tra modernità e tradizione," in K. Mezran, S. Colombo and S. van Genugten (eds.), *L'Africa mediterranea. Storia e futuro* (Rome: Donzelli, 2011).

Cubertafond, B., "La transition marocaine après le printemps arabe et la nouvelle Constitution," *Les Etudes et Essais du Centre Jacques Berque*, no. 5, November 2011, www.cjb.ma/images/stories/publications/Cubertafond_EE_5.pdf.

Dalmasso, E., "Surfing the Democratic Tsunami in Morocco: Apolitical Society and the Reconfiguration of a Sustainable Authoritarian Regime," *Mediterranean Politics*, vol. 17, no. 2, 2012.

de Esteban, J., "El proceso constituyente español, 1977–78," in J.F. Tezanos, R. Cortarelo and A. de Blas (eds.), *La transición democrática española* (Madrid: Editorial Sistema, 1989).

de Vergottini, G., *Diritto costituzionale comparato* (Padua: Cedam, 2011).

Dubay, C.A., "Morocco's 'Arab Spring' and Judicial Independence," *International Judicial Monitor*, spring 2011, www.judicialmonitor.org/archive_spring2011/sector assessment.html.

El Mesbahi, K., "La prévention de la corruption au Maroc, entre discours et réalité," *Pouvoirs*, no. 145, 2013.

Elster, J., "Arguing and Bargaining in Two Constituent Assemblies," *University of Pennsylvania Journal of Constitutional Law*, vol. 2, no. 2, 2000.

——, "Forces and Mechanisms in the Constitution-making Process," *Duke Law Journal*, vol. 45, 1995.

——, "Legislatures as Constituent Assemblies," in R.W. Bauman and T. Kahana (eds.), *The Least Examined Branch. The Role of Legislatures in the Constitutional State* (Cambridge: Cambridge University Press, 2006).

Fassi Fihri, B., *Le projet constitutionnel en 30 points essentiels*, Institut Amadeus, 2011, www.amadeusonline.org/images/stories/Le_projet_constitutionnel_en_30_points_essentiels.pdf.

Fernández Molina, I., "The Monarchy vs. the 20 February Movement: Who Holds the Reins of Political Change in Morocco?," *Mediterranean Politics*, vol. 16, no. 3, 2011.

Frosini, J.O., *Constitutional Preambles: At a Crossroads between Politics and Law* (Rimini: Maggioli, 2012).

Guédira, A.R., "Une constituante ni nécessaire ni possible," *Confluent*, no. 27, January 1963.

Harsi, A., "Séparation et équilibre des pouvoirs dans la nouvelle Constitution de 2011," in A. Bouachik, M. Degoffe, and C. Saint-Prot (eds.), *La Constitution marocaine de 2011. Lectures croisées*, Publications de la Revue marocaine d'administration locale et de développement, Série "Thèmes actuels", no. 77, 2012.

Hazan, P., *Judging War, Judging History. Behind Truth and Reconciliation* (Stanford: Stanford University Press, 2010).

Human Rights Watch, *Human Rights Watch 2013 World Report*, www.hrw.org/sites/default/files/wr2013_web.pdf, 2013.

——, *Maroc: les droits humains à la croisée des chemins*, vol. 16, no. 6, October 2004.

——, *Morocco's Truth Commission: Honoring Past Victims During an Uncertain Present*, vol. 17, no. 11, 2005.

International IDEA, *The 2011 Moroccan Constitution: A Critical Analysis* (Stockholm: International Institute for Democracy and Electoral Assistance, 2012).
Maghraoui, D., "Constitutional Reforms in Morocco: Between Consensus and Subaltern Politics," in G. Joffé (ed.), *North Africa's Arab Spring* (London: Routledge, 2013).
Maus, D., "L'exécutif dans la Constitution marocaine de 2011," in Centre d'Études Internationales (ed.), *La Constitution marocaine de 2011. Analyses et commentaires* (Paris: LGDJ, 2012).
Melloni, D., "La Constitution marocaine de 2011: une mutation des ordres politique et juridique marocains," *Pouvoirs*, no. 145, 2013.
——, "Le nouvel ordre constitutionnel marocain: de la 'monarchie gouvernante' à la 'monarchie parlementaire'?," in Centre d'Études Internationales (ed.), *La Constitution marocaine de 2011. Analyses et commentaires* (Paris: LGDJ, 2012).
Mezran, K., and Alunni, A., "Power Shifts in the Arab Spring: A Work in Progress," *The Bologna Center Journal of International Affairs*, vol. 15, spring 2012.
Ministère de la Justice, *Guide pratique du Code de la famille*, Association de Diffusion de l'Information Juridique et Judiciaire, Collection des guides pratiques, no. 6, Rabat, 2005.
Montabes Pereira, J. and Parejo Fernández, M.A., "Morocco," in D. Nohlen, M. Krennerich and B. Thibaut (eds.), *Elections in Africa: A Data Handbook* (Oxford: Oxford University Press, 1999).
Ottaway, M., "Morocco: Can the Third Way Succeed?," *Carnegie Endowment*, 31 July 2012, http://carnegieendowment.org/2012/07/31/morocco-can-third-way-succeed/d3op.
Ottaway, M. and Muasher, M., "Arab Monarchies: Chance for Reform, Yet Unmet," *The Carnegie Papers*, December 2011.
Ottaway, M. and Riley, M., "Morocco: From Top-down Reform to Democratic Transition?," *Carnegie Papers*, no. 71, 2006.
Perrault, G., *Notre ami le Roi* (Paris: Gallimard, 1990).
Pinelli, C., "La démocratisation par voie législative après la transition à la démocratie," in Commission de Venise – Association internationale de droit constitutionnel, *Processus constitutionnels et processus démocratiques: les expériences et les perspectives*, Marrakech, March 29–30, 2012, www.venice.coe.int/files/2012_03_29_MAR/Presentation_Pinelli.pdf.
Powell, C.T., *El piloto del cambio. El rey, la monarquía y la transición a la democracia* (Barcelona: Planeta, 1991).
Pruzan-Jørgensen, J.E., "Islam, Gender, and Democracy in Morocco: The Making of the Mudawana Reform," in M. Badran (ed.), *Gender and Islam in Africa. Rights, Sexuality, and Law* (Washington, DC, and Stanford: Woodrow Wilson Center Press and Stanford University Press, 2011).
Rosen, L., "Revision and Reality in the Family Law of Morocco," in R. Medhy, H. Petersen, E. Reenberg Sand and G.R. Woodman (eds.), *Law and Religion in Multicultural Societies* (Copenhagen: DJØF Publishing, 2008).
Rousset, M., "L'interprétation des pouvoirs du roi dans la nouvelle Constitution," in Centre d'Études Internationales (ed.), *La Constitution marocaine de 2011. Analyses et commentaires* (Paris: LGDJ, 2012).
Rouvillois, F., "Les règles relatives à la révision dans la Constitution marocaine de 2011," in Centre d'Études Internationales (ed.), *La Constitution marocaine de 2011. Analyses et commentaires* (Paris: LGDJ, 2012).
——, "Réflexions sur la monarchie démocratique à la marocaine," in A. Bouachik, M. Degoffe, and C. Saint-Prot (eds.), *La Constitution marocaine de 2011. Lectures*

croisées, Publications de la Revue marocaine d'administration locale et de développement, Série "Thèmes actuels", no. 77, 2012.

Saint-Prot, C., "L'islam au Maroc," in C. Saint-Prot and F. Rouvillois (eds.), *L'exception marocaine* (Paris: Ellipses, 2013).

Storm, L., *Democratization in Morocco: The Political Elite and Struggles for Power in the Post-independence State* (London: Routledge, 2007).

Tourabi, A., *Constitutional Reform in Morocco: Reform in Times of Revolution*, www.arab-reform.net/sites/default/files/Morocco_EN.pdf (Arab Reform Initiative, 2011).

Touzeil-Divina, M., "Printemps & Révolutions arabes: un renouveau pour la séparation de pouvoirs?," *Pouvoirs*, no. 143, 2012.

Tozy, M., *Monarchie et Islam politique au Maroc* (Paris: Presses de Sciences Po, 1999).

Traub, J., "The Reform of the King," *Foreign Policy*, October 2012, www.foreignpolicy.com/articles/2012/10/08/the_reform_of_the_king.

Notes

* Previous versions of this paper were presented at the International Congress "Constitutional Transformations in the Arab World following the Arab Spring: Comparative Models," Johns Hopkins University SAIS Bologna Center, Bologna, Italy, February 7–8, 2013, and at the Faculty Lecture Series, College of Law of the University of Illinois, Champaign-Urbana, USA, April 2, 2013. The author would like to thank the participants for their precious suggestions and comments.

1 Even if it should be noted that Algeria has remained to a large extent "immune" from the Arab upheavals (see J. Entelis, "Algeria: The Outlier State?" in this volume).

2 Mohammed V died in 1961.

3 S. Colombo, "Il Marocco tra modernità e tradizione," in K. Mezran, S. Colombo and S. van Genugten (eds.), *L'Africa mediterranea. Storia e futuro* (Rome: Donzelli, 2011), p. 82.

4 K. Mezran and A. Alunni, "Power Shifts in the Arab Spring: A Work in Progress," *The Bologna Center Journal of International Affairs*, vol. 15, Spring 2012, p. 29. On the "*makhzen*" see also M. Tozy, *Monarchie et Islam politique au Maroc* (Paris: Presses de Sciences Po, 1999), p. 40 ff.

5 A. Bouchkars, *Politics in Morocco: Executive Monarchy and Enlightened Authoritarianism* (London: Routledge, 2011), p. 42.

6 A. Tourabi, *Constitutional Reform in Morocco: Reform in Times of Revolution*, www.arab-reform.net/sites/default/files/Morocco_EN.pdf (accessed May 21, 2014).

7 B. Cubertafond, "La transition marocaine après le printemps arabe et la nouvelle Constitution," *Les Etudes et Essais du Centre Jacques Berque*, no. 5, November 2011, p. 7, www.cjb.ma/images/stories/publications/Cubertafond_EE_5.pdf (accessed May 21, 2014).

8 The main opposition parties were the Istiqlal and the Union Nationale des Forces Populaires (UNFP).

9 M. Ottaway and M. Riley, "Morocco: From Top-down Reform to Democratic Transition?," *Carnegie Papers*, no. 71, 2006, pp. 4–5.

10 Several Western countries, for example, strongly condemned the violent repression of the strikes that took place in Fez in December 1990 and called for democratic reforms.

11 G. Perrault, *Notre ami le Roi* (Paris: Gallimard, 1990).

12 In 1998 Hassan II appointed as prime minister Abderrahmane Youssoufi, the secretary of the Socialist Party Union Socialiste des Forces Populaires. However, this new policy did not significantly limit the powers of the king, especially because

the key ministries (Interior, Foreign Affairs, Justice and Religious Affairs, i.e., the so-called "sovereignty" ministries) continued to be directly appointed by the sovereign.

13 J.E. Pruzan-Jørgensen, "Islam, Gender, and Democracy in Morocco: The Making of the Mudawana Reform," in M. Badran (ed.), *Gender and Islam in Africa. Rights, Sexuality, and Law* (Washington, DC, and Stanford: Woodrow Wilson Center Press and Stanford University Press, 2011), p. 235. It should be noted that the author does not specifically refer to the Moroccan experience, but describes in more general terms a strategy used by authoritarian regimes.

14 First and foremost, the family is now placed under the authority of both parents, and no longer under the exclusive authority of the husband. Moreover, equal treatment for men and women was also established as regards the minimum age for contracting marriage, which is set at 18 years for both. Moreover, women over age 18 may conclude marriage agreements in person. Under the new code, monogamy became the rule, while polygamy became the exception, and was prohibited in numerous cases. Also the right of repudiation granted to men, which could previously be exercised freely, is now strongly limited and a series of conditions have been imposed in order to prevent its abuse. An article-by-article commentary on the code is contained in Ministère de la Justice, *Guide pratique du Code de la famille*, Association de Diffusion de l'Information Juridique et Judiciaire, Collection des guides pratiques, no. 6, Rabat, 2005. See also F. Biagi, "Il nuovo diritto di famiglia in Marocco," *Liberal Risk*, no. 7, October 2005 (supplement of *Liberal*, no. 32, October-November 2005), p. 72 ff.

15 See Pruzan-Jørgensen, op. cit., p. 233 ff.

16 Consider for example that although the text sets at 18 years the legal age for marriage, in 2007 the family courts accepted 85 percent of applications for underage marriage (see T. Rambaud, "La garantie des droits et des libertés dans la Constitution marocaine de 2011," in A. Bouachik, M. Degoffe and C. Saint-Prot (eds.), *La Constitution marocaine de 2011. Lectures croisées*, Publications de la Revue marocaine d'administration locale et de développement, Série "Thèmes actuels", no. 77, 2012, p. 83). More information on the real implementation of the code can be found in L. Rosen, "Revision and Reality in the Family Law of Morocco," in R. Medhy, H. Petersen, E. Reenberg Sand and G.R. Woodman (eds.), *Law and Religion in Multicultural Societies* (Copenhagen: DJØF Publishing, 2008), p. 8 ff.

17 Indeed, the Commission was not able to publish the names of the individuals responsible for committing the crimes, which do not appear in the final report. Moreover, this document does not provide any possible interpretation of the ideological and political reasons for the repeated and serious violations of human rights. However, the most glaring omission regarded the question of Western Sahara: the final report is silent in relation to that region, which had witnessed very severe repression from the regime (P. Hazan, *Judging War, Judging History. Behind Truth and Reconciliation* (Stanford: Stanford University Press, 2010), pp. 122–23).

18 Hazan, op. cit., pp. 122–23.

19 Bouchkars, op. cit., p. 1.

20 See in particular Human Rights Watch, *Maroc: les droits humains à la croisée des chemins*, vol. 16, no. 6, October 2004, p. 1 ff.

21 See Human Rights Watch, *Morocco's Truth Commission. Honoring Past Victims During an Uncertain Present*, vol. 17, no. 11, 2005, p. 24; L. Buskens, "Sharia and National Law in Morocco," in J.M. Otto (ed.), *Sharia Incorporated. A Comparative Overview of the Legal Systems of Twelve Muslim Countries in Past and Present* (Leiden: Leiden University Press, 2010), pp. 129–30; on the problem relating in particular to freedom of the press, see Bouchkars, op. cit., p. 22 ff.; A. Benchemsi, "Presse: le printemps perdu," *Pouvoirs*, no. 145, 2013, p. 99 ff.

22 See C.A. Dubay, "Morocco's 'Arab Spring' and Judicial Independence," *International Judicial Monitor*, Spring 2011, http://www.judicialmonitor.org/archive_spring2011/sectorassessment.html (accessed May 21, 2014).
23 T. Carothers, "The End of the Transition Paradigm," *Journal of Democracy*, vol. 13, no. 1, 2002, p. 9.
24 These regimes "fall in the sprawling middle of a political continuum anchored by democracy on one end […] and dictatorship on the other end" (V. Bunce and S. Wolchik, *Mixed Regimes in Postcommunist Eurasia: Tipping Democratic and Tipping Authoritarian*, Società per lo studio della diffusione della democrazia, Working paper no. 1/2008, p. 4, http://www.sumitalia.it/ITA/link/documenti/wp_bunce_wolchik.pdf (accessed 21 May 2014)).
25 See I. Fernández Molina, "The Monarchy vs. the 20 February Movement: Who Holds the Reins of Political Change in Morocco?," *Mediterranean Politics*, vol. 16, no. 3, 2011, pp. 436–7.
26 Ibid., p. 437.
27 For example, the demonstrations of February 20 that took place in 53 cities and towns were attended by 240,000–300,000 people according to the organizers, or 37,000 people according to the Interior Ministry. In any case, these figures are decidedly lower than those registered in Tunisia or Egypt.
28 In Egypt, Libya, and Tunisia on the other hand, there were immediate calls for their respective dictators to be replaced.
29 Mezran and Alunni, op. cit., p. 29. It should be stressed that a high degree of legitimacy is enjoyed not only by the Moroccan king, but also more generally by all monarchs and ruling families in the Arab world (see J.O. Frosini and F. Biagi, "Transitions from Authoritarian Rule following the Arab Uprisings: A Matter of Variables," in this volume).
30 The survey was conducted by the Moroccan newspapers *TelQuel* and *Nichane* and by the French newspaper *Le Monde* (see A. Benchemsi, "Mohammed VI, despote malgré lui," *Pouvoirs*, no. 145, 2013, pp. 25–6).
31 For a more detailed discussion of the reform process pursued by Mohammed VI, see Centre d'Études Internationales (ed.), *Une décennie de réformes au Maroc (1999–2009)* (Paris: Karthala, 2010). With the purpose of stressing the Moroccan "exceptionalism", the new government often emphasised that Morocco represents a "third way" compared to countries such as Tunisia, Libya, or Egypt since it "has not embarked on a limited process of reform from the top, driven and controlled by the King. Nor has it experienced a revolution brought about by angry citizens rising up against the regime. Rather, it has chosen an alternate path based on a genuine partnership between the King and the PJD that promises to bring about more far-reaching reform than what the palace alone would grant, without the disruption caused by uncontrolled popular upheaval" (M. Ottaway, "Morocco: Can the Third Way Succeed?," *Carnegie Endowment*, 31 July 2012, http://carnegieendowment.org/2012/07/31/morocco-can-third-way-succeed/d3op (accessed May 31, 2014)).
32 See Benchemsi, *Mohammed VI, despote malgré lui*, op. cit., p. 24.
33 On the notion of "surviving constitutionalism" see J.O. Frosini and F. Biagi, "Transitions from Authoritarian Rule following the Arab Uprisings: A Matter of Variables," in this volume.
34 L. Storm, *Democratization in Morocco: The Political Elite and Struggles for Power in the Post-independence State* (London: Routledge, 2007), p. 157.
35 Ibid.
36 Ibid.
37 See section "The 2011 constitution: the introduction of relevant democratic novelties."
38 The speech of March 9 is available, along with all other official speeches of the sovereign, online at www.maroc.ma/fr/discours-du-roi (accessed May 21, 2014).

39 A member of the High Council of the *oulema*.
40 However, it should be noted that given the strong tie between the king and Moatassim, this body *de facto* was also assigned the task of identifying what was "politically acceptable to the palace and what was not" (M. Rousset, "L'interprétation des pouvoirs du roi dans la nouvelle Constitution," in Centre d'Études Internationales (ed.), *La Constitution marocaine de 2011. Analyses et commentaires* (Paris: L.G.D.J., 2012), p. 60).
41 There were some exceptions, such as the request presented by the leftist Vanguard Party to eliminate the "old" Article 19 of the constitution, which granted unlimited powers to the king (see Tourabi, op. cit., p. 6).
42 D. Maghraoui, "Constitutional Reforms in Morocco: Between Consensus and Subaltern Politics," in G. Joffé (ed.), *North Africa's Arab Spring* (London: Routledge, 2013), p. 182.
43 Ibid.
44 It also appears that Moatassim had made certain changes to the draft constitution a few hours before the king's speech on June 17, and that as late as the day before the referendum three articles from the new constitution were "furtively corrected" (Fernández Molina, op. cit., p. 439).
45 See the data reported by J. Montabes Pereira and M.A. Parejo Fernández, "Morocco," in D. Nohlen, M. Krennerich and B. Thibaut (eds.), *Elections in Africa: A Data Handbook* (Oxford: Oxford University Press, 1999), pp. 632–3.
46 A.R. Guédira, "Une constituante ni nécessaire ni possible," *Confluent*, no. 27, January 1963, p. 67, cited by Tozy, op. cit., pp. 90–1.
47 Cubertafond, op. cit., p. 3.
48 On the use of referendums in Morocco see E.H. Abouchi, "La pratique référendaire dans le régime constitutionnel marocaine, 1962–2011: une analyse du contenu," in *Cinquante ans de vie constitutionnelle au Maroc. Quel bilan?*, Publications de l'Association marocaine de droit constitutionnel, 2013, p. 45 ff.
49 J. Blount, "Participation in Constitutional Design," in T. Ginsburg and R. Dixon (eds.), *Comparative Constitutional Law* (Cheltenham-Northampton: Edward Elgard, 2011), p. 50. On the differences between authoritarian plebiscites and democratic referendums see also G. de Vergottini, *Diritto costituzionale comparato* (Padua: Cedam, 2011), pp. 244–8.
50 J. Blount, Z. Elkins and T. Ginsburg, "Does the Process of Constitution-making Matter?," in T. Ginsburg (ed.), *Comparative Constitutional Design* (Cambridge: Cambridge University Press, 2012), p. 41. See also J.O. Frosini and F. Biagi, "Transitions from Authoritarian Rule following the Arab Uprisings: A Matter of Variables," in this volume.
51 J. Elster, "Legislatures as Constituent Assemblies," in R.W. Bauman and T. Kahana (eds.), *The Least Examined Branch. The Role of Legislatures in the Constitutional State* (Cambridge: Cambridge University Press, 2006), p. 191.
52 J. Elster, "Forces and Mechanisms in the Constitution-making Process," *Duke Law Journal*, vol. 45, 1995, p. 395. With regard to this aspect two diametrically opposed processes of constitution-making are the 1787 Federal Convention in Philadelphia (which met in complete secrecy) and the 1789 French Constituent Assembly (which was fully public). On this point see J. Elster, "Arguing and Bargaining in Two Constituent Assemblies," *University of Pennsylvania Journal of Constitutional Law*, vol. 2, no. 2, 2000, p. 345 ff.
53 Elster, "Forces and Mechanisms," op. cit., p. 395.
54 Initially in fact, the Constitutional Affairs and Public Freedoms Committee appointed a *Ponencia* (comprised of seven members from the main political parties) with the task of drawing up a draft constitution, and the decisions of this limited body were taken in secret. The draft constitution was only subsequently presented to the *Cortes* and discussed publicly in both houses of parliament (see

J. de Esteban, "El proceso constituyente español, 1977–78," in J.F. Tezanos, R. Cortarelo and A. de Blas (eds.), *La transición democrática española* (Madrid: Editorial Sistema, 1989), p. 275 ff.).

55 Tourabi, op. cit., p. 3; see also Tozy, op. cit., pp. 101–2.

56 However, it should be noted that part of the literature have praised the constituent procedure adopted in Morocco, defining the process of drafting the constitution through a constituent assembly as "cumbersome, ineffective and disappointing" (F. Rouvillois, "Réflexions sur la monarchie démocratique à la marocaine," in A. Bouachik, M. Degoffe and C. Saint-Prot (eds.), op. cit., p. 67).

57 For a commentary on the new constitution, see A. Bouachik, M. Degoffe and C. Saint-Prot (eds.), op. cit.; Centre d'Études Internationales (ed.), *La Constitution marocaine de 2011*, op. cit.; International IDEA, *The 2011 Moroccan Constitution: A Critical Analysis* (Stockholm: International Institute for Democracy and Electoral Assistance, 2012); A. Azzouzi and A. Cabanis, *Le néo-constitutionnalisme marocaine à l'épreuve du printemps arabe* (Paris: l'Harmattan, 2011); F. Biagi, "La Monarchia nella Costituzione del Marocco del 2011," *Percorsi costituzionali*, no. 3, 2012, p. 399 ff.

58 It should be pointed out that the preamble of the constitution enshrines the superiority of international conventions, but "within the framework of the provisions of the Constitution, the laws of the Kingdom, and respect for its *immutable national identity*" (emphasis added). Similarly, Article 19 of the constitution subjects the principle of equal rights for men and women to compliance with the "provisions of the Constitution and … the *immutable values* and the laws of the Realm" (emphasis added). In both cases it is evident the reference made by the constitution to the Islamic religion. On the legal validity of constitutional preambles, see J.O. Frosini, *Constitutional Preambles: At a Crossroads between Politics and Law* (Rimini: Maggioli, 2012).

59 See B. Fassi Fihri, *Le projet constitutionnel en 30 points essentiels*, Institut Amadeus, 2011, p. 2, www.amadeusonline.org/images/stories/Le_projet_constitutionnel_en_30_points_essentiels.pdf (accessed May 21, 2014).

60 See J.O. Frosini and F. Biagi, "Transitions from Authoritarian Rule following the Arab Uprisings: A Matter of Variables," in this volume.

61 N. Ba Mohammed, "Le Parlement dans la Constitution de 2011," in A. Bouachik, M. Degoffe and C. Saint-Prot (eds.), op. cit., p. 101.

62 See F-P. Blanc, "La régionalisation et la Constitution de 2011: genèse et prospective," in Centre d'Études Internationales (ed.) (2012), op. cit., p. 326 ff.

63 On the problem of corruption in Morocco see K. El Mesbahi, "La prévention de la corruption au Maroc, entre discours et réalité," *Pouvoirs*, no. 145, 2013, p. 83 ff.

64 A. Harsi, "Séparation et équilibre des pouvoirs dans la nouvelle Constitution de 2011," in A. Bouachik, M. Degoffe and C. Saint-Prot (eds.), op. cit., p. 55.

65 Similarly to the previous constitutions, the 2011 constitution does not distinguish between "ministries of sovereignty" and other ministries. However, this does not prevent the king from recommending "one particular individual rather than another" for a ministry of sovereignty "depending upon the political situation and his personal relations with the Head of Government" (D. Maus, "L'exécutif dans la Constitution marocaine de 2011," in Centre d'Études Internationales (ed.), *La Constitution marocaine de 2011*, op. cit., p. 73).

66 It should be pointed out that the 1996 constitution stipulated that the role of vice-president of the Higher Council of the Judicial Power was to be performed by the minister of justice, who exercised the functions of executive-president. Now on the other hand, the functions of executive-president (Article 115) are vested in the first president of the Court of Cassation, with the goal of "better highlighting the separation of powers", to quote the words used by the sovereign in his speech of June 17.

67 A. Benchemsi, "Morocco: Outfoxing the Opposition," *Journal of Democracy*, vol. 23, no. 1, 2012, p. 62. There are also other cases in which the French version differs from the Arabic text. For example, Article 2 of the constitution refers to the fact that "sovereignty" belongs to the "nation", while the equivalent word in Arabic is "*ummah*", which has a religious connotation (International IDEA, op. cit., pp. 16–17).
68 Rousset, op. cit., p. 60.
69 See section "The autocratic regime of Hassan II."
70 Fassi Fihri, op. cit., p. 7.
71 On the role played by the king as "Commander of the Faithful" see C. Saint-Prot, "L'islam au Maroc," in C. Saint-Prot and F. Rouvillois (eds.), *L'exception marocaine* (Paris: Ellipses, 2013), pp. 54–8.
72 D. Melloni, "Le nouvel ordre constitutionnel marocain: de la 'monarchie gouvernante' à la 'monarchie parlementaire'?," in Centre d'Études Internationales (ed.), *La Constitution marocaine de 2011*, op. cit., p. 40.
73 Ibid., pp. 38–40.
74 Ibid., pp. 38–39.
75 Ibid., p. 42.
76 Morocco experienced the state of emergency under Hassan II during the period 1965–70, when the 1962 constitution was suspended.
77 Melloni, "Le nouvel ordre constitutionnel marocain," op. cit., p. 44.
78 In fact, members of Parliament have a right of initiative, although proposals will only be adopted if approved by two-thirds of the members of each house. In turn, a proposed amendment presented by the head of government must be submitted in advance to the Council of Ministers which (as pointed out above) is chaired by the king (Article 173).
79 F. Rouvillois, "Les règles relatives à la révision dans la Constitution marocaine de 2011," in Centre d'Études Internationales (ed.), *La Constitution marocaine de 2011*, op. cit., p. 363.
80 Ibid., p. 364.
81 In particular, the Moroccan regime was defined by Hassan II as a "*monarchie gouvernante*", and by Mohammed VI as a "*monarchie agissante*" (see D. Melloni, "La Constitution marocaine de 2011: une mutation des ordres politique et juridique marocains," *Pouvoirs*, no. 145, 2013, p. 6).
82 Melloni, "La Constitution marocaine," op. cit., p. 10.
83 With little over 27 percent of the votes, the PJD obtained 107 out of 395 seats in the House of Representatives. In the light of the provisions of Article 47 of the constitution, the king appointed PJD leader Abdelilah Benkirane as head of government. After a series of negotiations, a coalition government was formed at the start of January 2012, comprised of members of the PJD, Istiqlal, the Mouvement populaire, the Parti du progrès et du socialisme and several independent members. Although the majority of ministers belonged to the Parti de la justice et du développement, the party was forced to leave some key government posts to other parties. A new ruling coalition (comprised of the PJD, the Mouvement populaire, the Parti du progrès et du socialisme, and the new entry Rassemblement national des Indépendants) was formed in October 2013 following the resignation of the Istiqlal from the previous coalition government in July 2013.
84 See E. Dalmasso, "Surfing the Democratic Tsunami in Morocco: Apolitical Society and the Reconfiguration of a Sustainable Authoritarian Regime," *Mediterranean Politics*, vol. 17, no. 2, 2012, p. 218 ff.
85 See J. Traub, "The Reform of the King," *Foreign Policy*, October 2012, www.foreignpolicy.com/articles/2012/10/08/the_reform_of_the_king (accessed May 21, 2014).
86 Ottaway, op. cit.
87 Traub, op. cit.

88 See M. Ottaway and M. Muasher, "Arab Monarchies: Chance for Reform, Yet Unmet," *The Carnegie Papers*, December 2011, p. 7.
89 See F. Abdelmoumni, "Le Maroc et le printemps arabe," *Pouvoirs*, no. 145, 2013, pp. 136–7.
90 Y. Belal, "L'Islam politique au Maroc," *Pouvoirs*, no. 145, 2013, p. 80.
91 C. Pinelli, "La démocratisation par voie législative après la transition à la démocratie," in Commission de Venise – Association internationale de droit constitutionnel, *Processus constitutionnels et processus démocratiques: les expériences et les perspectives*, Marrakech, March 29–30, 2012, p. 6, www.venice.coe.int/files/2012_03_29_MAR/Presentation_Pinelli.pdf (accessed May 21, 2014).
92 Ibid., p. 5.
93 It is important not to underestimate the fact that the presidency of the opening of the first session of parliament, which is reserved under Article 65 of the constitution to the sovereign, provides the king with the opportunity to provide inspiration for and to guide legislative action. To a certain extent, this speech given by the monarch has some analogies with the "message on the state of the Union" delivered by the president of the United States.
94 In relation to these four organic laws, see the commentary by M. Abdelaziz Lamghari, *Développements constitutionnels récents au Maroc (juillet – décembre 2011)*, 2 February 2012, www.venice.coe.int/webforms/documents/?pdf=CDL(2012)002-f (accessed May 21, 2014).
95 Moreover, in September 2013 the "High Authority for national dialogue on the reform of the justice system" (established by Mohammed VI on May 8, 2012) presented the results of its work, consisting of a "Charter on the Reform of the Judiciary System." This charter is a very long document containing a number of proposals aimed at implementing the constitutional provisions in the field of judicial independence, strengthening the judicial protection of fundamental rights, and improving judicial procedures.
96 *Human Rights Watch 2013 World Report*, p. 588, www.hrw.org/sites/default/files/wr2013_web.pdf (accessed May 21, 2014).
97 On this issue see J.O. Frosini and F. Biagi, "Transitions from Authoritarian Rule following the Arab Uprisings: A Matter of Variables," in this volume.
98 On the role played by other actors (in particular the ordinary judges and the Constitutional Court) in the process of constitutional implementation see F. Biagi, "The 2011 Constitutional Reform in Morocco: More Flaws than Merits," *Jean Monnet Occasional Papers*, Institute for European Studies (Malta), no. 7/2014, pp. 16–19, www.um.edu.mt/–data/assets/pdf_file/0020/208307/JM_Occasional_Paper_no._7_final,_5th_March_update.pdf (accessed May 21, 2014).
99 Tourabi, op. cit., p. 14.
100 On this topic see M. Touzeil-Divina, "Printemps & Révolutions arabes: un renouveau pour la séparation de pouvoirs?," *Pouvoirs*, no. 143, 2012, p. 39 ff.
101 International IDEA, op. cit., p. 50.
102 C.T. Powell, *El piloto del cambio. El rey, la monarquía y la transición a la democracia* (Barcelona: Planeta, 1991).
103 See J.O. Frosini and F. Biagi, "Transitions from Authoritarian Rule following the Arab Uprisings: A Matter of Variables," in this volume.

4 Actors and factors in Libya's revolution

Karim Mezran and Eric Knecht

Introduction

A bird's eye view of the Arab Spring presents a deceptive degree of contagion—Tunisian unrest spreads to Egypt, then Bahrain, Libya, Syria, and so on. Like dominos, seemingly fortified regimes appeared to be caving, one after the other, to sheer historical momentum. While a popular analogy for the Arab Spring, this is, as we know, a pure mischaracterization. To peel away the tissue of each revolt is to expose an entangled lattice of veins connecting present regimes to past histories, actors, and strategic interests. Nowhere was this perhaps more true than in Libya, where the 2011 uprising, and its ultimate success, rested on the weight of a diverse set of actors, their interests in seeing Qaddafi removed, and the rare—perhaps once-in-a-generation—window that opened amid the region's larger transformation to make this happen. Indeed, the Libyan story is one of disparate, loosely connected domestic and foreign actors, linking up harmoniously like the unlikeliest of symphony orchestras.

Taking this interconnectivity as its thread, the following chapter analyzes how Western engagement and "reform" ushered in by Saif al-Islam Qaddafi, the late-dictator's second eldest son, and the resultant actors, networks, and ideas that emerged in the decade before the revolution, set the stage for a revolt connecting an uncannily broad swath of the international community with a charged Libyan population set on regime change. By detailing the complex interaction of these disparate actors, a clearer picture emerges of how Libya's 42-year dictatorship was uprooted. This chapter will also provide an assessment of the constitutional drafting process.

This is not, it should be noted, a holistic assessment of the Libyan revolution, nor should it be interpreted as such. It is rather, as the title of this collection suggests, an analysis of the major actors and factors that greatly influenced the direction of Libya's uprising and political developments in its wake.[1]

Saif al-Islam and the shadow of reform

Saif al-Islam was, for a time, the reason many believed an uprising of the 2011 variant would never happen. The clean-cut, Western-educated, son of

Muammar Qaddafi emerged as a key interlocutor in 2003, when the regime renounced its nuclear weapons program—however rudimentary—and became a key ally of the West in its War on Terror, sharing intelligence and providing information that helped break up the A.Q. Khan nuclear proliferation network. Crippling UN sanctions in place since 1992 were also formally removed in 2003, after Libya agreed to make payments to the families of those killed in the infamous 1988 Lockerbie bombing.[2]

Almost overnight, and not without many raised eyebrows, the Qaddafi regime was radically reinterpreted, and Colonel Qaddafi, the leader President Reagan famously dubbed the "mad dog of the Middle East," was welcomed into the club of Western trade partners. In 2004, EU sanctions were removed,[3] and in 2006 the regime was removed from the United States' list of state sponsors of terror. With little mention of Qaddafi's still horrendous human rights record, the Libyan state was nearly free to engage in trade—including arms—with the West.

Saif al-Islam was, in part, a convenient way to argue that Libyan rehabilitation was genuine, and the days of rogue statehood were over. Few doubted the young Libyan's conviction that his country needed greater democracy, although most were highly skeptical of his ability, in the shadow of his mercurial father, to actually bring such change forward.

Nevertheless, even if Saif al-Islam's efforts were viewed by Qaddafi senior as mere window-dressing, a convenient sideshow that allowed for the regime to thrive economically while continuing its business as usual, the individuals and networks established by Saif during this period of rapprochement with the West (2003–10) planted the seeds for a successful revolution later on.

Mahmoud Jibril, for example, brought on to run the National Economic Development Board—essentially tasked with drawing up the country's liberalization plans—became during his tenure a friendly face to the West. Jibril would draw on these connections in 2011 when he served as the rebel council's *de facto* foreign minister, persuading Western countries to recognize and support the then-incipient National Transition Council.

Likewise, Saif's work during this period to reintegrate imprisoned Islamist jihadists into society proved highly counterproductive for regime stability the moment the uprising got underway. In the years leading up to the revolution, hundreds of Islamists, many of whom served in Afghanistan with the Libyan Islamic Fighting Group (LIFG), were released from prison after renouncing the use of violence and interpreting it as against the ethics of *sharia* law.[4] Not only would many of these experienced fighters take up arms against Qaddafi in the frontlines in 2011, but perhaps more crucially, the process' mediator, Doha-based Libyan cleric Ali al-Sallabi, like Jibril, would serve as a crucial rebel linkage to outside support, directly connecting Qatari government arms with many of the Islamist fighters he had come into contact with years earlier through the mediation program.

Seven years of such relatively radical reform efforts made Saif al-Islam, at the onset of Libya's uprising in February 2011, the only credible voice within the regime capable of steering the country in a different, decidedly less bloody or revolutionary, direction as protests got underway. On February 20, 2011, five days after bloody skirmishes had begun, Saif al-Islam addressed the Libyan people in arguably the most pivotal—and miscalculated—speech of the war's history.

The crucial February 20 speech itself came with context. In the months immediately prior to the Libyan revolution, Saif al-Islam's reform efforts appeared decidedly finished off by the more conservative elements of the Qaddafi regime. In November 2010 then prime minister, and regime hardliner, al-Baghdadi al-Mahmoudi, shut down all of Saif's reform-oriented media outlets (*Oea, Quryna,* and *Cyrene*) following an op-ed critical of the government that highlighted apparent corruption; upwards of 22 journalists affiliated with these outlets were arrested days later.[5] Around this time Saif retired to London, commenting that he no longer felt welcome in Tripoli. "I have too many enemies there right now," Saif told a colleague at the time.[6]

In mid-February Muammar Qaddafi called on his son's help. In what will likely forever be a much-debated chapter of Libyan history, Saif al-Islam allegedly discarded a prepared speech supposedly apologizing for violence in Benghazi and calling for a constitutional convention to bring together the Libyan people,[7] and instead delivered an off-the-cuff, rambling diatribe that presented Saif as little more than his father's son.[8] "They now want to transform Libya into a group of [Islamic] emirates—small states—and even [cause] separatism. They have a plot," Saif declared,[9] leaving the world to wonder what had happened to the friendly cosmopolitan who, not long ago, commented there was nothing to fear from American democracy promotion, and championed stronger civil society.

In any case, Saif's tumultuous February 20 speech horrified observers inside and outside of the country.[10] For Libyans, the last glimmer of hope for peaceful reform was veritably dead. At the country's zero hour, the individual many had hung their aspirations on revealed a complete inability to exert influence on the regime's major decisions. From this point forward, the proverbial lines were drawn, and political negotiation—although attempted, most notably by the African Union[11]—would never emerge as a viable option. Regime hardliners and revolutionaries geared up for a long conflict.

The fruits of Western engagement

Although the period of rapprochement set in motion forces that later helped take down the regime, for Qaddafi Western engagement also came with considerable perks, not least of which was his regime's ability to reinvigorate its ailing military. Prior to the removal of UN and EU sanctions, the colonel's armed forces were largely outfitted with obsolete Soviet-era arms and equipment, a product of being unable to procure much of anything during the prior decade. When UN and EU sanctions were removed, Qaddafi, at the behest of a number of more than willing partners, used this period to retool the armed forces. This pre-2011 military buildup is highly relevant, as it explains why the conflict wore on despite Western intervention, and also sheds light on some of the more taboo, even if subconscious, reasons certain Western countries were unusually proactive about involvement.

France, Italy, and the UK were among the most active lobbyists of ending the EU arms embargo in 2004. Coincidence or not, they were subsequently the largest EU suppliers of arms and training to the Qaddafi regime.

Just months after the EU embargo was lifted, then-French defense minister Michèle Alliot-Marie arrived in Tripoli, in part to discuss military contracts to refurbish aging Mirage fighter jets and provide training to Libyan pilots and technicians; in 2006 a $140 million deal along these lines was signed;[12] in 2007 an additional contract for 1,000 MILAN anti-tank missiles was inked.[13] France also tried, quite aggressively, to market Qaddafi its Rafale fighter jets in a deal worth several billion dollars.[14] Like every other country France approached for Rafale contracts, however, the Libyans rejected the deal.[15] In a fitting historical counterpunch, it was Rafale fighter jets that first entered Libyan airspace and dismantled an armed column headed for Benghazi at the very start of NATO's intervention.[16]

The United Kingdom, and Tony Blair in particular, was similarly eager to win contracts for General Dynamics. The British company ultimately earned a contract of upwards of $165 million to supply and train the Khamis brigade, the 10,000-person unit commanded by Qaddafi's son and directly responsible for the colonel's protection.[17] The Khamis brigade launched many of the most brutal assaults on Misrata.[18]

Italy provided upwards of €200 million-worth of helicopters and equipment, although ostensibly for the mutually shared interest of border control.[19] Although the German government was critical of France for so aggressively engaging Libya in arms deals, the Germans themselves trained Libyan police in counterterrorism techniques.[20]

Overall, the arms shipped to Libya during the rapprochement years were enough to have a sizeable impact on the conflict to come. From 2006 to 2009 alone, the West exported $1 billion in arms to Libya, the lion's share split between Italy, France, and the UK.[21] This was in addition to Tripoli's arms deals with China, Russia, and ex-Soviet states.[22]

Saif, as optimistic as ever during these years, told a reporter in 2008 "Why should we have an army? If Egypt invades Libya, the Americans are going to stop it."[23] His father was less sanguine. The Brother Leader, a perpetual pessimist, was always contemplating the worst-case scenario. To balance Western interests, the longtime stalwart of anti-imperialism offered in 2008 to host a Russian naval base in Benghazi.[24] In Libya's 2008 Friendship Treaty signed with Italy, Qaddafi was adamant about including a clause stipulating that Italy cannot participate in any EU or NATO-backed mission against Libya, or allow its land to be used as a base for such operations.[25] Where Saif al-Islam was bullish on the prospects of building lasting peace through economic integration, his more skeptical father was always careful to hedge all bets.

Regardless, the reconcilement, the economic opening led by Saif al-Islam, and the resultant arms deals had important consequences for the 2011 uprising, allowing Qaddafi senior to reconstruct a military that would have otherwise been far less effective against the NATO-backed rebels. Once the regime went rogue and began firing on its own people, European suppliers of arms—particularly France and the UK—immediately lost a key market for their defense industries, since the Qaddafi regime was sure to be subject to an arms embargo for the indefinite future. In this light, actively supporting regime change—at least for countries such as France that explicitly viewed exploiting the Libyan arms market as a top priority—made good economic sense (even before oil, gas, and other potential contracts are considered). In order to maintain their sales despite the loss of one particular market, the suppliers filled the gap, merely shifting their supply chains' destinations from the Libyan government to the Libyan rebels. While there were numerous other grounds for France taking a lead role in NATO operations as it did, it is difficult to separate this ancillary benefit given the French government's explicitly stated prior goals.

Coalition of the everyone

The world had no particular love for Muammar Qaddafi. In fact, no other contemporary Middle East dictator inspired the level of disdain among his Arab or Western cohorts quite like the so-called Brother Leader. His meddling in other country's affairs was legendary, his pompous speeches the stuff of fiction, his caricature as evil supervillain readymade. In a region comprised of out-of-touch strongmen, Qaddafi was in a class all his own, and when the historic opportunity to overthrow his regime arose, an unprecedented majority came out in favor of doing so.

By the end of February the eastern portion of Libya had essentially fallen out of the regime's control and into rebel hands. Some have attributed the rapid takeover to the tactical ploy of Qaddafi's then interior minister Abdul Fatah Younis, who before defecting on February 22, convinced Qaddafi to not send additional reinforcements to the East, arguing this would cause greater provocation.[26] Younis' role in the war remains a hotly disputed topic; nevertheless, his defection, and the large number of defectors from the East that followed him, allowed that part of the country to serve as the rebel safe zone for the entirety of the war.

The cover provided by the East was essential in allowing opposition forces to form a reasonably functioning governing council in breakneck time. In fact, one of the key factors in the opposition's success was its easily discernible leadership from the very beginning—particularly in comparison to the Syrian experience, for example. From the early days of revolt, Mustafa Abdul Jalil, the Qaddafi justice minister and one of the first defectors, was named as leader of the opposition movement. When Mahmoud Jibril and Ali al-Issawi, then ambassador to India, decided the opposition movement needed a clearer organizational structure to represent it abroad, they called Jalil, and together the three formed the National Transitional Council (NTC). The NTC comprised a mix of reformers, defected officials, exiled regime opponents, elites, academics, journalists, and lawyers, largely—at least initially—from the East.[27]

The rapid formation of the NTC was a stroke of public diplomacy genius with profound implications for the rebel war effort. Among its earliest acts was to write a statement specifically calling on the international community to impose a no-fly zone, rescinding a statement rebels had made earlier warning off outside intervention.[28] Communicating the core goals of the NTC and its demands to international policymakers was then taken up by Mahmoud Jibril, whose diplomacy in this regard has been described as masterful. A Belgian adviser who sat in on one of Jibril's EU meetings on March 8 noted:

> This unknown man was so short and precise in his description of the situation of the Libyan revolution and in his demands to the European Union that for the audience it was almost impossible not to be convinced. Jibril spoke with authority. Most of all, he made clear to everyone that there would be a serious alternative if Qaddafi would fall.[29]

Jibril subsequently met with French president Nicholas Sarkozy, then US secretary of state Hillary Clinton, and a range of other world leaders. A member in Clinton's entourage noted that Jibril proved highly influential in winning over the secretary to his position on the no-fly zone.[30] While true that Clinton may have already supported intervention by this point, returning to Washington with arguments from a credible Libyan source may have proven key in winning what was then a highly contentious debate over whether the US could afford to engage in yet another regional conflict.

Jibril and the NTC would get a key boost on March 12 when the Arab League unanimously called for a no-fly zone. *The New York Times* called it "an extremely rare invitation for Western military forces on Arab territory;"[31] Indeed, it was the first such occurrence in the league's 65-year history.[32]

The Arab League statement was in fact a clear indicator of just how poorly regarded Qaddafi's regime was, including by his regional community. Although Syria and Algeria lobbied successfully to have language added explicitly to denounce full foreign intervention,[33] it was quite remarkable that 21 Arab states, many concerned about a Libyan scenario erupting within their own borders, would call on the West to impede on Arab sovereignty. From Morocco to Sudan, Lebanon to Saudi Arabia, Qaddafi had directly interfered in the domestic affairs of numerous Arab states, and watching his regime now fall into crisis was likely pure *Schadenfreude*.

Just hours before the UN Security Council was set to vote on a no-fly zone on March 17, Qaddafi made a jarring tactical mistake, appearing on the radio to warn Benghazi residents of his forces' impending assault, telling them "we will find you in your closets" and "we won't show mercy."[34] As it were, the no-fly zone was being marketed, and justified, as the logical and necessary extension of the responsibility to protect doctrine (R2P), a relatively new idea that emerged in the UN only in 2005 and had never before been utilized to justify a case of intervention. In some ways then, Qaddafi's March 17 remarks strengthened the case for R2P justification for intervention to stop him.

The vote on UN Security Council Resolution (UNSCR) 1973, which authorized all necessary means to protect Libyan civilians and allowed for a no-fly zone, passed on March 17, ten in favor, and five abstentions: China, Russia, Brazil, India, and Germany. The UK and France had worked together to draft the resolution; Lebanon, the Security Council's only Arab member, worked out the provisions specifically pertaining to the no-fly zone.[35] As will be seen, although the NATO mission that operated under UNSCR 1973 tried to keep their operations in line with a literal interpretation of what the resolution allowed—only protecting civilians—individual member states would take greater latitude in their dealings with the Libyan opposition, acting overtly to overthrow Qaddafi.

NATO and friends

France initially opposed having the Libya mission fall under the auspices of NATO. As the country that had taken the lead in drumming up support for the civilian protection mission, they were loath to work with allies such as Turkey and Italy, which, from France's perspective had proven abundantly overcautious and were viewed as a possible hindrance to the war effort.[36] This helps to explain why the French, several hours before the official start of the NATO operation, unilaterally sent eight Rafale fighter jets into Libyan airspace on March 19, blowing up a number of regime tanks stationed outside Benghazi.[37] A European diplomat revealed months later that the French gambit "nearly broke up the coalition" before it even got off the ground. Italian prime minister Silvio Berlusconi threatened to cut NATO access to Italy's air bases, and only through aggressive behind-the-scenes diplomacy on the part of Clinton did the coalition get back on track.[38]

Ultimately, the opening days of the NATO mission, initially led by the US via Operation Odyssey Dawn—and however fraught with internal bickering—were highly successful. Over the course of ten days the coalition, led by the US, UK, and France, and with notable support from Belgium, Denmark, and Norway, flew more than 1,000 combat sorties, obliterating Qaddafi's air defenses, making the regime's recapture of the East untenable, and solidifying a massive green zone for the rebels to work in throughout the war.[39] Following this opening foray, and with the UN mandate accomplished in its most literal terms, the US pulled its strike aircraft from operations, assuming only a supporting role in subsequent missions and beginning what was later dubbed by an Obama official, not without great controversy, as "leading from behind."

With NATO protecting the skies, what the rest of the war entailed is perhaps best summarized as building up the rebel forces so they could do the impossible: overthrow the regime. The effort to do this was led first and foremost by a broad array of Libyan fighters across the country, the vast majority of whom had no prior fighting experience. With the help of external actors, delineated below, Libyan opposition fighters got remarkably stronger, more cohesive, and generally more impressive as the war went on. Although many believed the regime would crumble in no time at all with NATO intervention, this of course proved untrue.[40] The rebel fighters' responsibility was to continue to inflict damage—both physical and moral—on the regime loyalist forces, thereby provoking increased defections. The rebels held on, but gaining the upper hand required help. The massive outpouring of support from all corners of the international community, a no-fly zone protecting ports of entry for much of this assistance to be received, and an embargo slowly cutting the lifeline of the regime, contributed to the rebel forces' increased chances for success in what became a war of attrition.

Qatar

No Arab country did more for Libya's war efforts than Qatar. The tiny, gas-rich Gulf country assisted Libya so much that nearly everyone has an opinion on what their ulterior motives may have been.

Qatar was the first Arab country to recognize the NTC, on March 28, only the second country worldwide to do so following France's recognition two weeks earlier.[41] Moreover, the Gulf country was the first among its Arab cohorts to participate directly in NATO operations, sending several jets to help conduct air patrol. In fact, from the start of the uprising, Qatari assistance never ceased, often violating the provisions of UNSCR 1973.[42]

Through the end of combat Qatar sent more than 20,000 tons of weapons in at least 18 shipments, including French anti-tank weapon launchers (MILANs).[43] Beyond pure arms, they also flew entire contingents of fighters to Doha for training, provided the rebels with hundreds of millions in cash, and stepped in to market Libyan oil to help anti-Qaddafi forces circumvent UN sanctions, which were then preventing states from buying oil directly from Libya.[44] The Qataris also worked with Mohamed Shammam—an individual with strong ties to Doha later appointed NTC information minister—to establish Libya al-Ahrar, an influential media outlet that provided an alternative to state television, and more explicitly, served as a mouthpiece for the NTC.[45] Qatar-based channel al-Rayyan offered Libya al-Ahrar studio space and technical equipment so the channel could go live by the end of March 2011.

Qatar showed little concern for transmitting its assistance through the formal channels in place via UNSCR 1973 and almost no scruples for evading international norms generally. The Gulf state, for example, was found to have shipped Swiss ammunition explicitly marked for no re-exportation. The Qatari ambassador to Switzerland called it "misadventure in the course of his country's support of the NATO engagement in Libya."[46]

What's more, the Qatari government displayed an impressive amount of gall, and willingness to deny its level of involvement in Libya even in the face of overwhelming evidence. When a UN panel asked the Qataris to explain documented instances of arms provision, they responded with a letter explaining:

> The state of Qatar categorically denies the information reported by some media that the state of Qatar supplied the revolutionaries with arms and ammunition. It confirms that it did not supply them with any arms or military material. If some of the aforementioned ammunition found its way to some Libyan revolutionaries, the Qatari government has no explanation other than the conditions of fierce fighting taking place in most of the Libyan territory, which could have led to exceptional consequences that are difficult to assess.[47]

There were, moreover, widespread reports of actual Qataris—in addition to military advisers—participating on the ground in combat, particularly in the final assault on Tripoli in August 2011. In fact, following the end of the war, Qatari chief of staff Major-General Hamad Bin Ali al-Atiya admitted there were "hundreds" of Qatari forces dispersed throughout Libya. According to al-Atiya, training and communications were in Qatari hands, and the Gulf state "acted as the link between the rebels and NATO forces."[48]

Qatar's assistance was largely built on the back of personal networks formed long before the war. Besides crucial figures such as Shammam, there was also Ali Sallabi—the Doha-based cleric that ran Saif al-Islam's Islamist rehabilitation effort—who served as the primary interlocutor connecting rebels on the ground with Qatari largesse. Because of this, certain rebel leaders received a larger share of the country's assistance. The Libyan Islamic Fighting Group (LIFG) leader Abdel Hakim Belhadj, who had grown close to Sallabi during the Saif al-Islam reconciliation, was among the prime recipients. Belhadj received copious amounts of assistance as he trained forces in the eastern Nafusa Mountains leading up to the final assault on the capital.[49]

This is, yet again, a reminder of how the Saif al-Islam-led opening years earlier paved the way for networks that would facilitate opposition forces' successful conduct of the war—where Saif's economic opening gave birth to Jibril, the Western-friendly face of the NTC, Saif's Islamist détente empowered Ali Sallabi to play kingmaker of the Islamist fighters, themselves free and hungry for revenge.

Sudan

Little was known among outsiders of Sudan's efforts during the war, but as more comes to light, it is growing clear they were perhaps second only to Qatar in terms of direct bilateral assistance.[50]

Sudanese involvement, perhaps more so than that of any other party in the conflict, was directly tied to strategic national interests. Put simply, the

Sudanese government of Omar al-Bashir had accused Qaddafi of arming the fiercest Darfur rebel movements—the Justice for Equality Movement (JEM)[51] and the Sudan Liberation Army (SLA) since as early as 2003.[52] In fact, the head of security in the far southern city Kufrah under Qaddafi, Commander Belqasem al-Abaaj was said to be the coordinator of Libyan support to Darfur and Chad.[53] In this way, Libya, and its southern region in particular, had long established ties to Sudan's Darfur conflict. Sudanese President al-Bashir thus saw an opportunity to sever these ties once and for all with the outbreak of the Libyan uprising.

Unsurprisingly given this context, during March and April 2011 reports emerged that JEM was being armed by Qaddafi in order to defend the Libyan south.[54] According to a UN report, JEM forces participated in an attack on Kufrah between April 28 and May 5, 2011. Sudanese armed forces struck back and played a key role in removing Qaddafi's forces from the southern city.[55]

Put differently, for Sudan the Libyan uprising grew into a proxy war over the still ongoing conflict in Darfur. Consistent with this view, al-Bashir did everything in his power to support Libya's anti-Qaddafi forces, opening Sudanese airspace to NATO, facilitating strategic communication between NATO and Niger—which still largely supported Qaddafi—and more controversially, sending large shipments of arms to Benghazi and Misrata. In early April, when Misratan rebels were still badly underequipped compared to their loyalist opponents, Sudanese shipments were cited as a major factor in overcoming ammunition shortages.[56] Exaggerating or not, after the war al-Bashir noted that "the forces that liberated Tripoli were armed 100 percent by Sudan,"[57] suggesting, at the least, that his country's contribution to the war effort was not insignificant.

Sudanese involvement highlights yet again the extent to which the Libyan uprising was one defined by blowback for Qaddafi's policies of interference.

Creeping engagement

Most, if not all, parties to the Libyan conflict grew steadily more involved as the conflict wore on, especially as it became increasingly apparent that the NATO no-fly zone, in itself, would not strengthen rebels enough to take down the regime. In late April the United States reintroduced predator drones, which had been removed following the completion of Operation Odyssey Dawn in late March.[58] Also in April, Western military advisers began to pour in, primarily from the UK and France, to train some of the rebel units, especially those in the Nafusa Mountains.[59]

By this point the limitations of the NATO mission had become evident. Regime forces had learned to disguise themselves as rebels or civilians.[60] NATO was often unwilling, moreover, to go beyond its mandate of protecting civilians, angering rebel fighters that would ask for strikes on targets to no avail. Opposition forces would go as far as trying to provoke

Qaddafi troops to fire in the direction of civilians in order to instigate a NATO response.[61]

Around this time, at the start of May, the French stepped up their unilateral involvement, going ahead without their allies "because there was no other way to proceed," according to a senior source at the time. France began airdropping weapons directly into the eastern mountains, sending in rocket launchers, assault rifles, machine guns, and anti-tank missiles.[62]

The fall of Tripoli

By most accounts, the fall of Tripoli in late August 2011 reveals a regime hollowed out by defections, low in morale, and drained of resources. The NATO-enforced embargo had by then been in place for six months, and although weapons transit from the south was still a realistic option for the regime, the northern coast was totally blocked off—even access to fuel was becoming a serious issue.[63] Regime officials made a trip to China around this time to secure new arms, but the deal was reportedly never completed.[64] Conversely, NATO protection of key northern ports allowed tugboat shipments destined for rebels to move freely into Misrata.

Daily life in the capital, moreover, had become miserable. Journalist William Wheeler describes a desperate situation:

> Life in the capital had by then become the stuff of nightmares […] There were widespread rumors, accepted as fact, that the regime had planted bombs throughout the sewer system. Security forces were conducting nightly raids, arresting anyone suspected of activism, and distributing weapons to their supporters ahead of an expected rebel assault. "Every individual will be armed," Qaddafi announced. "Libya will become a hell."[65]

The date for the final rebel assault on Tripoli was pushed back twice, ultimately called for on August 20. Some sources believed on September 1 a massive execution was set to take place at Abu Selim, making the August 20 date even more crucial.[66] Regardless, for months, rebels had been training in the Nafusa Mountains preparing for the final battle, and weapons had been smuggled in to rebels residing in the capital. Inside Tripoli, fighter cells were clandestinely formed so that they would rise up against Qaddafi's troops as opposition forces would move in and attack the city in a double offensive.

Internal defections by those still within Qaddafi's forces were key to the success of the operation. In the weeks before the attack, army officers began issuing special permits to Tripoli residents seeking to "defend against rebels," which enabled these residents to obtain weapons from depots in the capital. Contrary to its intended purpose, many officers knew, and allowed for, weapons to be given to those who were planning to attack the regime.[67]

The marquee defector in waiting for the rebels, however, was Brigadier al-Barani Ishkal, Qaddafi's cousin and head of an important brigade charged with protecting an entrance to Tripoli. In the weeks leading up to the siege he had been coordinating with the NTC, and, unbeknownst to the regime, was ready to stand down and let opposition forces enter the city when they made their move.[68] In fact, by this point intelligence prowess may have finally shifted in favor of the rebels, as the regime appeared legitimately surprised by the August 20 attack.

Various observers described Qaddafi's forces on the night of August 20 as simply "melting away" when the rebels marched into Tripoli. Rather than stand their ground as the siege got underway, a large swath of Qaddafi's fighters simply removed their uniforms—revealing jeans and T-shirts they had worn just in case—and ran.[69]

As NTC Information Minister Mohamed Shammam said:

> The plan was very successful. Our assumption was that it would take a few days but the results were clear in a few hours. We were expecting more resistance from Gaddafi's troops. We thought they were determined to fight to the last moment but it seems like they got tired or lost the cause.[70]

The final rebel campaign on the capital was in many ways emblematic of how and why the Libyan war was won—what actors and factors combined to push Qaddafi out of power. In the weeks leading up to the attack, Libyan forces—some seasoned by their days fighting with the LIFG, many armed, and some trained by Qatar (if not Sudan or France)—strategized with British and French advisers in the Nafusa Mountains. NATO airstrikes took out key targets in the city once the assault began, and frustration with Qaddafi and a massive wave of defections among loyalists as the operation got underway made success all the more likely. While the war was undoubtedly won by Libyans, it must be recognized that the revolution's success was largely determined by the intervention of a diverse set of foreign actors motivated by myriad interests but united by the strong desire to see a world without Qaddafi.

Security implications of the revolution

During the uprising, the NTC and its allied revolutionary brigades encouraged liberated towns to set up their own military councils. The councils provided a modicum of hierarchical structure to the disparate armed groups in the various localities. They also, in theory at least, organized the groups for basic police activity in the absence of the state.[71] Some of these groups, however, used newly sanctioned authority for less benign purposes: engaging in smuggling and drug trafficking, taking control of major industries, and even starting conflicts with neighboring communities. Thus, in many cases, armed groups were beyond the control of the loosely state-affiliated security councils entrusted to oversee them.

In October of 2011, the interior ministry formed the Supreme Security Committee (SSC) as a temporary solution to the long-term problem of building a stable police force. By offering a lucrative salary the SSC rapidly attracted new recruits, and by spring 2012 there was upwards of 85,000 individuals serving.[72] The Ministry of Defense used a similar tactic a few months later, bringing together various armed brigades to form the Libyan Shield Force (LSF) to supplement the paltry national army.

The common thread running through all of these NTC security solutions—whether the formation of military councils, the SSC, or the LSF—was that these parallel institutions were formed via the wholesale adoption of existent brigades. In other words, units remained tied to specific communities but now operated with state sanction. This proved to be a fatal flaw. The central government was too weak, and perhaps simply too understaffed, to bring all militia members together, train them, and disperse them in such a way as to build national, as opposed to regional, loyalties and command structures.[73]

The discord engendered by hyper-local groups carrying out national government objectives has continued to place the security of the state on tenuous ground. In some instances local biases, historic alliances, or personal prejudices have prevented notionally state approved forces from carrying out their missions in a neutral manner. Famous examples abound: LSF units deployed to the south to break up communal warfare exacerbated the conflict by taking the side of their historic allies; in the west, a state-sanctioned brigade in Zintan similarly used its force to wreak havoc on its weaker traditional rival, the Mashashiya, who had no meaningful avenue for recourse; when Sufi shrines were desecrated by Islamist extremists, sympathetic SSC members allegedly refused to intervene and stop the destruction.

The fragmented nature of the war's conduct was a manifestation of an organic uprising against a regime that ruled over a state with no cohesive national identity and in fact exacerbated that characteristic. It was a war won by local militias rather than a national liberation army. The consequence in the post-conflict phase is such that disparate militias continue to operate with no unifying national vision, creating an environment conducive to violent competition that takes place as a new state struggles to emerge and build legitimacy.

The fractious politics of the post-revolutionary phase[74]

The handover of power from the unelected NTC to an elected institution marked the opening salvo of Libya's experiment in representative democracy. Elections for Libya's legislative body, the General National Congress (GNC), held in July 2012, were widely considered free and fair. They yielded a body in which 80 seats were allocated to political parties while 120 went to independent candidates. Two political forces, Mahmoud Jibril's National Forces Alliance (NFA) and the Muslim Brotherhood's Justice and Construction Party (JCP), dominated competition for the party list seats with the NFA coming out on top with a plurality (39 out of 80) of seats.

International media hailed the NFA's electoral victory as a surprising success by liberal secularist forces, but that was a misleading conclusion. As Mahmoud Jibril himself reiterated many times, the NFA coalition is neither liberal nor secular, but rather nationalist and non-ideological. Moreover, the 120 candidates who won independent seats did not initially align themselves with either of the two main groups, opting instead to support either of the two groups on an issue-by-issue basis.

In the end, the July 2012 elections produced a strong (but not dominant) non-Islamist faction led by the NFA, and a statistically weaker (but more cohesive) and ideologically motivated Islamist opposition led by the JCP. Given this ideological polarization and the fragmentation of independent members and smaller parties, no majority coalition was formed. Thus, early into the GNC's tenure, Libyan politics moved behind the curtain and politicking became increasingly opaque.

The results of the July 2012 GNC elections and somewhat misguided media coverage obscured the relative strengths of the parties involved. Jibril's NFA obtained an admittedly impressive 39 of the 80 seats available to party lists, while the Muslim Brotherhood's JCP came in a distant second with only 19. This led many commentators to proclaim a liberal victory in the elections. However, this hasty assessment ignored the fact that it was unclear how the remaining 120 independents would align themselves, and whether the loosely connected NFA members would follow Jibril's marching orders or pursue different agendas.

A noteworthy opinion poll conducted by the Libyan Center for Research and Development just after the elections found that 81 percent of those who voted for NFA did so because it was headed by Mahmoud Jibril. Among the primary reasons for his selection, voters noted the absence of prominent leaders from other political movements that could compete with him, or match his experience and qualifications. Votes for Jibril and, by extension, the NFA were based less on the nuance of his ideology or party platform and more on the perceived competency of his leadership. Hasty media analysis proclaiming a liberal sweep made incorrect assumptions about voters' intentions. Moreover, Jibril himself often noted that his party was neither secular nor liberal, but rather on ideological and nationalist. He stressed the fact that everybody in Libya is Muslim, and the words "secular" and "liberal" are understood to be incompatible with Islam.

As it turned out, the NFA was unable to win over enough of the 120 independent members or to form a strong coalition with other political forces to grant them control of key items on the GNC's agenda. Although its primary rival, the JCP, was also unable to form a coalition it would begin to demonstrate its ability to rally independents—largely Islamist sympathizers—in order to prevent Jibril's hegemony within the GNC. In the early months of the GNC, the Muslim Brotherhood was twice able to block the NFA's top candidates from key positions: first, in the race for speaker, and subsequently in the race for prime minister.

These early political confrontations immediately demonstrated two key points about GNC politics that collectively set the stage for political gridlock. First, the NFA did not have enough votes to unilaterally set the agenda. Second, the Brotherhood would exert great effort to avoid working with Jibril and the NFA.

This extreme polarization was exemplified by the struggle over the highly controversial political isolation law, a piece of legislation aimed at preventing individuals who worked for the Qaddafi regime from serving in any public position for a period of ten years. Because of its direct impact on many members then in government and the assembly, it was fought bitterly. The law's approval was stalled in parliament for several months until those who supported it (mostly Islamist groups and some of the militias) orchestrated a quasi-*coup d'état* by besieging several institutional buildings with armed militias and vociferously calling for the immediate adoption of the law. Immediately after passage of the law in May 2013, it became clear that it was simply an attempt to cover a bid for power by groups inside and outside the GNC. Their goal was to reach a result they did not have the legal means to obtain otherwise: the overthrow of the Ali Zidan government and the installation of a prime minister more sympathetic to their values and reasons.

Although it never successfully removed Zidan, the political isolation law controversy put the country's post-revolution divides on full display and highlighted the latent dangers of the country's powerful lingering revolutionaries. One of the key questions following the war and during the political rebuilding process was how best to include the thousands of *thuwwar*, or revolutionary fighters. The *thuwwar* were largely left out of the political process from the GNC's inception. They remain restless and angry, asserting that the revolution's goals of change have not been fulfilled, and are critical that too much attention is given to former members of the regime who defected only at the last moment (many of whom now associate with Jibril's NFA).

The GNC's fragmentation and the collision between the two main blocs—loosely defined as Islamists (led by the JCP) and non-Islamists (led by the NFA)—essentially paralyzed the decision-making process throughout the year following the body's formation and brought about a dangerous polarization of the political landscape. This, along with the *thuwwar*'s perception of their marginalization, collectively produced a highly polarized and mistrusted GNC that, instead of addressing the country's woes and driving reconstruction, became a microcosm of its poor health: a weak, fragmented, politically stalled body. The GNC practically lost its legitimacy and its protracted inactivity put the entire transition process at serious risk. In the spring of 2014, the crisis reached its peak, and, while the GNC succeeded to overthrow Zidan, public pressure forced the legislative body to accept resignation and to call for new elections.

The Constitutional Committee and the National Dialogue

On February 20, 2014, Libya held elections to form the Constitutional Committee that is responsible for drafting the country's new constitution. An incremental step forward, the electoral law guiding the vote nevertheless raised serious questions about the inclusiveness of the overall process. It called for equal representation for Libya's three historical provinces (20 for Cyrenaica, 20 for Tripolitania, and 20 for Fezzan), despite great disparities in population sizes between the provinces. Moreover, the law allocated only six seats for women and only six seats altogether for the three minority groups (the Tebu, Tuareg, and Amazigh). In protest, the Amazigh effectively boycotted the process by refusing to put forth any candidates. Even the Tebu minority, who at the beginning seemed to be willing to participate, withdrew their support in the days leading up to election day.

In a sign of growing apathy and frustration with Libya's ineffective political institutions, only a little more than one million voters registered to cast their ballots, significantly lower than the 2.7 million voters who registered for the GNC elections in 2012. According to official figures from the Higher National Elections Commission, only around 45 percent of registered voters participated in the elections, raising further questions about the legitimacy of the Constitutional Committee. Security concerns deterred polling centers in certain cities from opening at all, resulting in only 47 of the 60 seats being filled. Efforts to organize additional rounds of election over the following months have proven ineffective.

According to the timetable outlined in the Temporary Constitutional Declaration (TCD), the Constitutional Committee has four months from its first meeting to draft a constitution. In a symbolic move, the committee held an inaugural session in Bayda in April 2014, but a second meeting will only be held after the remaining vacant seats are filled. Given challenges to forming the body, the drafting phase will most likely take longer than planned, raising questions and concerns about the mechanisms in place to relax the drafting deadline without losing the public's faith in the committee's productivity.

Beyond inclusiveness, deadlines, and security threats to the committee's operations, there are several other big-picture questions that deserve careful consideration to ensure that the constitutional drafting process moves forward effectively. If the Constitutional Committee drafts a constitution that the GNC or its successor body approves, then the constitution will be put to a popular referendum within 30 days. If rejected by the GNC or the people, however, then the committee will have to rework a new draft. As the committee is itself elected, it may chaff at the GNC or successor body's rejection of its first draft, leading to competition for jurisdictional territory and eventual brinksmanship. Moreover, little consideration has been given to which elected body is in charge of public outreach to ensure transparency and inform citizens of the committee's deliberations—an important ingredient for restoring the body's legitimacy after a shaky start.[75]

The one parallel track that provides the best answer to the outstanding questions delineated above is the National Dialogue.[76] In August 2013, Prime Minister Ali Zidan belatedly endorsed the idea. With the absence of a state functioning ably enough to provide much-needed services to its citizens, the initiative was meant to convene the collective Libyan polity and citizenry to have a shared national discussion exploring what it means to be Libyan and what the country's direction ought to be. The independent Preparatory Commission established to define a framework for the dialogue has since been traveling throughout the country in an outreach campaign to gauge public opinion on the issues they would like to see addressed in the National Dialogue.[77] While the criteria and process for selecting delegates for the National Dialogue conference remain undetermined, upon selection they will debate the drafting of a national charter. There is significant collaboration with and support from the United Nations in building a model that will ensure representation of Libya's many stakeholders. In theory, the six-month timeframe for the dialogue would culminate in proposed solutions to be taken up for ratification.

At present, there is no legal framework in place that would guarantee that the findings and proposals of the National Dialogue would be legally binding. By extension, it is unclear how, if at all, the output of the National Dialogue might feed into the constitution-drafting process. A constitution is intended to be reflective of national values and priorities. Especially given the inherent difficulty of making the constitution-drafting process both participatory and inclusive, connecting it to the National Dialogue could help restore the population's sense of investment in the country's political direction and future. As such, an idea appears to be taking root within Libya to include the Constitutional Committee members in the National Dialogue, although the parameters of such an arrangement are not yet clearly defined. This would lend the necessary legal weight to the dialogue process and create a mechanism by which its findings would be absorbed into the constitutional-writing process, such as the principles derived from the dialogue serving as a basis for the constitutional preamble.

Political implications of the revolution

At the end of May 2014, the security and political situation in Libya is nearing collapse. Targeted assassinations of officials, car bombs, and attacks against foreign delegations, widespread criminal activity, increased smuggling of weapons, drugs, and alcohol through the porous borders of the country, and the lack of any improvement in the actions of the elected institutions all give the impression of Libya quickly becoming a failed state. Nevertheless, it has to be pointed out that current events in Libya are the result of a series of causes, rooted in the revolution. While there is much focus on how to address the deteriorating security situation, it is in fact the *effect* of other policies and not the cause of the crisis.[78]

In hindsight, one can pinpoint two original causes that have been overlooked and misunderstood by analysts and policymakers and that are the reason for much of today's turmoil. First, there was no recognition by the Libyan elites and the international community that the revolution was indeed a "civil war." Libyans fought against Libyans; this was not just a case of popular revolution against the foreign mercenaries of a dictator (as the opposition's initial propaganda wanted to convey). The consequence of this mischaracterization has been the oversight of the necessity of a national reconciliation program in order to mend the increasing rift between the various parts of society and to establish a political and social vision for the new Libya based on shared basic principles. It has been almost three years since the fall of the dictatorship; the fact that the National Dialogue has not yet taken place is one of the reasons why large parts of the society still feel marginalized and are probably taking measures to destabilize the state, which they view as an enemy since it is an entity that they have no role in building.

The second reason is the lack of recognition that foreign support was important in winning the war and overthrowing Qaddafi. The rhetoric employed by the former leaders of the NTC (Jibril, Abdul Jalil, and others) about Libyans having achieved such feats all by themselves created expectations in the population of a capable new leadership and instilled a sense of "mission accomplished" among the foreigners who were more than happy to leave the country immediately after the liberation. This resulted in the Western countries' premature departure, rather than their harnessing of the Libyans' good will in order to support the nascent Libyan institutions, strengthen them *vis-á-vis* their opponents, and create a security climate more conducive to the reconstruction of the state. This has left the country in the hands of the militias, which formed at the beginning of the revolution to conduct the war. The powerlessness of the central government allowed for their entrenchment and turned them *de facto* into a force with interests fundamentally at odds with the state.

These two root causes were compounded by the new Libyan elites' lack of capacity to act, as both the government and the elected General National Congress (GNC) were composed of inexperienced politicians and bureaucrats. These institutions blocked each other in a series of quarrels regarding distribution and exercise of power that produced a paralysis. The inaction, ineffectiveness, or both of the state has gradually chipped away at the Libyan institutions' legitimacy in the eyes of the population. This has opened ample space where the enemies of the revolution—from former Qaddafians to members of the deep state, from criminal organizations to jihadi terrorists—thrive in a climate of perennial state weakness and paralysis. Even the Egyptian military's *coup d'état* against the Islamist-led government in Cairo has exacerbated tensions between Libya's Islamists and non-Islamists, revealing the existence of interests—domestic and foreign—further undermining the democratic stabilization and institutional development of the Libyan state.

Despite all of these negative developments, the success of the democratic transition in Libya is by no means doomed. There are a few factors that still play an instrumental role in preventing Libya from the verge of collapse.

A good example of this happened recently. In early May 2013, Islamist groups and some aligned militias exerted unprecedented pressure on the state institutions in order to pass the law of political isolation, which they saw as favorable for their bid to power. These groups besieged government institutions and forced the GNC to pass the law. While this was surely a negative development, on the other hand, it is important to notice that something prevented these groups from carrying out their objective in an egregious push against the state to take power entirely. They did not, for example, storm the ministries and force the current leadership to step down with the butt of their guns. That is because they realize that the international community would immediately condemn such action and that the Libyan people would not accept being relegated once again to the role of a pariah state through political and economic isolation by the international community. Therefore, militias and political groups know that their battle for political hegemony has to be carried out through "legal" or semi-legal means.

Given all of this, it is of utmost importance that the international community pay attention to and maintain a strong stance against any deviation from the transition to democracy. So far the international community, and particularly the United States, has been very staunch in this position and has not bowed to any pressure. If this support remains active, and the government of Libya can begin to function and carry out policies that restore the confidence of its citizens, the risk of an overtly aggressive and extralegal push will be repelled. More recently, the election of the Constitutional Committee, as well as the initiation of the National Dialogue process, constitute an example of a step forward and reason for optimism. If the Constitutional Committee and the National Dialogue conference can involve the Libyan people and its civil society in an inclusive and transparent way, the road to democracy, albeit bumpy, will have taken a major step forward. Just as the success of the Libyan revolution was the culmination of measures taken by a range of actors, so too will Libya's democratic transition require robust assistance from the international community working side by side with the Libyan people as the country faces numerous obstacles ahead.

References

Barakat, S., "The Qatari Spring: Qatar's Emerging Role in Peacemaking," London School of Economics and Political Science Kuwait Programme on Development, Governance, and Globalisation in the Gulf States, no. 24, July 2012, www2.lse.ac.uk/government/research/resgroups/kuwait/documents/The-Qatari-Spring%20-%20Qatars-Emerging-Role-in-Peacemaking.pdf.

Bronner, E. and Sanger, D.E., "Arab League endorses no-flight zone over Libya," *The New York Times*, 12 March 2011, http://www.nytimes.com/2011/03/13/world/middleeast/13libya.html?pagewanted=all.

CBS News, "UN Security Council Mulls Libya No-Fly Zone," *CBS News*, March 16, 2011, www.cbsnews.com/2100–2202_162–20043868.html.

Chivvis, C., "Libya and the Future of Liberal Intervention," *Survival: Global Politics and Strategy*, vol. 54, no. 6, 2012.

Chivvis, C., *Toppling Qaddafi: Libya and the Limits of Liberal Intervention* (New York: Cambridge University Press, 2013).

Chorin, E., *Exit Gaddafi* (London: Saqi, 2012).

CNN.com, "CNN Factsheet: Libya Sanctions", February 10, 2004, www.cnn.com/2004/WORLD/africa/02/10/libya.sanctions.facts.

Coker, M., "Qatar Recognizes Libyan Rebel Council," *Wall Street Journal*, March 28, 2011, http://online.wsj.com/article/SB10001424052748704559904576228341860730126.html.

Coker, M., Dagher, S., and Levinson, C., "Tiny Kingdom's Huge Role in Libya Draws Concern," *The Wall Street Journal*, October 17, 2011, http://online.wsj.com/article/SB10001424052970204002304576627000922764650.html.

De Waal, A., "African Roles in the Libyan Conflict of 2011," *International Affairs*, vol. 89, March 2013, www.chathamhouse.org/sites/default/files/public/International%20Affairs/2013/89_2/89_2deWaal.pdf.

Dempsey, J., "Berlin Denies it Approved Training for Libyan Police," *The New York Times*, April 7, 2008, www.nytimes.com/2008/04/07/world/europe/07iht-germany.4.11740759.html?_r=2Rebels Say Qatar Ready to Market East Libyan Oil," *Reuters*, March 27, 2011, www.reuters.com/article/2011/03/27/us-libya-rebels-oil-idUSTRE72Q1ON20110327.

Elhag, A., "The Sudanese Role in Libya 2011," *Reinventing Peace*, 2011, http://sites.tufts.edu/reinventingpeace/2012/12/17/the-sudanese-role-in-libya-2011.

Emsden, C., "Italy's 'Unusual' Friendship Treaty with Libya," *The Wall Street Journal*, February 25, 2011, http://blogs.wsj.com/source/2011/02/25/italys-unusual-friendship-treaty-with-libya.

EU Observer, "The Untold Story of Libya's Mahmud Gebril," *EU Observer*, May 18, 2013, http://blogs.euobserver.com/debeuf/2013/05/18/the-untold-story-of-libyas-mahmud-gebril.

The Guardian, "EU Arms Exports to Libya: Who Armed Gaddafi?," *The Guardian*, March 1, 2011, www.guardian.co.uk/news/datablog/2011/mar/01/eu-arms-exports-libya.

——, "EU Lifts Libya Sanctions," *The Guardian*, October 11, 2004, www.guardian.co.uk/world/2004/oct/11/libya.eu.

——, "Gaddafi Son: 'We Will Eradicate Them All,'" *The Guardian*, February 21, 2011, www.guardian.co.uk/world/2011/feb/21/gaddafi-son-muammar-libya.

——, "Saif al-Islam Gaddafi: LSE-educated Man the West Can No Longer Deal With," *The Guardian*, February 21, 2011, www.guardian.co.uk/world/2011/feb/21/saif-al-islam-gaddafi.

Freeman, C., "How Britain Courted, Armed and Trained a Libyan Monster," *The Telegraph*, September 25, 2011, www.telegraph.co.uk/news/worldnews/africaand indianocean/libya/8786897/How-Britain-courted-armed-and-trained-a-Libyan-monster.html.

France 24, "Gaddafi Offers to Host Russian Naval Base," *France 24*, October 31, 2008, www.france24.com/en/20081031-gaddafi-offers-host-russian-naval-base-libya.

Grech, H., "Gaddafi Threatened Oil Spill off Malta in 2011," *Times of Malta*, April 28, 2013, www.timesofmalta.com/articles/view/20130428/local/Gaddafi-threatened-oil-spill-off-Malta-in-2011.467465.

Hilsum, L., *Sandstorm: Libya in the Time of Revolution* (London: Faber and Faber, 2012)

International Crisis Group, "Divided We Stand: Libya's Enduring Conflicts," September 14, 2012.

Jeune Afrique, "Libye: la France parachute des armes pour les rebelles," *Jeune Afrique/AFP*, June 29, 2011, www.jeuneafrique.com/Article/ARTJAWEB20110629151544.

Kirkpatrick, D.D., Erlanger, S., and Bumiller, E., "Allies Open Air Assault on Qaddafi's Forces in Libya," *The New York Times*, March 19, 2011, www.nytimes.com/2011/03/20/world/africa/20libya.html?pagewanted=all.

Lutterbeck, D., "Arming Libya: Transfers of Conventional Weapons Past and Present," *Contemporary Security Policy*, vol. 30, no. 3, 2009.

McQuinn, B., "After the Fall," Small Arms Survey, October 2012, www.smallarmssurvey.org/fileadmin/docs/F-Working-papers/SAS-WP12-After-the-Fall-Libya.pdf.

Mezran, K., "Libya in Transition: From *Jamahiriya* to *Jumhuriyyah*?", in F.A. Gerges (ed.), *The New Middle East: Protest and Revolution in the Arab World* (New York: Cambridge University Press, 2014).

Mezran, K. and Pickard, D., "Negotiating Libya's Constitution," January 2014, www.atlanticcouncil.org/images/publications/Negotiating_Libyas_Constitution.pdf.

Mezran, K., Lamen, F., and Knecht, E., "Post-revolutionary Politics in Libya: Inside the General National Congress," Atlantic Council Rafik Hariri Center for the Middle East, May 2013, www.atlanticcouncil.org/images/publications/postrevolutionary_politics_libya.pdf.

Pack, J. (ed.), *The 2011 Libyan Uprisings and the Struggle for the Post-Qadhafi Future* (New York: Palgrave Macmillan, 2013).

Pack, J., Mezran, K., and Eljarh, M., "Libya's Faustian Bargains: Breaking the Appeasement Cycle," *Atlantic Council Report*, May 5, 2014, http://libya-al-mostakbal.org/uploads/files/Libyas_Faustian_Bargains.pdf.

Pargeter, A., *Libya: The Rise and Fall of Qaddafi* (New Haven and London: Yale University Press, 2012).

Rayner, G., "Libya: Secret Role Played by Britain Creating Path to the Fall of Tripoli," *The Telegraph*, August 22, 2011, www.telegraph.co.uk/news/worldnews/africaandindianocean/libya/8716758/Libya-secret-role-played-by-Britain-creating-path-to-the-fall-of-Tripoli.html.

Reuters, "Gaddafi tells Benghazi his army is coming tonight," *Reuters*, March 17, 2011, http://uk.reuters.com/article/2011/03/17/libya-gaddafi-address-idUKLDE72G2E920110317.

Sands, P., "The Accomplice," *Vanity Fair*, August 2011, www.vanityfair.com/politics/features/2011/08/qaddafi-201108.

Shuster, S., "The Tyrant of Belarus: Gaddafi's Friend Far, Far to the North?," *Time*, March 2, 2011, www.time.com/time/world/article/0,8599,2056420–22,00.html.

SIPRI Arms Transfer Database, http://armstrade.sipri.org/armstrade/page/trade_register.php.

Solomon, A., "Circle of Fire," *The New Yorker*, May 8, 2006, www.newyorker.com/archive/2006/05/08/060508fa_fact_solomon.

"Turmoil in Libya and the Darfur Conflict," Sudan Human Security Baseline Assessment, Chr. Michelsen Institute, April 2011, www.cmi.no/file/?1235.

Sudan Tribune, "Bashir Says Sudan Armed Libyan Rebels," *Sudan Tribune*, October 27, 2011, www.sudantribune.com/spip.php?article40547.

The Telegraph, "Libyan Islamic Fighting Group Revises Jihadist Ideology," *The Telegraph*, January 31, 2011, www.telegraph.co.uk/news/wikileaks-files/libya-wikileaks/8294700/LIBYAN-ISLAMIC-FIGHTING-GROUP-REVISES-JIHADIST-IDEOLOGY. html.

United Nations Security Council, *Final Report of the Panel of Experts Established Pursuant to Security Council Resolution 1973 (2011) Concerning Libya*, 2012, www.securitycouncilreport.org/atf/cf/%7B65BFCF9B-6D27-4E9C-8CD3-CF6E4FF96FF9%7D/Libya%20S%202012%20163.pdf, 2012.

UN Panel of Experts on Libya, "Final Report," March 20, 2012, www.securitycouncilreport.org/atf/cf/%7B65BFCF9B-6D27-4E9C-8CD3-CF6E4FF96FF9%7D/Libya%20S%202012%20163.pdf.

UN Panel of Experts on Libya, "Report," www.securitycouncilreport.org/atf/cf/%7B65BFCF9B-6D27-4E9C-8CD3-CF6E4FF96FF9%7D/s_2013_99.pdf.

Verini, J., "The Good Bad Son," *New York Magazine*, May 22, 2011, http://nymag.com/news/politics/saif-qaddafi-2011-5.

Warrick, J., "Clinton Credited With Key Role in Success of NATO Airstrikes, Libyan Rebels," *The Washington Post*, October 30, 2011, http://articles.washingtonpost.com/2011-10-30/world/35277483_1_brega-misurata-benghazi.

Wehrey, F., "The Hidden Story of Airpower in Libya," *Foreign Policy*, February 11, 2013, http://mideast.foreignpolicy.com/posts/2013/02/11/the_hidden_story_of_airpower_in_libya.

Wheeler, W., "Zero Hour," *McSweeney's Quarterly Concern*, vol. 43, 2013.

Wollenberg, A. and Pack, J., "Rebels with a Pen: Observations on the Newly Emerging Media Landscape in Libya," *The Journal of North African Studies*, vol. 18, no. 2, 2013, www.tandfonline.com/doi/abs/10.1080/13629387.2013.767197#.UZ5tjiuuszQ.

Notes

1 For a general overview of the Libyan transition and its developments, see K. Mezran, "Libya in Transition: From *Jamahiriya* to *Jumhuriyyah*?," in F.A. Gerges (ed.), *The New Middle East: Protest and Revolution in the Arab World* (New York: Cambridge University Press, 2014).

2 CNN.com, "CNN Factsheet: Libya Sanctions," February 10, 2004, www.cnn.com/2004/WORLD/africa/02/10/libya.sanctions.facts (accessed May 20, 2014)

3 *The Guardian*, "EU Lifts Libya Sanctions," *The Guardian*, October 11, 2004, www.guardian.co.uk/world/2004/oct/11/libya.eu (accessed May 20, 2014).

4 *The Telegraph*, "Libyan Islamic Fighting Group Revises Jihadist Ideology," *The Telegraph*, January 31, 2011, www.telegraph.co.uk/news/wikileaks-files/libya-wikileaks/8294700/LIBYAN-ISLAMIC-FIGHTING-GROUP-REVISES-JIHADIST-IDEOLOGY.html (accessed May 20, 2014).

5 E. Chorin, *Exit Gaddafi* (London: Saqi, 2012), p. 158.

6 J. Verini, "The Good Bad Son," *New York Magazine*, May 22, 2011, http://nymag.com/news/politics/saif-qaddafi-2011-5 (accessed May 20, 2014).

7 P. Sands, "The Accomplice," *Vanity Fair*, August 2011, www.vanityfair.com/politics/features/2011/08/qaddafi-201108 (accessed May 20, 2014).

8 See www.youtube.com/watch?v=eL6I5hktEs0 (accessed May 20, 2014).

9 *The Guardian*, "Gaddafi Son: 'We Will Eradicate Them All,'" *The Guardian*, February 21, 2011, www.guardian.co.uk/world/2011/feb/21/gaddafi-son-muammar-libya (accessed May 20, 2014).

10 The London School of Economics, where Saif had completed graduate work and given generous donations, immediately cut off their relationship and rejected upcoming tranches of aid previously scheduled by Saif. Other individuals on the board of Saif's charitable foundation immediately resigned. See *The Guardian*, "Saif al-Islam Gaddafi: LSE-educated Man the West Can No Longer Deal With," *The Guardian*, February 21, 2011, www.guardian.co.uk/world/2011/feb/21/saif-al-islam-gaddafi (accessed May 20, 2014).

11 For an in-depth discussion of African Union attempts at political settlement and their ultimate failure, see A. De Waal, "African Roles in the Libyan Conflict of 2011," *International Affairs*, vol. 89, March 2013, pp. 365–79, www.chathamhouse.org/sites/default/files/public/International%20Affairs/2013/89_2/89_2deWaal.pdf (accessed May 20, 2014).

12 D. Lutterbeck, "Arming Libya: Transfers of Conventional Weapons Past and Present," *Contemporary Security Policy*, vol. 30, no. 3, 2009.
13 SIPRI Arms Transfer Database, http://armstrade.sipri.org/armstrade/page/trade_register.php (accessed May 20, 2014).
14 For France, selling Rafale jets remains a key strategic interest, as it is produced almost entirely by French defense contractors Dassault, Thales, and Safran, and succesful deals imply thousands of French jobs. During the rapprochement period France considered Libya a key strategic market for its declining defense industry.
15 The Rafale jet has never been successfully integrated into a military outside of France. It is often considered overpriced with its competitors, and not battle tested. This has led some to accuse France, unfairly or not, of using the conflicts in Libya and Mali to market their Rafale jets.
16 D.D. Kirkpatrick, S. Erlanger, and E. Bumiller, "Allies Open Air Assault on Qaddafi's Forces in Libya," *The New York Times*, March 19, 2011, www.nytimes.com/2011/03/20/world/africa/20libya.html?pagewanted=all (accessed May 20, 2014).
17 Chorin, op. cit., p. 136.
18 C. Freeman, "How Britain Courted, Armed and Trained a Libyan Monster," *The Telegraph*, September 25, 2011, www.telegraph.co.uk/news/worldnews/africaandindianocean/libya/8786897/How-Britain-courted-armed-and-trained-a-Libyan-monster.html (accessed May 20, 2014).
19 *The Guardian*, "EU Arms Exports to Libya: Who Armed Gaddafi?," *The Guardian*, March 1, 2011, www.guardian.co.uk/news/datablog/2011/mar/01/eu-arms-exports-libya (accessed May 20, 2014).
20 J. Dempsey, "Berlin Denies it Approved Training for Libyan Police," *The New York Times*, April 7, 2008, www.nytimes.com/2008/04/07/world/europe/07iht-germany.4.11740759.html?_r=2& (accessed May 20, 2014).
21 Chorin, op. cit., p. 139.
22 Belarus is believed to have stocked Qaddafi with arms just as the uprising was getting underway in the final two weeks of February, right up until the UN arms embargo was in place. See S. Shuster, "The Tyrant of Belarus: Gaddafi's Friend Far, Far to the North?," *Time*, 2 March 2011, www.time.com/time/world/article/0,8599,2056420–22,00.html (accessed May 20, 2014).
23 A. Solomon, "Circle of Fire," *The New Yorker*, May 8, 2006, www.newyorker.com/archive/2006/05/08/060508fa_fact_solomon (accessed May 20, 2014).
24 *France 24*, "Gaddafi Offers to Host Russian Naval Base," *France 24*, October 31, 2008, www.france24.com/en/20081031-gaddafi-offers-host-russian-naval-base-libya (accessed May 20, 2014).
25 C. Emsden, "Italy's 'Unusual' Friendship Treaty with Libya," *The Wall Street Journal*, February 25, 2011, http://blogs.wsj.com/source/2011/02/25/italys-unusual-friendship-treaty-with-libya (accessed May 20, 2014).
26 Chorin, op. cit., p. 200.
27 J. Pack (ed.), *The 2011 Libyan Uprisings and the Struggle for the Post-Qadhafi Future* (New York: Palgrave Macmillan, 2013), pp. 71–2.
28 Chorin, op. cit., p. 205. The earlier, pre-NTC statement made by members of the February 17 Coalition was itself noteworthy. It called for a democratic, unified Libya, and, more importantly, was interpreted by Ambassador Chris Stevens at the time as meaning there were legitimate interlocutors that could be worked with (see Chorin, op. cit., p. 197).
29 *EU Observer*, "The Untold Story of Libya's Mahmud Gebril," *EU Observer*, May 18, 2013, http://blogs.euobserver.com/debeuf/2013/05/18/the-untold-story-of-libyas-mahmud-gebril (accessed May 20, 2014).
30 Chorin, op. cit., p. 224.

31 E. Bronner and D.E. Sanger, "Arab League Endorses No-flight Zone Over Libya," *The New York Times*, March 12, 2011, www.nytimes.com/2011/03/13/world/middleeast/13libya.html?pagewanted=all (accessed May 20, 2014).
32 Pack, op. cit., Chapter 4.
33 Algeria is believed to be the only Arab country to directly support Qaddafi during the uprising, sending arms and supplies to bolster loyalist forces. Though Algerian President Bouteflika did not hold Qaddafi in high regard, he likely wanted to prevent Libya from becoming an unstable zone ripe for jihadist operations, a fear brought to life by the In Amenas hostage crisis in January 2013.
34 "Gaddafi Tells Benghazi His Army is Coming Tonight," *Reuters*, March 17, 2011, http://uk.reuters.com/article/2011/03/17/libya-gaddafi-address-idUKLDE72G2E920110317 (accessed May 20, 2014).
35 *CBS News*, "UN Security Council Mulls Libya No-fly Zone," *CBS News*, March 16, 2011, www.cbsnews.com/2100–2202_162–20043868.html (accessed May 20, 2014).
36 For a detailed overview of the Western intervention in Libya, see C. Chivvis, *Toppling Qaddafi: Libya and the Limits of Liberal Intervention* (New York: Cambridge University Press, 2013) and C. Chivvis, "Libya and the Future of Liberal Intervention," in *Survival: Global Politics and Strategy*, vol. 54, no. 6, 2012, pp. 69–92.
37 Chorin, op. cit., p. 228.
38 J. Warrick, "Clinton Credited With Key Role in Success of NATO Airstrikes, Libyan Rebels," *The Washington Post*, October 30, 2011, http://articles.washingtonpost.com/2011-10-30/world/35277483_1_brega-misurata-benghazi (accessed May 20, 2014).
39 For an excellent graphic tracking the progressive military movements of the war see Chivvis, "Libya and the Future of Liberal Intervention," op. cit., p. 73.
40 As noted earlier, many likely underestimated the extent to which Qaddafi had upgraded his armed forces in the years prior. The regime's ability to attract large numbers of mercenaries, many from Sudan, Niger, Chad, and Mali, was also a key factor.
41 M. Coker, "Qatar Recognizes Libyan Rebel Council," *Wall Street Journal*, March 28, 2011, http://online.wsj.com/article/SB10001424052748704559904576228341860730126.html (accessed May 20, 2014).
42 According to the UNSCR 1973, which, in addition to a no-fly zone also imposed an arms embargo on Libya, member states wishing to provide military assistance were required to notify the UN secretary general and specify the assistance granted, which Qatar largely did not do. According to a UN panel of experts tasked with following up on the matter, "Qatar denied that it had ever transferred any materiel to the revolutionaries … The Panel therefore considers that [Qatar] never intended to utilize the provisions of the sanctions regime to deliver arms and ammunition and therefore provided this materiel to the Libyan opposition in breach of the arms embargo." See UN Panel of Experts on Libya, "Report," p. 15, www.securitycouncilreport.org/atf/cf/%7B65BFCF9B-6D27–4E9C-8CD3-CF6E4FF96FF9%7D/s_2013_99.pdf (accessed May 20, 2014).
43 Pack, op. cit., Chapter 4.
44 A. Dziadosz, "Rebels Say Qatar Ready to Market East Libyan Oil," *Reuters*, March 27 2011, www.reuters.com/article/2011/03/27/us-libya-rebels-oil-idUSTRE72Q1ON20110327 (accessed May 20, 2014).
45 For an in-depth analysis of media proliferation during the revolution see A. Wollenberg and J. Pack, "Rebels with a Pen: Observations on the Newly Emerging Media Landscape in Libya," *The Journal of North African Studies*, vol. 18, no. 2, 2013, www.tandfonline.com/doi/abs/10.1080/13629387.2013.767197#.UZ5tjiuuszQ (accessed May 20, 2014).
46 UN Panel of Experts on Libya, "Final Report," March 20, 2012, p. 25, www.securitycouncilreport.org/atf/cf/%7B65BFCF9B-6D27–4E9C-8CD3-CF6E4FF96FF9%7D/Libya%20S%202012%20163.pdf (accessed May 20, 2014).

47 Final Report of the Panel of Experts established pursuant to Security Council Resolution 1973 (2011) concerning Libya, Annex V.
48 S. Barakat, "The Qatari Spring: Qatar's Emerging Role in Peacemaking," London School of Economics and Political Science Kuwait Programme on Development, Governance, and Globalisation in the Gulf States, no. 24, July 2012, www2.lse.ac.uk/government/research/resgroups/kuwait/documents/The-Qatari-Spring%20-%20Qatars-Emerging-Role-in-Peacemaking.pdf (accessed May 20, 2014).
49 M. Coker, S. Dagher, and C. Levinson, "Tiny Kingdom's Huge Role in Libya Draws Concern," *The Wall Street Journal*, October 17, 2011, http://online.wsj.com/article/SB10001424052970204002304576627000922764650.html (accessed May 20, 2014).
50 Sudan itself was a theater of diplomatic conflict and animosity between Qatar and Libya as each sought to be the key mediator in the Darfur conflict.
51 At the time of the uprising JEM leader Khalil Ibrahim was based in Tripoli after being expelled from Chad in 2010.
52 A. Elhag, "The Sudanese Role in Libya 2011," *Reinventing Peace*, http://sites.tufts.edu/reinventingpeace/2012/12/17/the-sudanese-role-in-libya-2011 (accessed May 20, 2014).
53 Final Report of the Panel of Experts established pursuant to Security Council Resolution 1973 (2011) concerning Libya.
54 "Turmoil in Libya and the Darfur Conflict," Sudan Human Security Baseline Assessment, Chr. Michelsen Institute, April 2011, www.cmi.no/file/?1235 (accessed May 20, 2014).
55 Elhag, op. cit.
56 B. McQuinn, "After the Fall," Small Arms Survey, October 2012, p. 44, www.smallarmssurvey.org/fileadmin/docs/F-Working-papers/SAS-WP12-After-the-Fall-Libya.pdf (accessed May 20, 2014).
57 "Bashir Says Sudan Armed Libyan Rebels," *Sudan Tribune*, October 27, 2011, www.sudantribune.com/spip.php?article40547 (accessed May 20, 2014).
58 Chivvis, "Libya and the Future of Liberal Intervention," op. cit., p. 77.
59 A UN report shows that on April 26, 2011, the UK, France, Italy, and US together all made large shipments, sending thousands of helmets, uniforms, body armor, sandbags, hescos, and tens of military advisers each. See Final Report of the Panel of Experts established pursuant to Security Council Resolution 1973 (2011) concerning Libya, p. 22.
60 Chivvis, "Libya and the Future of Liberal Intervention," op. cit., p. 74.
61 F. Wehrey, "The Hidden Story of Airpower in Libya," *Foreign Policy*, February 11, 2013, http://mideast.foreignpolicy.com/posts/2013/02/11/the_hidden_story_of_airpower_in_libya (accessed May 20, 2014).
62 *Jeune Afrique*, "Libye: la France parachute des armes pour les rebelles," *Jeune Afrique/AFP*, June 29, 2011, www.jeuneafrique.com/Article/ARTJAWEB20110629151544/ (accessed May 20, 2014).
63 While imposing its arms embargo, NATO hailed 3,100 ships, boarded 300 and denied 11 vessels access to Libyan ports—no breach of the arms embargo was reported. See UN Final Report 2012, p. 16 (44–5). In one of the more extreme examples, 30,000 tons of fuel desperately needed by the regime was held off the coast of Malta and kept from reaching loyalist forces in late July 2011. See H. Grech, "Gaddafi Threatened Oil Spill Off Malta in 2011," *Times of Malta*, April 28, 2013, www.timesofmalta.com/articles/view/20130428/local/Gaddafi-threatened-oil-spill-off-Malta-in-2011.467465 (accessed May 20, 2014).
64 Rebel military leader Omar Hariri claims to have seen some of the allegedly purchased Chinese weapons on the battlefield during August 2011 clashes in the Nafusa Mountains and Tripoli. See www.theworld.org/2011/09/documents-reveal-chinas-arms-connection-with-libya (accessed May 20, 2014). The Chinese Ministry of Foreign affairs acknowledged the trip by Qaddafi officials had taken place but

expressly denied that any deal was signed. See UN Panel of Experts Final Report 2012, p. 17 (54–5).

65 W. Wheeler, "Zero Hour," in D. Eggers (ed.), *McSweeney's Quarterly Concern*, vol. 43, 2013, p. 110.

66 Ibid., p. 118.

67 Ibid., p. 110.

68 A. Pargeter, *Libya: The Rise and Fall of Qaddafi* (New Haven and London: Yale University Press, 2012), p. 241.

69 L. Hilsum, *Sandstorm: Libya in the Time of Revolution* (London: Faber and Faber, 2012), p. 248.

70 G. Rayner, "Libya: Secret Role Played by Britain Creating Path to the Fall of Tripoli," *The Telegraph*, August 22, 2011, www.telegraph.co.uk/news/worldnews/africaandindianocean/libya/8716758/Libya-secret-role-played-by-Britain-creating-path-to-the-fall-of-Tripoli.html (accessed May 20, 2014).

71 These councils and the armed groups they presided over existed separately from the revolutionary brigades engaged in active combat with Qaddafi's forces. In other words, many of these local groups never fought in the war and should thus be thought of more as rogue police forces.

72 International Crisis Group, "Divided We Stand: Libya's Enduring Conflicts," September 14, 2012, p. 12.

73 A notable attempt to centrally train and employ former and active militia members did occur under the Warrior Affairs Committee (WAC), which held several training sessions for former brigade leaders throughout early 2012 before being shut down.

74 For more on this, see K. Mezran, F. Lamen, and E. Knecht, "Post-revolutionary Politics in Libya: Inside the General National Congress," Atlantic Council Rafik Hariri Center for the Middle East, May 2013, www.atlanticcouncil.org/images/publications/postrevolutionary_politics_libya.pdf (accessed May 20, 2014).

75 K. Mezran and D. Pickard, "Negotiating Libya's Constitution," January 2014, www.atlanticcouncil.org/images/publications/Negotiating_Libyas_Constitution.pdf (accessed May 20, 2014).

76 For a more in-depth analysis of these political processes, see J. Pack, K. Mezran, and M. Eljarh, "Libya's Faustian Bargains: Breaking the Appeasement Cycle," *Atlantic Council Report*, May 5, 2014, http://libya-al-mostakbal.org/uploads/files/Libyas_Faustian_Bargains.pdf (accessed May 20, 2014).

77 Karim Mezran personal interview with Fadeel Lamen, chairman of the National Dialogue Preparatory Commission.

78 For a deeper discussion on post-revolution political developments, see J. Pack, K. Mezran, and M. Eljarh, op. cit.

5 Algeria: The outlier state?

John P. Entelis

Preface

> Thousands of people took to the streets fueled by years of anger and frustration against a government viewed by many as unresponsive to populist aspirations in the areas of economic opportunity, social justice, and political freedom. Initial police response was unable to halt the riots and stem the unrest that were sweeping the country's major cities as young men and boys took to the streets, targeting major symbols of the state including the national party headquarters and state-owned economic enterprises. For many of the frustrated, unemployed, and angry youth concentrated in over-crowded cities, the governing elite were deemed as hopelessly corrupt, a political class intent on exploiting the country's massive hydrocarbon wealth to maintain and advance its powers, privileges, and perks at any cost. In desperation, the government called in the army that resorted to shooting at the demonstrators, killing hundreds of unarmed protestors in the process. As a consequence, the very foundation of the authoritarian, one-party state was shaken to its core forcing the regime to reassess the durability of its political legitimacy. In less than a year an amended constitution was promulgated that introduced a multiparty democratic system of rule that saw up to sixty different political parties register for participation in upcoming competitive elections. For the first time in the history of the modern Arab world, a popular uprising led to the elimination of one-party authoritarian rule to be replaced by a genuinely democratic and transparent multiparty system; one that included participation by a wide range of ideological formations and political groupings.[1]

The above quotation is a description of Algeria in 1988–90, not Tunisia, Egypt, Libya, or Yemen in 2011–13. It suggests that, rather than having escaped the Arab Spring democratic revolutions, Algeria in fact was the first Arab country to have experienced one. It also provides insight into the multiple conditions—historical, political, socioeconomic—that have regularly separated, but not "exceptionalized," Algeria from its North African neighbors. This chapter seeks to explain the causes, conditions, and consequences of Algeria's "outlier" status in the context of post-Arab Spring developments. While having escaped the first wave of authoritarian overthrows, Algeria cannot be guaranteed that it will not succumb to a second or third wave.

For their part, Algerian authorities have repeatedly stressed their "exceptional" status based on their "traditionally strong nationalist sentiments."[2] On the eve of the May 2012 parliamentary elections and one full year after the Arab Spring was launched in Tunisia, for example, then Prime Minister Ahmed Ouyahia expressed the sentiment of many in his government when he declared that "[Algeria does not] need lessons from outside."[3] He went on to describe the Arab Spring as a "plague" and the political upheavals that followed it as the "work of Zionism and NATO," while adding that "our spring is Algerian, our revolution of 1 November 1954."[4]

Yet, whatever Algerian ruling elites may want to believe, the multitude of social, economic, political, and cultural grievances that combined to create the revolutionary upheavals associated with the Arab Spring have long been present in Algeria as well. Like its neighbors to its east and west, Algeria experienced mass protests and demands for fundamental changes to existing political arrangements. Yet, unlike the cases of Tunisia, Egypt, and Libya, the Algerian state has managed to contain and ultimately suppress popular challenges to its rule. What explains this anomaly? I will argue that Algeria constitutes an "outlier" in the Arab world explained by a combination of factors that serve to immunize it, in the short and intermediate term at least, from sudden mass-based overthrow. However, whether this immunity can serve to protect the state from future challenges or ensure its durability in its present form remains problematic.

Algeria confronts the Arab Spring

The uprisings that swept away the authoritarian regimes in Tunisia and Egypt in early 2011 did not so much inspire similar acts in Algeria as intensify and extend long-festering socioeconomic and political grievances that found almost daily expression in street demonstrations, political protests, and labor strikes. To be sure, the conditions that led to the uprisings in other parts of North Africa including those in Libya—massive youth unemployment, legions of underemployed and overeducated young people, an atmosphere of political suffocation, and widespread corruption at the highest levels of power—have long existed in Algeria. Yet these system challenges have rarely threatened the regime's existence as long as *le pouvoir*[5] remained united in its determination to safeguard the state's coercive, economic, and technocratic assets. What cannot yet be determined, however, is the extent to which the dramatically altered regional environment, in which the state-society equilibrium has shifted significantly in favor of democratic forces within civil society and at the expense of regime legitimacy, will strain the already fragile fabric of Algerian politics. Clearly pressures have been building up since the beginning of 2011 as wave after wave of protests, demonstrations, strikes, and other forms of public contestation have swept over the country almost on a daily basis.[6]

In early January 2011 disturbances over rising food prices and chronic unemployment spiraled out from Algiers with youths setting government buildings on fire and shouting, "bring us sugar!" Security forces were brought in to block off streets in the working class neighborhoods of Bab el Oued and the Casbah as areas outside the capital were swept up in the rampages. The violence followed price increases for milk, sugar and flour in the previous days, and amid simmering frustration that Algeria's abundant gas and oil resources had not led to broader prosperity. Despite a heavy police presence following Friday prayers, rampaging youth continued their attacks that now spread to the east and west of the capital in cities like Oran, Bouira, Annaba, and Bejaia. By the end of the month and following the departure of President Ben Ali from power in Tunisia on January 14, events in Algeria began taking a more confrontational turn as riots, demonstrations, and protests began to sweep the capital and other cities defying the ban on public gatherings put into place following the coup of 1992, also in January. This pattern of civil disobedience and popular protest accelerated following the fall of the Mubarak regime in Egypt on February 11, almost a month after Ben Ali's removal in Tunisia. Emboldened by the successes of their neighbors to the east, Algerians began to articulate their grievances in explicitly political terms as placards, banners, and slogans appeared declaring "no to the police state," "give us back our Algeria," "Boutef[7] out," and "*le pouvoir* assassins."

Riots and protests have long been a regular feature of Algerian political life given the widespread socioeconomic grievances held by large swaths of Algeria's population and the elite's seeming indifference to such grievances and generally contemptuous attitude (*hogra*) towards the mass public.[8] Public sector strikes occur almost daily in a wide variety of professions from medical personnel, schoolteachers, oil and gas industry workers, municipal guards, and so on. When such strike activity becomes overwhelming, the regime has the ability to meet some of the short-term economic demands of the protestors by rescinding, for example, the price hikes that initially brought protestors to the streets. The country's large oil stabilization fund (*Fonds de régulation des recettes*) makes such policy reversals possible.

The prevalence of abundant hydrocarbon resources has long been considered a "curse" for many developing countries like Algeria. Yet while the "oil curse" may serve to undermine long-term development,[9] it can also be the very bulwark against regime change especially where oil and gas are controlled by and exploited for the benefit of a military-industrial complex. Such is the case with Algeria where Sonatrach, the massive national oil and gas company, is the goose that lays the golden eggs. Sonatrach remains firmly under the control of the state serving to direct the country's mineral wealth to the key stakeholders within the military-industrial complex, thereby ensuring sufficient resources both to buy off socioeconomic discontent as well as enriching high army officers and their counterparts in the intelligence services.[10]

The depth and scope of anti-regime activity occurring in a dramatically changed regional environment in the first quarter of 2011 forced the regime into broader concessions than those usually made under similar conditions. For the first time since coming to power in 1999, Bouteflika convened the National Security Council (*Haut conseil de securité*), the body established to advise the president on security matters especially those concerning terrorist threats by GSPC (Salafist Group for Preaching and Combat) and AQIM (Al-Qaida in the Islamic Maghreb). Its first decision was to lift the emergency laws imposed in 1992 that limited political activities, demonstrations, protests, and other forms of public contestation not authorized by the state. For its part, a loosely coordinated group of opposition figures formed the National Coordination for Democratic Change (Coordination nationale pour le changement et la démocratie, CNCD) to serve as a spearhead for political change using mass demonstrations, political protests, and other forms of public contestation to achieve fundamental changes in the country's political economy reflecting the popular demand, over many years, for such changes.[11]

Having kept virtually silent throughout the first three months of 2011 as the country was being rocked by public unrest echoing the protests taking place in other parts of the Arab world, President Bouteflika finally went on state television in mid-April to announce a series of constitutional changes intended to "strengthen democracy." Speaking in a low and hoarse voice reflecting the fragile state of the president's health, he declared that it was important to introduce the necessary amendments to the constitution that would "crown the institutional edifice with the aim of strengthening democracy."[12] He went on to state that "active political currents" would join constitutional law experts in drawing up the amendments. In addition, the electoral law would be "revised in depth," with the participation of "the political parties, whether present [in parliament] or not."[13] A new information law would also be introduced to replace existing legislation under which journalists have been jailed after writing articles critical of the president. The new law would include "regulations for responsible blogging," he added.[14]

Given the intensity and longevity of public demands for major political change, most observers felt that Bouteflika's speech did not go far enough in responding to those demands, especially since no clear timeline was provided regarding the implementation of these constitutional reforms. Opposition groups such as the CNCD have all along been calling for deeper changes including the dissolution of the current government and parliament as well as the creation of a constitutional council that brings together all of the country's political forces in advance of organizing genuinely free and democratic presidential and legislative elections.[15] Other critics of the president's proposals referenced the intrigues and machinations surrounding the struggle for power currently underway between the president's office and the military-industrial complex highlighted by back-to-back Sonatrach scandals and their political aftermath.[16]

To what extent, therefore, do the conditions in place in Algeria today forecast a fundamental change in the political system *à la* Tunisia and Egypt or are the calls for reform little more than symbolic gestures that leave political power centralized in the military-industrial complex? Or, given the many distinctive if not unique features of the Algerian political experience, will a hybrid form emerge that is neither fully democratic nor fully authoritarian but whose oil-generated wealth can sustain into an indefinite future?

As of this writing, the chronic protests in Algeria have not coalesced into a nationwide opposition movement seeking the overthrow of the Bouteflika regime in the manner that happened in Tunisia, Egypt, and Libya. By hiking food subsidies, doubling the salaries of state workers, offering free land, and ending the emergency laws, the regime has contained the most excessive aspects of the unrest. Additionally, the recent memory of the civil war in the 1990s that nearly tore the country apart and left nearly 200,000 people dead hangs over the national consciousness serving as a brake to large-scale domestic violence. Indeed, to the extent that the chaos in neighboring Libya festers or deepens, with all the implications this has on national security concerns and the fight against the Al-Qaida insurgency in the country and outside it, this may serve to dampen the support for those calling for violence against the regime. However, "were Algerians to protest forcefully and coherently against the structure of the government, particularly the concentration of power in the executive and the military, the regime lacks the flexibility or credibility among the people to meet their demands through constitutional means."[17] Given its recent history, there is little doubt that the security forces and the army would intervene in a forceful if not deadly way to prevent any attempt at an extra-constitutional transfer of power that is not engineered by *le pouvoir* itself.

Bouteflika, no Qaddafi

Other distinctive features serve to diminish the potential threats to regime stability in the near future. Among them is the absence of a regime "culprit," one so despised and detested that ordinary Algerians would be willing to sacrifice their lives to see his removal. Unlike Ben Ali, Mubarak, and Qaddafi, Bouteflika has never been as dominant a figure within the Algerian political system. The Algerian deep state or *le pouvoir* has always enjoyed power independent of the president, and in many respects eclipses the office in critical respects. The Algerian presidency, therefore, rarely engendered the kind of contempt directed at the Tunisian, Egyptian, and Libyan leaders. As such he could not serve as a lightning rod sparking widespread, revolutionary upheaval. Unlike his counterparts in Tunisia, Libya, and Egypt, Bouteflika has never inspired the kind of deep hatred directed at those dictators. More often than not, Bouteflika has been the subject of ridicule, rarely an object of contempt. While the leaders of the other North African dictatorships served as the focus of mass-based opposition, inasmuch as each was viewed both as the symbolic representative of the corrupt state but also as its very embodiment, this has not been the case in Algeria where the opaque powers of *le pouvoir* are deeply embedded within impermeable institutions of the military-industrial complex—the DRS

(*Département du renseignement et de la sécurité*) or intelligence service, the national oil and gas company or Sonatrach, and the state bureaucracy.

Political geography matters

A rarely noted but critically important variable in the ability of revolutionaries to overthrow incumbent regimes is the nature of a country's geography and the political implications of its topographical features. As the largest country on the African continent, Algeria consists of an immense territory featuring an expansive Mediterranean coast, a vast Saharan desert, and a multitude of mountains, plateaus, and valleys across which nearly 40 million people live in diverse regional, rural, nomadic, and urban settings. Unlike Egypt and Tunisia whose relatively homogeneous populations—virtually all Arabic-speaking and Sunni Muslims—live along fairly identifiable and restricted geographical zones (along the Nile in Egypt, along the Mediterranean coast in Tunisia), Algeria's population is widely dispersed in diverse regional, linguistic, and cultural zones, some with deep distinctive identities whether they be Berbers in Kabylia, Mozabites in Ghardaia, or Tuaregs deep in the southern Sahara.

These ethnolinguistic disparities spread across an enormous physical landscape have forever served to frustrate central authority's ability to fully control, contain, and coerce its diverse population. The same obstacles of geography and population have also applied for those seeking to mobilize counter-regime opposition. Even Algeria's largest cities—Algiers, Oran, and Constantine—possess very distinctive personalities and propensities. Not only is there not a counterpart to Tahrir Square (Cairo) or Avenue Habib Bourguiba (Tunis) in Algeria, there's not even a "Cairo" or "Tunis" to serve as the urban center around which large-scale demonstrators can mobilize sufficient in size that regime forces cannot easily encircle, contain, and defeat. As the French learned during their nearly eight-year war (1954–62) against Algerian nationalist fighters and the Algerian military learned as well in their fight against an Islamist insurgency that began in 1992 and still continues until today, Algeria's rugged and expansive terrain serves explicit political purposes. A failure to appreciate this reality of political geography has been and continues to be a distinctive factor in explaining why the Algerian state has never been able to fully enforce its political will and why those seeking the state's overthrow confront the same challenge. In short, geography neutralizes incumbents and insurgents alike in their quest to alter the political status quo.

Whither Islamism?

What role has political Islam or Islamism played in "immunizing" Algeria from the Arab Spring aftershocks? Three competing ideological orientations characterized Algeria's pre-independence politics: liberal assimilationism of Ferhat Abbas, Islamic reformism of Abdelhamid Ben Badis, and radical anticolonial nationalism of Messali Hadj. Ultimately all three were superseded by a synthetic alternative that fused secular nationalism with strong socialist strains yet rhetorically tied to Islamic belief. More so than its Maghrebi neighbors, Algeria comes closest to representing the metamorphosis described above: hydrocarbon-generated wealth served as the springboard for a state-led developmental strategy that was intended to rapidly and thoroughly modernize Algeria. With the help of oil rent, the Algerian state achieved considerable social progress: the creation of jobs, the increase of purchasing power, low prices for consumer goods through government subsidies, universal healthcare, and an education system ensuring the schooling and training of many young Algerians. Thus throughout the 1960s and 1970s the country witnessed the emergence of a broad middle class with the enormous public sector serving as a launch pad for upward mobility, with the added possibility of being directly coopted into the ranks of the state class. Welfare benefits were being assured at the expense of political freedoms; a condition most Algerians accepted in the name of institutionalizing "the revolution for the people and by the people."

The socialist experiment came crashing down with the collapse of oil prices in the mid-1980s. The crisis of the rentier state put an end to the distribution of wealth strategy upon which Algeria had heavily relied to maintain loyalty amongst its citizens. The share of socially marginalized youth was growing rapidly and demands of the middle class for more economic and, subsequently, political freedoms became more insistent. The culmination of these conflicting trends was the nationwide riots of October 1988 that opened the gates for Islamism's formal entry into politics. Such an entrance represented the institutionalization of a process of re-Islamization that had long been underway but remained of secondary significance in an environment of relative economic well-being.

The principle beneficiary of the political opening up was the Islamic Salvation Front (Front Islamique du Salut, FIS) although nearly 60 other parties were legalized with the amending of the Algerian constitution in 1989 that formally abolished the one-party state that had been under the control of the National Liberation Front (FLN) since independence in 1962. At all levels of local, regional, and national elections held in 1990 and 1991, the FIS far out performed its competitors especially the now disgraced FLN.

The FIS attracted a wide range of followers but especially present were two diverse social forces—members of the blocked middle class and groups representing the marginalized urban lower class. While the movement's Islamist credentials appealed to both social groups long disillusioned by the rampant corruption, opaqueness, and manipulation of the governing class, it was the opportunity to advance economic interests that most attracted followers to the FIS. While the middle classes hoped to wrench reforms from the government by joining the FIS, lower-class groups had a more radical agenda directed at eliminating the ruling class altogether. Inevitably, these diverse social classes with opposing political agendas hindered the FIS' ability to develop a coherent party structure enabling it to permanently challenge the power of the state. Yet when it appeared that the FIS was on the verge of a decisive electoral victory at the polls in January 1992, the Algerian army high command staged a *coup d'état*, cancelled the election results, banned the FIS, imprisoned thousands of its followers, suspended the constitution, and imposed martial law that was only lifted in the aftermath of the Arab Spring on February 22, 2011. For its part, the more radical wing of the FIS regrouped in the countryside to begin an insurgency struggle that morphed into several different stages of violence and terrorism that has left more than 200,000 dead.

The Algerian experience in which a non-violent and widely popular Islamist movement that appears on the verge of achieving political power through constitutional and democratic means thereby wrenching authority from the governing class which then employs armed force to re-establish its hegemony has served as an exemplar of what authoritarian regimes must never allow to happen if they value their incumbency and all the power, perks, and privileges associated with it. It is a lesson that leaders in Cairo learned belatedly but those in the Maghreb have long recognized.

The alternative to a purely coercive response to an Islamist challenge has been a policy of cooptation of the Islamist idiom and the incorporation of "moderate", i.e., pliable Islamist groups within the existing political system but outside the regime structure. This has been the case in Algeria where alternative Islamist groups have been propped up to serve as visible alternatives to the FIS. The best known of such movements is the Movement for a Society of Peace (MSP). The MSP has been the most visible partner in the regime's efforts to pacify and integrate the Islamist current by offering the MSP's middle-class base remunerative economic options while fostering its political ambitions through active participation in electoral politics and parliamentary life. The overall result has been an "Islamist" party that differs little from its secular competitors—all seeking access to the rent-seeking activities of the state. The MSP and its middle class base shows little interest in democratic development but more so in a state-run capitalization that enhances its economic status by attaching its political fortunes to state structures.

For its part the regime has continued its policy of promoting a more religious society by constructing more mosques, certifying more imams, expanding the powers and responsibilities of the ministry of religious affairs, broadcasting more religious programming on television and radio, and generally permeating Algerian society with an Islamic identity in the belief that if its policy of "out terrorizing the terrorists" directed against the Islamic insurgency in the 1990s succeeded so would "out Islamizing the Islamists" achieve the same results.

Algeria: between myth and reality

The news that Colonel Qaddafi's wife and three of his children found political refuge in neighboring Algeria following the fall of the Libyan regime in 2011 came as no surprise to regular Algeria watchers given the country's long-standing effort to reaffirm its revolutionary heritage drawn from 132 years of colonial occupation and nearly eight years of a war of national liberation.

Yet this historically rooted association with revolutionary struggle has long ago been routinized into a bureaucratically defined and elitist directed nationalist myth intended as much to sustain the political status quo as to serve as an exemplar of peoples' revolt against hegemonic rule whether foreign imposed or domestically conspired.

Algeria's reluctance to abandon its fellow revolutionary in Libya flows from an outdated yet still dominant ideological frame of reference through which Algeria sees the world and wants to be seen by it. It also reflects an unwillingness to accept the new geopolitical and strategic realities that the Arab Spring has brought to North Africa and the Middle East. This "stand pat" perspective exists in the context of fundamental challenges currently confronting the Algerian political system along three different but related axes: (1) an intra-elite struggle for power between the governing class and the all-powerful intelligence services (DRS) at a time when the presidential succession is being contested; (2) the battle for economic supremacy between resource nationalists and economic reformers revolving around control over the "goose that lays the golden eggs," Sonatrach, the country's gargantuan national oil and gas company; and (3) the intergenerational divisions plaguing state-society relations as the discontented, disillusioned, and desperate youth, often overeducated but underemployed, have taken to the streets in repeated wildcat strikes, public demonstrations, and other forms of anti-regime protest signaling a permanent rupture with the grand social contract implied in the post-independence ideological mantra, "the revolution for the people and by the people." The Islamist-secular divide, so prominent a divisive force in the battle for political power in Tunisia and Egypt, is less salient a feature in the context of the greater challenges facing Algerian state and society today. Even the terrorist threat posed by AQIM is viewed more as an instrumental rather than existential challenge.

Bouteflika versus Mediène

Although the many challenges confronting the Algerian state preceded the Arab Spring events, the latter have exposed the country's political precariousness at a time of uncertain transition. The intra-elite struggle for political dominance is best represented by the unending struggle between executive authority and *le pouvoir*. In early January 2010 there was a political upheaval of national proportions affecting the highest levels of the Sonatrach senior management team. The president of Sonatrach, Mohammed Meziane, and three of the company's four vice-presidents, were sacked from their positions, the result of a public corruption investigation initiated by the DRS (still widely referred to by its previous incarnation, la Sécurité Militaire, SM), Algeria's top security and intelligence agency headed by the influential

General Mohammed "Toufic" Medième. Given the direct relationship between Sonatrach's Meziane and his boss, minister of energy, mines, and industry, Chakib Khelil, it was not long after the scandal broke out that Khelil himself was indirectly implicated, although not charged, and removed from his important position in a government reshuffle. A subsequent Sonatrach-related scandal, separate from the Meziane affair but more directly implicating Khelil in corruption charges, occurred in early 2013 that came to be known as "Sonatrach II." Living with his American-born wife and children in the United States where he has American citizenship, Khelil is currently being sought by the Algerian authorities under an international arrest warrant. The origin of this latest corruption episode is related to bribes that were allegedly paid to Khelil and other Algerian officials by the Canadian group SNC Lavalin to secure oil contracts from Sonatrach. The Sonatrach II scandal has stirred up indignation among the political class, community groups, and civil society in Algeria at a time when the country is facing severe regional security challenges and awaits the uncertain outcome of the presidential succession.

The major shifts in key cabinet appointments followed another significant event with major political consequences, namely the assassination of Ali Tounsi, the head of the national police or Direction Générale de la Sûreté Nationale (DGSN), in late February 2010.

Tounsi was no mere *flic* (cop), but a key figure in the government security apparatus having been head of the DGSN for more than ten years. Under the direction of President Bouteflika, Tounsi was instrumental in modernizing the national police force, overseeing a rapid expansion in personnel, and constructing dozens of new police stations across the country as part of the government's anti-terrorism program. According to many analysts, Bouteflika's strong support for Tounsi's efforts were part of a larger strategy of the president to create a powerful security force loyal to the presidency and independent of the DRS. Although Tounsi himself was once a colonel in the army, he had been a civilian for many years. Thus some analysts saw a connection between the DRS investigation of Sonatrach officials close to Bouteflika and the murder of the police chief.

Although *le pouvoir* was instrumental in securing the Algerian presidency for Abdelaziz Bouteflika in 1999, since that time and following two successful back-to-back presidential re-elections in 2004 and 2009, Bouteflika had succeeded in gradually reasserting his authority over his military patrons.[18] Through a combination of forced retirements, ambassadorial assignments, and the age-related deaths of many key high army officers, he was able to concentrate ultimate power within the executive office with him at its head. This evident attempt at shifting the balance of power away from *le pouvoir* in favor of civilian authority did not sit well with the country's ultimate power broker, the aging but still powerful head of the DRS, General Medième.

For many analysts of the Algerian political scene, however opaque and inscrutable its functioning, all these developments point to a power struggle at the highest levels of state authority involving the three pillars of the Algerian state—*le pouvoir* or the military and intelligence agency, Sonatrach, representing the economic engine of the country, and the ruling elite in the governing party (Front de Libération National, FLN) and its ally, the RND (Rassemblement National Démocratique).

Resource nationalists/rent-seekers versus economic/budget reformers

The full political implications of the corruption scandal that ultimately led to the indictment of 14 men, the majority of them now-former senior officials of Sonatrach, for their involvement in the direct awarding of contracts to international service companies, was played out with the cabinet reshuffle announced by President Bouteflika at the end of May 2010. Three key members of Bouteflika's government associated with reformist economic policies in the energy and other high value sectors were removed from their influential cabinet positions and replaced by individuals identified more closely with "resource nationalists," old line political conservatives, and *le pouvoir*.

The removal of Chakib Khelil from the energy ministry, Abdelhamid Temmar from the investment promotion ministry, and Nourredine Zerhouni from the interior ministry constituted a blow to Bouteflika's efforts to redirect the Algerian economy and polity away from its overly authoritarian and centralized past into a more liberal, pluralistic future. While this transition from a liberal to a more conservative political economy orientation has been long coming, the confluence of the dramatic events described above, concluding with new cabinet appointments, virtually assured that hard line resource nationalists would be determining the direction of the national economy, including the legal, administrative, and financial status of Sonatrach, in the immediate and intermediate future.

These governmental changes were significant because all three of the men removed from their high profile positions were professionally, politically, and personally close to the Algerian president. Khelil and Temmar, for example, were central to Bouteflika's efforts early on in his second term to open up the country to increased foreign investment, especially in the energy sector. These efforts were consistently being opposed by *le pouvoir*. For his part, as interior minister Zerhouni was instrumental in trying to exercise the full powers of the presidency. His current status as "deputy prime minister," a new and undefined position behind the increasingly powerful premier, Abdelmalek Sellal, pales in importance to that of the ministry of interior where he had control of the DGSN, the police agency that had been significantly strengthened ostensibly to reinforce the "war on terror," but also as a means of counterbalancing the power of *le pouvoir*, the army and the DRS.

The changes in personnel reflected a broader policy shift in key areas of the economy, especially the energy sector. Both Khelil and Temmar came to represent the liberal moment in recent Algerian economic history, with the former tasked with the liberalization of the hydrocarbons industry in which foreign companies were to be allowed majority ownership in upstream oil and gas licenses and related downstream industry. For his part, Temmar was given responsibility for implementing a privatization policy intended to sell off more than 1,000 state-owned enterprises (SOEs). But in the past five years, the two ministers have been undermined by an increasingly conservative government strategy and in any case had long since ceased to promote market-oriented reforms.

No understanding of Algeria's ability both to withstand internal domestic challenges and maintain a hegemonic position in regional affairs can be had separate from the crucial role played by Sonatrach in its relationship with ruling elites and the country's key power brokers in the military.

The unending contest between 'budget reformers' and 'rent-seekers'

For more than two decades, the Algerian political elite has been aware that for the country to meet the challenge of globalization it would have to accelerate the transition to a market economy and work towards the integration into the world economy. In this regard, fear of losing an edge to its immediate neighbors has put pressure on the regime to conclude the ongoing negotiations for an association agreement with the European Union and membership into the World Trade Organization (WTO), both of which are expected to offer new opportunities for greater access to capital, markets, and low-cost supplies, as well as the economic benefit of introducing information technology into business. However, even when there has been apparent unanimity in recent years about the appropriate reforms to be undertaken in the non-oil economy, there is still a lack of consensus on when, how, or even if the hydrocarbons sector should be reformed.

The reality of Algerian politics, of course, has made it virtually impossible to undertake serious reforms in this rent-seeking sector without alienating deeply entrenched interests and powerful forces in the military-industrial complex (*le pouvoir*). Since the early 1980s successive "reformist" and "restructuring" initiatives have been undertaken intended to clarify the relationship between politics and business as, for example, with the institutional and energy policy framework put in place in 1998. This framework put forward by the then president Liamine Zéroual was intended to demarcate the roles and clarify the responsibilities of the president in his capacity as chairman of the National Energy Council (NEC), the Minister of Energy, and Sonatrach's new statutory bodies. The resulting arrangements were expected to give the national oil company more freedom and provide for some separation between politics and business. In reality, no such separation ever occurred reflecting the fundamental dilemma faced by government reformers in reconciling their commitment to reform with domestic political constraints especially those revolving around the power, patronage, and privileges of the ruling elite within the military-industrial complex. The latter have always voiced concerns about control of a strategic natural resource with its enormous rent-seeking capacity, fear of losing some element of sovereignty, and the potential dominance of the national economy by foreign interests. For their part, budget-reformers put forward the view that a constructive debate should move beyond the issue of sovereignty that nobody questions and focus, instead, on how to substitute genuine productive efforts for rent-seeking behavior. They see liberalization as capable of restraining the power of those who influence the distribution of the rent (the powerbrokers), and discouraging those whose only effort consists of seeking to benefit from this largesse.

The fact that Sonatrach was not going to be "denationalized" or "privatized" anytime soon was made perfectly clear early on in the "reformist" process when President Bouteflika in 2000 moved to directly appoint all senior managers within Sonatrach. From a managerial point of view, this decision weakened the company's new statutory bodies, undermined efforts to improve its governance, and signaled once again the government's "insincerity" about "reform." In the Algerian context, however, politics has always trumped good management, efficiency, and sound administration. Following his uncertain and highly controversial election as the republic's president in 1999, Bouteflika was determined to gain control of Sonatrach. The move was meant to deprive the president's opponents within the regime of support within Sonatrach and to neutralize the opposition within the company itself. A similar process occurred in 2005–6 when the president reversed his support for Sonatrach's incipient "denationalization" in favor of continued control of the goose that lays the golden eggs. In both periods, unexpectedly high oil-generated revenues unleashed intra-elite conflicts over the distribution of the windfall profits. Interest groups of all stripes lobbied in order to undermine the government's objective of channeling excess budget revenues into a newly established stabilization fund designed as a buffer against future fiscal crises. The resulting tug-of-war between rent-seekers and budget-formers has deflected the government from its intention to tackle the country's pressing socio-economic problems.

The move to neutralize Sonatrach and to influence the distribution of the rent are among many instances of the still unsettled struggle for political and economic control. Unchanged since independence, the divisive issues continue to be those of *power* (who will make the key decisions affecting the economy) and of *distribution* (which social groups will be favored by those who hold power). Until this struggle is settled through genuine representative institutions, factional conflict and persistent violence will continue to characterize the pattern of the Algerian transition to democracy and a market economy. As a consequence of the dilatory movements to date, the pace of economic reform has been slow, even protracted. In the hydrocarbons sector, where reforms are more complex and politically sensitive, the process of implementation, already long and laborious, has virtually halted as the recent "reintegration" of Sonatrach within the state apparatus has made abundantly clear.

Rent-seeking hinders reforms

Privatization efforts and IMF-inspired institutional improvements needed to nurture the private sector in an environment that rewards innovation and growth rather than rent-seeking opportunities continue to face enormous challenges in the face of Algeria's opaque political system. Despite repeated declarations to the contrary, the emphasis remains very much on rent-seeking, hence the military's and unions' desire to protect the main source of rent—the state hydrocarbons company, Sonatrach—from restructuring and privatization.

In a broader sense, flawed institutions have held private-sector growth back. Sound institutions and laws, together with effective law enforcement improve economic interactions among economic agents and reduce transaction costs. If institutions are not well-developed and in particular if there is a lack of accountability and transparency, the business environment is not conducive to growth. One of the chief criticisms of the Algerian state is its secrecy. The shadowy military elite and its civilian counterparts in the hierarchy of power (*le pouvoir*) have an enormous influence on political and economic decisions, but remain accountable only to themselves. They in turn can influence the bureaucracy and the judiciary, resulting in a situation where only businessmen that are "connected" can prosper. The patronage network linking key elite groups within the military-industrial complex or *le pouvoir* is dense and widespread, with its tentacles reaching into every key sector of national economic activity the most important being the hydrocarbons.

Why transparency is absent in Algeria—and its economic implications

In theory, introducing greater transparency to the Algerian government's fiscal operations should be a relatively straightforward exercise. In fact, it is a politically challenging task that has yet to be undertaken in any serious or sustained way. To document and disaggregate the financial status of every public sector company and the degree of state support that each is receiving would be to lay bare the consequences of the culture of cronyism that has gripped the Algerian state for nearly three decades. The industrial output of public enterprises has declined by around 25 percent over the past ten years. Their financial plight is parlous: in fact most are technically bankrupt, supported by a public banking sector that has become riddled with non-performing loans. According to one UN report, Algeria is, with the exception of the Comoros Islands, the Arab country with the lowest level of physical capital productivity (that is, investment efficiency). In addition, labor productivity is low and is falling.

The cause of this malaise is multifaceted. First, public enterprises (including public banks) have been viewed as a means of channeling oil revenues around the economy, not as a means of adding value or making profits.

Second, this channeling is based largely on cronyism, which compounds the inefficiency of the process. Regime insiders, often members of, or persons closely connected to, the military, control the public enterprises (without necessarily having technical ownership of them) and staff them with their own supporters. Third, the political "protection" that these firms consequently enjoy has prevented their privatization. Privatization would, in effect, require the reshaping of the entire political economy. This is not something that anyone or any group, from President Bouteflika on down, will likely attempt.

Successive Algerian administrations have talked boldly about the need for reform and the importance of privatization. Indeed, specific targets for divestment have been drawn up. Yet there has been virtually no movement on this, while the unions, who have strong support within the military elite, have fiercely opposed any suggestion of labor market reform.

Legal reform is another area that is much needed (contract enforcement leaves much to be desired) but about which the government has done very little. This was one of the three great reform areas proclaimed by President Bouteflika at the outset of his first term in office in 1999. An initial surge of press interest was followed by a period of preparing "expert" reports, upon which future government action would be based. Yet again, however, there was no follow-through, and the reports either failed to materialize or were not released—let alone acted upon—by the government. The case of Sonatrach's alternating financial, administrative, and legal status *vis-à-vis* the state over the past two decades represents the quintessential case study of such government flip-flopping.

Who controls Sonatrach?

Despite the alternating and at times confusing if not misleading positions taken by high level Algerian officials in the executive as well as legislative branches of government regarding Sonatrach's "true" legal and corporate status, it is very clear that the country's national oil and gas company remains 100 percent under the control of the state. Sonatrach's governing administrative council is currently headed by Youcef Yousfi, the minister of energy and mines, who is appointed directly by the Algerian president, Abdelaziz Bouteflika, through his prime minister, Abdelmalek Sellal, also chosen by the president. Other government representatives on the council include the minister of finance, Mouloud Medelci, and Mohammed Lakssasi, the central bank governor. Khelil's selection as energy minister in 1999 until 2010, who also served for two years as Sonatrach CEO (2001–3), reflected his close association with Bouteflika and support for the latter's goal of consolidating his authority, following his successful presidential re-election in April 2004, over virtually all other counter-centers of power whether in the bureaucracy, polity, military, or economy. Khelil was given the authority to staff all high-level appointments within Sonatrach including its two vice-presidents. Bouteflika's direct control was most evident when he decided, for political as well as economic reasons, to overturn the Hydrocarbons Reform Bill of 2005 that Khelil had devoted so many years to promoting. If there was ever any doubt about who controls and manages Sonatrach, Bouteflika's unilateral political decision-making and enhanced standing in the hierarchy of state power has effectively eliminated that doubt.

That power in Algeria is under the unitary control of one leader is not surprising given the country's authoritarian practices. For example, Algeria does not practice a separation of powers nor operate under a system of constitutional checks and balances. The country's judiciary, for example, is not independent from the executive branch. The lack of impartiality and independence of judicial authorities, a key foundation of any democratically-constituted political order, is widely criticized both within and outside Algeria. The judiciary's serious deficiencies including its blatant politicization weaken the rule of law. Public perception of corruption and bribery in the judicial system is widespread. Since the country's legislative bodies are themselves politically subordinated to the executive, there are no effective legislative or judicial checks on presidential authority. Simply put, until the current regime resolves fundamental constitutional questions—the armed forces' political role, presidential prerogatives, judicial independence, and the problem of establishing law-bound government—its claim that Algeria's democratic transition is moving forward on a step-by-step basis will remain hollow.

What the above reflects is that in the ongoing intra-elite conflicts between "rent-seekers" and "budget reformers," political survivalist strategies of the former have triumphed over the imperatives for economic reform advocated by the latter. What emerges most clearly in this regard is that despite surface appearances and public commitments to the contrary, in late 2013 Sonatrach remains as firmly integrated within the Algerian state apparatus as it has ever been. A kind of "pendulum effect" reveals a clear pattern of putative liberalization measures in the economy and polity quickly being overtaken by the survivalist strategies of the ruling elites who are themselves ensconced within a military-industrial complex that serves to maintain Algeria's "robust authoritarianism." The various "hard" and "soft" phases of political-economic reform reflect alternating tactical choices made to ensure the same strategic outcome—the further empowerment of the national security state. Given the resource wealth embedded in the hydrocarbon sector, it seems very unlikely that the fused nature of the Sonatrach-state relationship will unravel, diminish, or significantly be altered anytime soon.

The state-society divide has never been wider

The gap between state and society in Algeria has never been wider than it is today. Labor strikes and popular demonstrations are near-daily occurrences throughout the country highlighting a deep social malaise and resentment of what Algerians say is an increasingly corrupt government that deserves little trust. The list of grievances held by the majority of ordinary Algerians cuts across every category of society, economy, and polity; grievances that have found expression in virtually daily acts of protests and other forms of civil disobedience. While anti-state behavior has not reached the proportions experienced in Tunisia, Libya, Egypt, Syria, or Yemen, it does reflect a deep cleavage within the body politic between a deeply discontented mass public and an apparently indifferent if not contemptuous ruling elite best captured in the widely used term, *hogra.*

While the state's repressive capacity, especially its security apparatus, has expanded significantly in recent years aided by the surplus flow of hydrocarbon-generated revenues and the military assistance provided by powerful outside actors like the United States in its pursuit of the war on terrorism, civil society has suffered repeated reversals in the areas of socioeconomic development, quality of life, and political opportunities. These latter conditions have obtained despite the significant reduction in the violence associated with the decade-long civil war.

Population pressures have long bedeviled Algeria's social development as the country's birth rates were among the highest in the world in the 1970s and 1980s. More recent population data, however, reveal a long-term slowdown in population growth as the result of improved access to contraceptives and the implementation of family planning policies. Yet as Algeria is about to make its demographic transition from an average annual population growth rate of 3.06 percent in the preceding ten years to 1.17 percent in 2011, its extremely youthful population (40 percent of Algerians are under 15 and 70 percent are under 30) will apply severe demographic pressures on the economy and society over the next two decades as those born in the 1970s and 1980s reach working age.

Adding to the problems of an excessively youthful society, is the geographic misdistribution of Algeria's population. More than 90 percent of Algerians live in the north of the country, where massive migration from the countryside since 1962 has contributed to the current overcrowding in such large cities as Algiers, Oran, and Constantine. The percentage of the urban population has increased from 31 percent in 1966 to 65 percent in 2009. While birth rates have dropped noticeably in the past ten years, the legacy of past population growth policies in which "birth spacing" substituted for "birth control," is a youthful, urbanized population, with a significant percentage having only limited opportunities within the formal sector of the economy. As many have been forced to look for work in the parallel *trabendo* (from "contrabande," the French word for smuggling) economy, this has fueled widespread popular discontent leading many urban youth to seek alternatives in political Islam.

Pressures to open up the Algerian economy have existed for nearly two decades following the nationwide riots of October 1988 after which "liberalization" substituted for "socialism" as the regime's new political economy mantra. Yet, despite repeated promises from a variety of different political leaders, little substantive reform has been actually legislated or promulgated.

Paradoxically, "Algeria has never been better placed in macroeconomic terms, as it is today, to promote the structural and fiscal reforms that the IMF and others have recommended for years. Even at the height of the violence in the middle 1990s in northern Algeria, the oil and gas sector of the southern Sahara continued to attract capital from multinational oil companies, compensating for the dearth of local and foreign direct investment in other sectors."[19] Because the Saharan oil and gas fields are far from populated centers, "exploration and exploitation deals have all along been sheltered from the conflict, operating as if they were offshore. For their part, European customers have increased their demand for Algerian gas in the past decade,"[20] making this as much a strategic resource for such European neighbors as Spain, Portugal, Italy, and France as for Algeria's political-military leadership.

However, "the apparently positive macroeconomic picture disguises a much grimmer micro economic reality.[21] In contrast to the booming hydrocarbon sector (the price of a barrel of oil reached over $70 in mid 2006 and over $100 in early 2013), which today generates 97% of foreign export earnings, the domestic economy is stagnating under a lack of both private and public sector investment,"[22] leading to official unemployment of nearly 30 percent in 2002, 24 percent in 2003, 17.7 percent in 2004, and 21 percent in 2009, of which more than 70 percent are under the age of 30. Unofficial estimates put current unemployment rate at above 30 percent. "Under the influence of reform plans promoted by the IMF, World Bank, and the European Union, thousands of workers have been laid off as a consequence of restructuring industries for privatization. Yet few investors have taken over inefficient heavy industry plants running at around 40 percent of capacity for more than a decade. Social investment in housing, welfare, infrastructure, and transport has been neglected in favor of importing basic goods. The access of newcomers to the market is severely restricted despite agreements with international financial institutions and the EU that full trade liberalization will be implemented by 2012."[23]

Despite more than two decades of economic reform, Algeria has yet to make the transition to a stable market economy. The state maintains a leading role in the economy as an employer, investor, and regulator. Although the private sector has significantly increased its contribution to gross domestic product, particularly in the retail, construction, and transportation sectors, it still accounts for less than a quarter of total industrial production outside the hydrocarbon sector. Bureaucratic regulations pose a major impediment to the efficiency of the market, and laws governing economic activities are piecemeal, poorly implemented, and largely inconsistent with the demands of a market economy.

Bureaucratic red tape permeates all aspects of business activity in the country. Bureaucracy's role as a "sponge" to soak up unemployment means that it is heavily overstaffed. The bureaucracy is also deeply influenced by political interests with various departments often housing the supporters of different "strong men," and is infused with clan and tribal factionalism, which in turn undermines notions of promotion based on merit. It is widely believed, for example, that military officers have abused their authority by controlling a wide range of economic activities. They are accused of forming alliances with civilians to control the importing and distribution of foodstuffs and medicine, to siphon off the output of public enterprises, and to steal public funds. The phrase "political-bureaucratic mafia" has often been used to describe government officials and army officers who utilize their public offices for private economic gain. Such individuals are accused of using sanitary inspections, customs regulations, and their influence with magistrates to harass private companies that compete with their clientelist economic networks creating an environment of widespread corruption.

Corruption is pervasive in Algeria constituting the most serious barrier to fundamental economic reform. Algeria scored 2.9 out of 10, ranking 105th out of 159 countries in Transparency International's 2010 Corruption Perceptions Index, putting it just behind Egypt, Mexico, and Zambia, and placing it among the five most corrupt countries in the Middle East and North Africa (MENA).[24] The CPI score for Algeria in 2013 reveals the depth with which citizens perceive corruption's influence on the country's institutions. On a score scale of 1–5, where 1 means not at all corrupt and 5 means extremely corrupt, the following Algerian institutions received the following perceptions of corruption scores: political parties 3.9; legislature 3.8; business/private sector 4.1; and the judiciary 4.1.[25] These scores are reflective of the widespread disenchantment that most Algerians have towards the majority of state institutions.[26] One result has been a consistent pattern of civil and political disengagement Algerians have towards both state institutions and civil associations. As one attitudinal survey after another has revealed, Algerians do not identify with political parties, avoid participating in elections, show little confidence in civil society, and generally regard the choices available to them as conspired from above with little real opportunity for influencing decision making whether at the national or local levels. Yet, as the vibrant protest activity has repeatedly shown, "Algerians are not apolitical; they are unhappy with their political and civic choices."[27]

In the absence of effective, market-based financial intermediation, government spending—either on civil service jobs or on large infrastructure projects—is the main mechanism for distributing hydrocarbons wealth around the economy. This opens up considerable opportunities for kickbacks and embezzlement, particularly when parliamentary oversight is negligible at best. Most independent observers remain skeptical about the regime's willingness to root out corruption among senior officials particularly members of the military officer corps and the ruling FLN. More generally, anti-corruption drives, which tend to tackle the symptoms rather than the root causes of bureaucratic shortcomings and often serve political ends, are liable to be used as an alternative to more challenging structural reform. The most dramatic recent examples of politically motivated anti-corruption drives are the Sonatrach I and Sonatrach II scandals that have cut across a wide spectrum of Algerian officialdom, political classes, and business interests.

The numerous qualitative indicators measuring Algeria's poor record of economic, social, and political performance find parallel results in several quantitative indexes. The 2010 Revenue Watch Index, for example, an annual product of the Revenue Watch Institute and Transparency International that measures and compares 41 resource-rich countries that are the top producers of petroleum, gold, copper, and diamonds, ranks Algeria at number 38 with a score of 22.8 (out of 100), placing in the lowest of three categories ("scant revenue transparency") and just above the Democratic Republic of the Congo, Equatorial Guinea, and Turkmenistan.[28]

The Global Competitiveness Index published in *The Arab World Competitiveness Report* for 2013, a collaborative project of the World Economic Forum and the European Bank for Reconstruction and Development, ranks Algeria 110th out of 144 countries worldwide and next to last among the other North African countries behind Morocco (70th), Egypt (107th), and only slightly ahead of an unstable Libya (113th).[29] Algeria's global ranking in the 12 categories used to derive the competitiveness index is abysmal except for the macroeconomic stability pillar in which it ranks fifth overall.[30] The wide gap between a high performing macroeconomy and dismal microeconomy is confirmed by both qualitative and quantitative evidence.

This macro–micro gap is translatable into another quantifiable indicator that measures people's happiness, a category in which Algeria performs poorly. According to the 2009 World Database of Happiness, Algeria ranks 5.2 out of a possible score of 10, outdistanced by other Arab countries such as Tunisia, Mauritania, United Arab Emirates, Kuwait, and Saudi Arabia. According to this survey, Algeria respondents indicated that only 37 years of their expected lifespan of 71 are considered to be "years of happy living."[31] The assessment of these findings by a respected and independent Algerian daily newspaper best captures their importance. "En dépit des richesses et des milliards accumulés dans les reserves, la qualité de la vie est toujours aux abonnés absents."[32]

The above pessimism is confirmed by additional statistical evidence gathered in Algeria by its National Center for Population and Development Studies and Analysis (CENEAP) in its most recent study (2009) on Algerian youth. According to this report, 60 percent of its sample complains about their uncertain future while 73 percent criticize their current status. More tellingly, one out of three of respondents dream of living overseas, 58 percent "turn their back on sports," and 90 percent indicate "no interest in associational life or any political party."[33]

Possibly a more objective set of indicators provided by the Economist Intelligence Unit's quality of life index ranks Algeria 75th out of 160 countries assessed with a score of 5.59 out of 10 in 2009. While comparable to its non-oil producing North African neighbors (Morocco 5.57; Egypt,5.61; Tunisia 5.6), Algeria ranks well below those of the oil-rich states of the Gulf Cooperation Council (GCC), such as Saudi Arabia with 6.45 and the UAE with 7.15.[34]

In the more explicit political category, Algeria again performs poorly as recorded, for example, in Freedom House's annual *Freedom in the World* report for 2010. Of the three categories in which a country can be ranked—Free, Partly Free, Not Free—Algeria has consistently been categorized as "not free" ever since the coup of 1992. In both the Political Rights and Civil Liberties categories, Algeria scored 6 and 5 respectively where "1" represents the highest guarantees and "7" the lowest.[35]

Finally, the annual US State Department report on human rights in Algeria provides a bleak picture, one that underlines Algeria's continuing failure to address the many problems in society, the polity, and the economy. In its report published in March 2011, the State Department summarized the situation in Algeria in the following way:

> Principal human rights problems [in 2010] included restrictions on freedom of assembly and association, which significantly impaired political party activities and limited citizens' ability to change the government peacefully through elections. There were reports of arbitrary killings. Failures to account for persons who disappeared in the 1990s and to address the demands of victims' families remained problematic. There were reports of official impunity, overuse of pretrial detention, poor prison conditions, abuse of prisoners, and lack of judicial independence. Additionally, widespread corruption accompanied reports of limited government transparency. Authorities used security grounds to constrain freedom of expression and movement. Women faced violence and discrimination, and the government maintained restrictions on workers' rights.[36]

To be sure there are numerous factors that limit the degree of political change via populist protest that Algeria can experience given the size of the country, the diversity of its population, the oil-generated wealth that can be used to placate aggrieved classes, the recent memory of a bloody civil war that left 200,000 people dead along with the continued attacks by the terrorist group, Al-Qaida in the Islamic Maghreb (AQIM), hangs over the national consciousness serving as a brake to large scale domestic violence, and the ferocity of a militarized apparatus determined to maintain itself in power at any cost. Yet, the generational gap reflects more than demographic differences as Algeria's youthful majority population articulates a political vision far removed from the country's aging ruling elite; an elite still trapped in an ideological time warp whose political comeuppance is perceived as occurring sooner rather than later. The emergence of a loosely coordinated group of opposition figures such as the National Council for Democratic Change (CNCD) that spearheaded a populist revolt against the regime in early 2011, inspired in great measure by the *intifadas* taking place in North Africa and the Middle East, serves as one indication that while an Arab Spring-like revolt may not overturn the current regime or its political system, Algerian civil society will remain forever vigilant.

Do legislative elections matter?

Within this relatively neutralized political environment, the regime moved forward with its promise to hold parliamentary elections. Instead of serving as an institutional mechanism for voicing popular discontent, however, the May 2012 elections reaffirmed the Algerian state's primacy. The pro-regime FLN (National Liberation Front) received a whopping 208 parliamentary seats, despite being more out of touch than ever with the electorate. Its coalition partner, the RND (National Rally for Democracy), won 66 seats. Together, the two parties garnered nearly 60 percent of the newly expanded parliament, where 462 seats were up for grabs.

The government claimed the electoral results constituted a popular mandate for its continued rule. Headlines in pro-government newspapers attempted to paint the results as a victory for stability, drawing contrasts with the "chaos" of the Arab Spring. Opposition parties cried foul play, and noted that election results had contradicted all pre-electoral predictions. Ignoring these arguments, Europe and the United States congratulated the regime for conducting "transparent" elections intended as a "first step towards genuine democracy."

Do presidential elections matter?

Bouteflika is Algeria's longest serving post-independence president. In 1999, *le pouvoir* brought Bouteflika back from self-imposed exile to stand for presidential elections. He easily won the contest thanks to a boycott by all major opposition candidates who viewed the election as a blatant, military-imposed effort at achieving legitimacy for the regime.

Bouteflika was reelected in 2004. After persuading the pliable national assembly to amend the constitution and extend presidential term limits from two five-year terms to unlimited terms, Bouteflika was elected again in 2009 with more than 90 percent of the vote. Despite suffering a series of debilitating illnesses since late 2005, he ran in the April 2014 presidential elections as the FLN's favored candidate.

Reflecting Algeria's political opaqueness, independent analysts have interpreted Bouteflika's presidential power in diametrically opposed ways. For some, his cabinet reshuffle and removal of high-level DRS figures from key positions of authority in September 2013 was part of an ongoing attempt, that first became evident following his 2004 election victory, to consolidate power within the presidency. It also appeared that the disastrous failure by the security forces to prevent the bloody attack at the Tigantourine gas facilities in In Amenas in January 2013 by Al-Qaida-affiliated terrorists that left 39 foreign hostages dead undermined the army's reputation that played to Bouteflika's strength. For others, however, the fact that the president was rarely seen in public in 2013 and 2014 indicated that he had been both physically and politically incapacitated, propped up by the military-industrial complex in its unending effort to maintain the political status quo at any cost.

The chaos, violence, and instability crisscrossing North Africa and the Middle East in the aftermath of the Arab Spring have served to advance *le pouvoir*'s goal of containing revolutionary forces within Algeria. The military-industrial complex supported the 2014 candidacy of Bouteflika, a man virtually on his deathbed, because it remained unwilling to allow the elections to become an instrument for institutional change. Bouteflika spent several months in 2013 in France's premier military medical facility after suffering a series of mini strokes that left him virtually unable to speak or act. It appeared, therefore, that as a "living corpse," the Algerian president would be unable to challenge *le pouvoir* in any effective or consistent way, thus making him the perfect candidate to lead Algeria, from *le pouvoir*'s perspective.

Yet, in an interview on February 2, 2014, two months prior to the vote, Amar Saadani, the FLN's secretary-general and a close ally of Bouteflika, boldly demanded DRS head Toufik Mediène's resignation, insisting the military and intelligence services remove themselves from Algerian political life. Political mobilization on behalf of Bouteflika's candidacy reached such ludicrous proportions that one pro-government politician went so far as to declare: "I will vote for him [Bouteflika] dead or alive because he has done so much for the country."[37]

Clearly a battle has been raging at multiple levels of state power. It is evident within the political classes, where those who favored and opposed Bouteflika's candidacy were pitted against each other. It is similarly clear both within the military, where high-ranking officers are attempting to unseat Toufik Mediène, who has long wielded significant power, as well as in struggles between civilian and military poles of authority.

Bouteflika declared his candidacy by proxy on February 22, 2014, with his close ally and current prime minister Abdelmalek Sellal making the formal announcement. It had been clear to most Algerians that Bouteflika would coast to an easy victory as no announced or likely opponent could muster enough votes in a competition that everyone believed had been fixed from the start. As ludicrous as it sounded, promises to vote for the Algerian president whether he was "alive or dead," seemed to have come true. While only 51 percent of the electorate participated in the election, compared to 74 percent in 2004, Bouteflika received an incredible 81.5 percent of the vote albeit less than the 90 percent he received five years earlier.

It is a testament to the extreme disconnect between the country's formal political structure and its civil society that the overwhelming majority of ordinary Algerians have been completely unaffected by the virtual absence of presidential authority these many months, while real decision-making power has lain elsewhere. Yet the response to Bouteflika's candidacy and inevitable victory in the April 17 presidential elections has aroused a new level of national protests encompassing a wide variety of political groups and social classes who have declared "enough" (*barakat*) of the old corrupt, manipulated, and clandestine style governance, which Bouteflika's candidacy represented.

Fearing the *barakat* movement, however disorganized, small, and spontaneous, could erupt into an Arab Spring-like revolutionary movement, police used extreme and excessive force against protesters, which has caused a public relations nightmare for the regime after footage was transmitted worldwide via social media. Given its past history of severe brutality in dealing with overt public protests, it seems unlikely, however, that *le pouvoir* would ever allow an incipient populist protest movement to delay or detour the politically inevitable—the re-election of Abdelaziz Bouteflika to a fourth five-year term as president.

The future: status quo, peaceful transition, or revolution?

As acute as are the institutional challenges, probably more threatening to regime stability is the defiant nature of a civil society that remains in a state of unending turbulence. While chronic socioeconomic discontent has yet to coalesce into a nationwide movement of organized political opposition, the bottom up ripple effect cannot but leave regime incumbents insecure and uncertain about the efficacy and long-term durability of their strategy of "managed instability."[38]

The Arab Spring has arrived at a critical juncture in Algeria's modern history as a state and society are in the midst of great uncertainty with a physically weakened president now re-elected for a fourth five-year term, a constitutional system that does not provide a clear mechanism for political succession, an emboldened national security apparatus headed by an individual who is himself, at 77, exhibiting signs of physical weakness, a politically manipulated and economically mismanaged hydrocarbon industry from which virtually all sources of state revenues derive, and an increasingly animated civil society no longer willing to be placated by either rhetorical promises or short-term economic rewards as condition for political compliance. However these conflicting forces ultimately resolve themselves, what is clear is that the previous modes of rule-making and rule-enforcement will have to be fundamentally reconfigured in ways that respond to populist demands for social advancement, economic opportunity, and political freedoms. Whether this process develops peacefully or violently is ultimately in the hands of *le pouvoir*—as it has been since the founding of the republic.

References

2009 World Data Base of Happiness (Rotterdam: Erasmus University).

Aïda Ammour, L., "Algeria's Role in the Sahelian Security Crisis," *Stability: International Journal of Security & Development*, vol. 2, no. 2 (Art. 28), 2013.

BBC News, "Algeria Leader Bouteflika Pledges Constitutional Reform," *BBC News Africa*, April 15, 2011, www.bbc.co.uk/news/world-africa.

Economist Intelligence Unit, *Algeria: Country Report*, December 2009.

El Watan, "Appel pour une transition démocratique en Algérie," *El Watan*, February 10, 2011.

Entelis, J.P., "Algeria: Democracy Denied, and Revived?," in G. Joffé, *North Africa's Arab Spring* (London: Routledge, 2013).

Entelis, J.P., "Civil Society and the Authoritarian Temptation in Algerian Politics: Islamic Democracy vs. the Centralized State," in A.R. Norton (ed.), *Civil Society in the Middle East*, vol. 2 (Leiden: E.J. Brill, 1996).

Entelis, J.P., "Sonatrach: The Political Economy of an Algerian State Institution," in D.G. Victor, D.R. Hults and M. Thurber (eds.), *Oil and Governance: State-Owned Enterprises and the World Energy Supply* (Cambridge: Cambridge University Press, 2012).

Freedom House, *Freedom in the World 2010* (NY: Freedom House, 2010).

International Crisis Group, "Algeria's Economy: The Vicious Circle of Oil and Violence," *ICG Africa Report*, no. 36, October 26, 2001.

Jeune Afrique, "Les sept plaies de l'Algérie," *Jeune Afrique*, December 29, 2010, www.jeuneafrique.com.

Liverani, A., *Civil Society in Algeria: The Political Functions of Associational Life* (London: Routledge, 2008).

Malti, H., *Histoire Secrète du Pétrole Algérien* (Paris: La Découverte, 2010).

Nossiter, A., and Williams, T., "Security Forces Halt Protest in Algeria," *The New York Times*, February 12, 2011, www.nytimes.com.

Parks, R.P., "Algeria and the Arab Uprisings," in C.M. Henry and J. Ji-Hyang (eds.), *The Arab Spring: Will It Lead to Democratic Transitions?* (Seoul: Asian Institute for Policy Studies, 2012).

Revenue Watch Institute, *2010 Revenue Watch Index* (New York: Revenue Watch, 2010).

Roberts, H., "Demilitarizing Algeria," *Carnegie Papers*, no. 86 (Washington: Carnegie Endowment for International Peace, May 2007).

Ross, M.L., *The Oil Curse: How Petroleum Wealth Shapes the Development of Nations* (Princeton: Princeton University Press, 2012).

The Economist Intelligence Unit, *Country Report: Algeria*, April 2011.

Tlemcani, R., "Le discours de Bouteflika confirme qu'il n'y a pas une volonté politique de sortie de crise," *El Watan*, April 18, 2011.

Transparency International, *Global Corruption Barometer 2010*, www.transparency.org.

US Department of State, *2010 Human Rights Practices: Algeria* (Washington: United States Department of State, 2011).

Werenfels, I., *Managing Instability in Algeria: Elites and Political Change Since 1995* (London: Routledge, 2007).

World Economic Forum and European Bank for Reconstruction and Development, *The Arab World Competitiveness Report 2013* (Geneva: World Economic Forum, 2013).

Notes

1 J.P. Entelis, "Algeria: Democracy Denied, and Revived?," in G. Joffé, *North Africa's Arab Spring* (London: Routledge, 2013), pp. 149–50. With the permission of the publisher, portions of this chapter are derived from the chapter cited.

2 L. Aïda Ammour, "Algeria's Role in the Sahelian Security Crisis," *Stability: International Journal of Security & Development*, vol. 2, no. 2 (Art. 28), p. 1.

3 Ibid.

4 Ibid.

5 *Le pouvoir* ("the power") is a very commonly used term in the Algerian context to refer to the "powers behind the throne," meaning the key members of the independence-era old guard within the army high command of the ANP (Armée Nationale Populaire) and the intelligence services (Département du Renseignement et de la Sécurité, DRS) often working in conjunction with high level elites in the party and bureaucratic apparatus of the state, constituting a kind of "military-industrial complex." *Le pouvoir* operates behind closed doors, its activities opaque and unknown to the overwhelming majority of Algerians.

6 In 2011 alone, for example, the Algerian minister of interior reported that 10,000 protests and demonstrations had taken place in the country. The unofficial figure is probably closer to ten times that number.

7 The diminutive for Bouteflika widely used by Algerians in a critical not complimentary sense.

8 Symptomatic of the frustration held by so many of the youth is the statement by one out-of-work 29-year old Algerian, Bilal Boudamous, who declared to a *New York Times* reporter during one large demonstration in the capital that saw as many security forces as protesters, that the police forces "can't kill us because we are already dead. We live with our parents, and we have no future." A. Nossiter and T. Williams, "Security Forces Halt Protest in Algeria," *The New York Times*, February 12, 2011, www.nytimes.com (accessed May 21, 2014).

9 See M.L. Ross, *The Oil Curse: How Petroleum Wealth Shapes the Development of Nations* (Princeton: Princeton University Press, 2012).

10 See J.P. Entelis, "Sonatrach: The Political Economy of an Algerian State Institution," in D.G. Victor, D.R. Hults, and M. Thurber (eds.), *Oil and Governance: State-Owned Enterprises and the World Energy Supply* (Cambridge: Cambridge University Press, 2012), pp. 557–98; H. Malti, *Histoire Secrète du Pétrole Algérien* (Paris: La Découverte, 2010).

11 Numerous petitions in favor of such democratic change have circulated nationally and internationally by respected Algerian scholars, lawyers, human rights activities, journalists, and others including Mohammed Harbi, Madjid Benchikh, Aïssa Kadri, and Ahmed Dahmani. See "Appel pour une transition démocratique en Algérie," *El Watan*, February 10, 2011, www.elwatan.com (accessed May 21, 2014).

12 BBC News, "Algeria Leader Bouteflika Pledges Constitutional Reform," *BBC News Africa*, April 15, 2011, www.bbc.co.uk/news/world-africa (accessed May 21, 2014).

13 Ibid.

14 Ibid.

15 See *El Khabar*, April 17, 2011. See also *El Watan*, April 18, 2011, which described the president's proposals as another way by which the system "wants to keep things in hand while making it appear that it is reforming – which it is not."

16 For a broader analysis of the political sclerosis currently confronting the Algerian regime, see R. Tlemcani, "Le discours de Bouteflika confirme qu'il n'y a pas une volonté politique de sortie de crise," *El Watan*, April 18, 2011, www.elwatan.com (accessed May 21, 2014).

17 The Economist Intelligence Unit, *Country Report: Algeria*, April 2011, p. 5.

18 See H. Roberts, "Demilitarizing Algeria," *Carnegie Papers*, no. 86 (Washington: Carnegie Endowment for International Peace, May 2007), pp. 1–28.

19 International Crisis Group, "Algeria's Economy: The Vicious Circle of Oil and Violence," *ICG Africa Report*, no. 36, October 26, 2001, p. i.

20 Ibid.

21 A recently published report by Algeria's human rights commission makes clear, in bold and honest fashion, the many challenges facing Algerians in their daily lives with seven areas highlighted for their severity and importance: disaffected youth,

violence against women, corruption, judicial abuses, status of the disappeared, public health, and the handicapped. See Jeune Afrique, "Les sept plaies de l'Algérie," *Jeune Afrique*, December 29, 2010, www.jeuneafrique.com (accessed May 21, 2014).

22 *Jeune Afrique*, December 29, 2010.

23 Ibid.

24 Transparency International, *Global Corruption Barometer 2010*, www.transparency.org (accessed May 21, 2014).

25 Ibid.

26 See R.P. Parks, "Algeria and the Arab Uprisings," in C.M. Henry and J. Ji-Hyang (eds.), *The Arab Spring: Will It Lead to Democratic Transitions?* (Seoul: Asian Institute for Policy Studies, 2012), pp. 102–25.

27 Ibid.

28 Revenue Watch Institute, *2010 Revenue Watch Index* (New York: Revenue Watch, 2010), p. 3.

29 World Economic Forum and European Bank for Reconstruction and Development, *The Arab World Competitiveness Report 2013* (Geneva: World Economic Forum, 2013), Table 2. Tunisia was not listed in the 2013 report.

30 Algeria's global ranking among 134 countries along the 12 categories constituting the Global Competitiveness Index are as follows: Institutions = 102; Infrastructure = 84; Macroeconomy = 5; Health and Primary Education = 76; Higher Education and Training = 102; Goods Market Efficiency = 124; Labor Market Efficiency = 132; Financial Market Sophistication = 132; Technological Readiness = 114; Market Size = 51; Business Sophistication = 132; Innovation = 113.

31 2009 World Data Base of Happiness (Rotterdam: Erasmus University).

32 *El Watan*, November 2, 2010.

33 *Jeune Afrique*, December 29, 2010.

34 Economist Intelligence Unit, *Algeria: Country Report*, December 2009, pp. 14–15.

35 Freedom House, *Freedom in the World 2010* (New York: Freedom House).

36 US Department of State, *2010 Human Rights Practices: Algeria* (Washington: United States Department of State, 2011), p. 1.

37 *The New York Times*, February 3, 2014.

38 See I. Werenfels, *Managing Instability in Algeria: Elites and Political Change Since 1995* (London: Routledge, 2007); A. Liverani, *Civil Society in Algeria: The Political Functions of Associational Life* (London: Routledge, 2008); J.P. Entelis, "Civil Society and the Authoritarian Temptation in Algerian Politics: Islamic Democracy vs. the Centralized State," in A.R. Norton (ed.), *Civil Society in the Middle East*, vol. 2 (Leiden: E.J. Brill, 1996), pp. 45–86.

6 Transitions from authoritarian rule following the Arab uprisings: A matter of variables

*Justin O. Frosini and Francesco Biagi**

Premise

The transformations that are taking place in the Arab world, like every transitional process, are undoubtedly extremely complex: they are not straightforward or rational. Rather they are dynamic processes characterized by a number of variables, that one can refer to as *actors* (i.e., subjects involved in the transitional process) and *factors* (i.e., facts that influence the transitional period).[1]

The actors that take part in these processes are manifold: the government, the parliament, the judiciary, the head of state, constitutional courts, the military, electoral management bodies, truth commissions, political parties, interest groups, civil society, elites, and so forth.

The factors that play a role in determining the success or failure of transitions are also numerous and heterogeneous: these are the nature of the outgoing non-democratic regime, the electoral system, the existence of a political democratic culture and tradition, the level of social and economic development, the form of government, the "stateness,"[2] the international context, the spirit of the times ("*Zeitgeist*"[3]) …

In the previous chapters the role of some of these actors/factors was analyzed and, as we underlined in our introduction, each of them is indicative of specific *trends* taking place in transition processes in North Africa and in the Middle East. Al-Nahda in Tunisia is an example of one of the Islamist parties that came to power following the Arab uprisings, and that now have to face a number of sensitive and difficult challenges; the Egyptian Supreme Constitutional Court is indicative of the trend consisting of the emergence and strengthening of constitutional courts following the Arab upheavals; the role played by Mohammed VI in Morocco reflects the resistance of Arab monarchies to the wind of change; the key role played by external actors in Libya highlights that the outcome of the processes of transition not only depends on internal variables; the case of Algeria shows that, despite the profound changes taking place in the MENA region, there are numerous and heterogeneous factors that hinder reform processes. In the following paragraphs we will examine each of these trends from a comparative constitutional standpoint by making reference to and comparing similar experiences that took place in other regions of the world.

The rise to power of the Islamist parties and their approaches to constitution-making

One of the most evident characteristics that is common to many of the countries involved in the Arab upheavals is the rise to power of Islamist movements. In fact, the Parti de la justice et du développement won the November 2011 parliamentary elections in Morocco, Al-Nahda came out as the party with a relative majority in Tunisia and the Muslim Brotherhood (through its Freedom and Justice Party) won the parliamentary and presidential elections in Egypt. As Karim Mezran and Alice Alunni have emphasized, the reason why these political parties and movements won the elections is because of

> their appeal to the Islamic religious and cultural identity of people that are no longer afraid to invoke Islamism. In a period of profound social upheavals in societies characterized by deep conservatism, one cannot expect a sudden "liberal turn," at least not in the short run. On the contrary, we are currently witnessing a return to the basic values of Islam that demonstrates the continued relevance of the identity question in these countries in the 21st century.[4]

From a constitutional standpoint, having acknowledged this success of Islamist movements in various countries in North Africa, the two cases that are interesting to examine and compare are those of Tunisia and Egypt (i.e., Al-Nahda and the Muslim Brotherhood) given their diametrically opposed approach with regard to one of the main challenges of the transition that is to say the constitution-making process.[5]

Leaving aside the textual analysis of the 2014 constitution of Tunisia and the 2012 constitution of Egypt, from a procedural standpoint, one can identify four important differences between the two Islamist parties: first, Al-Nahda adopted a consensual approach to the drafting of the constitution while the Muslim Brotherhood basically assumed a winner-takes-all attitude; second, Al-Nahda (together, of course, with other parties in the Tunisian constituent assembly) decided to put aside the 1959 constitution and start afresh, while the Muslim Brotherhood opted to use the 1971 constitution as a basis for the drafting of the new fundamental law; third, Tunisia's constitution-making process had a duration that is quite standard for the drafting of a modern constitution (just over two years), on the contrary the Muslim Brotherhood accepted the six-month timeframe imposed by the Supreme Council of the Armed Forces (SCAF); fourth, Al-Nahda has shown no opposition to seeking the advice of international experts, while the Muslim Brotherhood preferred an inward-looking constitution-making process.

Let us examine the first difference. As Duncan Pickard clearly explains in his chapter, from the very outset Al-Nahda's stance has been that of obtaining a carefully drafted consensual document through an inclusive process. Despite having a relative majority, Al-Nahda has constantly aimed at reaching compromises with the other secular political parties within the constituent assembly. Indeed as Pickard has emphasized "it has been Al-Nahda's compromises that have driven Tunisia's constitutional bargain, such as in its omission of Islamic *sharia* from the draft constitution."[6]

Here an interesting comparison can be made with a constitutional transition of the past, i.e., that of Italy. In fact one cannot escape noticing some unexpected similarities between the role of Al-Nahda in Tunisia today and Italy's Christian Democratic Party (Democrazia Cristiana, DC) during the transition period (and beyond). Indeed, as their name reveals, just like Al-Nahda, the Christian Democrats were a religiously denominated political party with strong backing from the Catholic Church, furthermore they also obtained a relative majority of approximately 40 percent of the seats in the Constituent Assembly elected on June 2, 1946, and they too insisted on governing in a coalition that (up until June 1, 1947[7]) included the Communist and Socialist Parties. Most importantly, again like Al-Nahda, they embraced an inclusive process for drafting the Italian constitution that came into force in 1948. In fact, Italian constitutional legal scholarship talks about the constitution being based on a "historical compromise" (*compromesso storico*). Testimony of the many compromises made by the Christian Democrats occurred on December 22, 1947, during the very last session of the Constituent Assembly, when Christian Democrat Giorgio La Pira made a proposal to include a preamble with a reference to the Holy Trinity; however, when it became apparent that this proposal would have provoked a serious split within the Constituent Assembly, La Pira withdrew it and this did not stop him from later commenting that the work of the assembly had been "blessed by God."[8] This episode constitutes an interesting comparison in particular with Al-Nahda's decision not to push for the inclusion of *sharia* in the constitution.

The Muslim Brotherhood, on the contrary, assumed a winner-takes-all attitude with regard to the drafting of the constitution. "It is in some ways strange to entrust one party, especially one with a particular religious ideology, with leading the process of drafting a document that has such broad obligations to fulfill."[9]

After the election of a new parliament at the beginning of 2012, the lower chamber appointed a 100-member constituent assembly to draft the constitution. It should be noted that there was a heated debate about the way these members were chosen. The Muslim Brotherhood was of the opinion that, given that they had won the elections, they should have the majority of seats in the constituent assembly, whereas the opposition insisted that, considering the task assigned, i.e., that of drawing up the "rules of the game," "the assembly's makeup should reflect all aspects of Egyptian society."[10]

The second difference, in terms of the procedure followed to draft the constitution, is related to the fact that Al-Nahda (in agreement with the other members of the constituent assembly) decided that the 1959 Constitution contained numerous flaws and that they should start from scratch. In Egypt the Muslim Brotherhood did the opposite. As Zaid Al-Ali has pointed out,

> Fatally, the assembly opted to use the 1971 constitution and existing traditions as a starting point for its deliberations. The effect is that while the new constitution claims to be a product of the people's will, it is heavily influenced by the preceding decades of autocratic rule. So much so that many articles have simply been reproduced verbatim in the final text.[11]

This means that although the 2012 constitution does address some of the underlying problems of the previous fundamental law (for example it introduces a term limit for the president and gives more powers to parliament) the fact that technically the 1971 constitution was used as the basis for drafting the constitutional provisions many of the technical flaws of the previous constitution have been embedded into the new one. A prime example of this can be seen in the section of the constitution that deals with decentralization, which has been defined as one of the "darker sides" of the 2012 constitution.[12]

The third important difference between Tunisia's and Egypt's constitution-making process is related to the timeframe. In coherence with the consensual approach adopted from the very start Al-Nahda has never tried to impose ultimatums with regard to the final approval of the constitution. On the contrary,

> Perhaps one of President Morsi's biggest mistakes was the decision to maintain the drafting process that had been established by the Supreme Council of the Armed Forces (SCAF) in March 2011. The SCAF, clearly not expert in democratic transition, imposed a 6-month timeframe for the entire constitutional drafting process, precisely because it did not understand the challenges that Egypt was faced with or because it preferred not to see those challenges met.[13]

From the perspective of comparative constitutional law, there is no doubt that six months[14] is far too short a period to draft a constitution, but despite this the Muslim Brotherhood appeared to consider meeting this deadline more important than ensuring that the constitution was adequately written thus leading Nathan Brown to rightly define some of the drafting "sloppy."[15] This also signified that the document that was approved in December 2012 was the Constitution *of the Muslim Brotherhood* rather than the Constitution *of Egypt*.

Fourth and finally, while Al-Nahda has constantly sought the advice of international experts, the Muslim Brotherhood preferred an inward-looking constitution-making process.

In particular, Tunisia has benefited from the assistance of the Venice Commission, due to the fact that the latter started intensive cooperation with the Tunisian constituent assembly regarding the constitution-making process. In fact, the commission was involved in a number of meetings and exchanges of views with the constitution drafters and established constructive working relations with the constitutional commissions of the assembly.[16] It is important to stress the fact that on June 3, 2013, the Speaker of the National Constituent Assembly requested the opinion of the Venice Commission on the final draft constitution of Tunisia. The observations of the commission were made public on July 17, 2013.[17]

On the contrary, another distinctive factor of the drafting process followed by the Muslim Brotherhood was the rejection of international assistance. The drafters worked alone and essentially refused to cooperate with the United Nations, the United States, and with scholars from outside. Of course the lack of involvement of international experts is, in part, related to the tight timeframe imposed by SCAF and is also one of the reasons that led to the plethora of technical imperfections mentioned above.[18]

In conclusion, the comparison between the role played by these two Islamist parties in the constitution-making process highlights strong divergences. Al-Nahda has adopted a more democratic approach compared to the Muslim Brotherhood. We believe the attitude of the latter was one of the elements that contributed to the fall of the Morsi government in July 2013. Having said this, the Tunisian constituent process was not free from perils. There is no doubt that six months is far too short for drafting a constitution; however, one should not forget that even very long constitution-making processes are symptomatic of non-democracies.[19] At a certain point, it was far from certain that the negotiating parties would be able to reach a final agreement especially given the influence of the changes that took place in Egypt during July 2013 and also because of the assassination of important opposition politicians in Tunisia itself. In the autumn of 2013, the opposition called for the government to resign and for the Constituent Assembly to be dissolved. Fortunately, a series of negotiations (involving the trade unions, the lawyers association and human rights movements) were able to avert the political crisis without the outbreak of widespread violence and in January 2014 the constitution was finally approved and came into force.

It has been rightly pointed out that

> By successfully negotiating a final agreement, the Tunisians have led the way in proving that ideological differences need not lead to conflict or stalemate and that they can survive in the context of a modern Arab state and society. The pragmatic and result-based approach that the Tunisian negotiators adopted will serve as a positive example of successful constitution-making and conflict resolution not just for the Arab region, but for much of the rest of the world as well.[20]

The emergence and strengthening of constitutional courts following the Arab uprisings

As mentioned above, one of the most significant trends following the Arab uprisings was the emergence and strengthening of constitutional courts in North Africa and in the Middle East.[21] In the following paragraphs, we will analyze the major novelties in the field of constitutional adjudication adopted in Morocco, Tunisia, Egypt, and Jordan, as well as the proposal to set up an International Constitutional Court. Moreover, we will identify some important lessons that Arab constitutional courts can learn from their institutional equivalents that have already experienced a transition from authoritarian rule.

Major novelties in the field of constitutional adjudication

Among the most relevant democratic novelties introduced in the constitutions of the countries involved in the Arab upheavals, one has to mention those related to constitutional adjudication.

In Morocco, for example, the new 2011 constitution replaced the Constitutional Council provided for in the 1996 constitution. The new court, besides deciding on the validity of the election of the members of parliament and that of referendum operations, has to make sure that organic laws, ordinary laws, and regulations of both houses of parliament are not at odds with the constitution (Article 132). Moreover, it is important to stress that in addition to *ex ante* review (already provided for under the previous constitution), the new constitution introduced concrete constitutional review.[22]

"The introduction of such *ex post* review […] thus appears to be extremely important in order to enable the Constitutional Court to reinforce its position as a counter-majoritarian body, and may thus contribute to the process of democratisation in a more effective manner compared to the past."[23] Indeed, the Moroccan Constitutional Council, which was established for the first time under the 1992 Constitution, had powers to review the constitutionality of laws and regulations. This body, however, has not "fulfilled the expectations in the field of protection of fundamental rights:"[24] this is due to the fact that the parliamentary opposition has appealed to the council only in a very limited number of cases, in spite of the fact that the constitutionality of a whole series of laws was more than doubtful.[25] Precisely for this reason, in the field of constitutional review the Constitutional Council has been compared to the "sleeping beauty castle."[26] Therefore, several scholars had expressed their hopes that a mechanism of *ex post* review would be introduced: evidently their requests have been listened to. However, it should be noted that the organic laws regulating the organization and functioning of the Constitutional Court, as well as the regulation of concrete constitutional review, have not been adopted yet. Therefore, as provided for by Article 177 of the constitution, the Constitutional Council will continue to carry out its functions until the new Constitutional Court has been set up.

Similarly to Morocco, Tunisian drafters have decided to improve the protection of the new constitution by replacing the previous Constitutional Council with a new Constitutional Court.[27] The major novelties introduced by the 2014 constitution refer to the composition and appointment of constitutional justices, as well as to the procedural gateways to the court. As far as the composition and appointment are concerned, one has to remember that the previous Constitutional Council was composed of nine members: four of them were appointed by the president of the republic, and two by the president of the Chamber of Deputies; the first president of the Court of Cassation, the first president of the Administrative Court, and the first president of the Court of Auditors were *ex officio* members of the Council (Article 75 of the 1959 constitution). This appointment procedure *de facto* granted to the president of the republic the control over the council: indeed, "as the President of the Republic [was] also the chief of the dominant party in Parliament, it [was] improbable that the President of the Chamber of Deputies [would] appoint members of the constitutional council who [did] not enjoy the trust of the President of the Republic."[28] The 2014 constitution has changed the appointment procedure of constitutional justices, as it grants a key role to each branch of government. Indeed, the Constitutional Court is composed of 12 members: the president of the republic, the Assembly of the Representatives of the People, and the Supreme Judicial Council each appoints four members.

As mentioned above, the second major novelty refers to the procedural gateways to the court. The 2014 constitution has maintained *ex ante* review, which was already provided for in the 1959 constitution. The Constitutional Court is competent to oversee the constitutionality of draft laws (upon the request of the president of the republic, the head of government, or 30 members of the Assembly of the Representatives of the People), constitutional draft laws (submitted by the president of the Assembly of the Representatives of the People), and treaties presented to it by the president of the republic before their legislative ratification. However, similarly to Morocco, the 2014 constitution has also introduced concrete constitutional review: therefore, the Constitutional Court has the power to check the constitutionality of "laws referred to it […] as a result of a request filed by a court, in the case of the invocation of a claim of unconstitutionality by one of the parties in litigation […]" (Article 120 of the Constitution).

In the past, the Maghreb countries followed the French model of constitutional review by setting up bodies (constitutional councils) competent to oversee the constitutionality of laws *before* they came into force. It should be underlined, however, that the French influence seems quite strong even today. Indeed, the introduction of concrete constitutional review in Morocco and Tunisia was probably influenced by the 2008 French constitutional reform, which gave the possibility to the Cour de Cassation and the Conseil d'Etat to submit legislative provisions to the Conseil Constitutionnel for a review of their constitutionality.[29] Therefore, these bodies are getting closer to the model of constitutional review adopted in countries such as Germany, Italy, and Spain.[30]

As we saw in Nathan Brown's chapter, the case of Egypt is of particular interest given the fact that in the last few decades the Supreme Constitutional Court (SCC) has been a very powerful and influential body. In the first place one has to stress that—as far as the composition and functions of the SCC are concerned—the 2012 and the 2014 Egyptian constitutions differ significantly. As regard the composition, according to Law 48 of 1979 on the SCC, the chief justice was appointed by the president at his discretion, and even associate justices were appointed by presidential decree. However, in appointing them, the president had to choose between two nominees, one chosen by the chief justice and one by the general assembly of the court. It should be noted that neither the 1971 constitution nor Law 48 of 1979 specified the number of the members of the court. The consequence of this "silence" was that there could be an infinite number of justices. Therefore, "if a Chief Justice and President both dislike[d] the decisions of majority on the Court, they [could] collude to pack the court with justices sympathetic to their views."[31] This is precisely what happened in the early 2000s, when "the executive did seek to control the Court by packing it with friendly justices."[32] The 2012 constitution had put an end to this practice, since it stated that the Supreme Constitutional Court was composed of the president and ten members (Article 176). This change—although probably aimed also at ousting justice Tahani al-Gebali from the Court, as underlined by Nathan Brown[33]—was of particular relevance. Indeed, in order to try to prevent the executive from controlling the court, a fixed number of justices is to be preferred, especially in countries undergoing a transition from authoritarian rule such as Egypt.

Another important change refers to the functions of the SCC. The 2012 constitution stated that the Supreme Constitutional Court carried out its review function not only *ex post* (for laws and regulations, as occurred in the past) but also *ex ante*. Indeed, the president of the republic or the House of Representatives had the power to submit bills on political rights and elections to the court. Article 177 also specified that the laws referred to the court for *ex ante* review were not eligible for *ex post* review. This provision was probably a reaction to the decision made by the SCC in July 2012, when the court declared parts of the law governing the parliamentary elections unconstitutional, and this led to the dissolution of parliament. As stressed by Nathan Brown, the intent of the constitutional provision "was clear: the SCC would review such laws before elections were held; if it upheld the law then it could not come back and strike it down later."[34]

The abovementioned changes to the composition and the functions of the SCC, however, were short-lived. In fact, not surprisingly, the 2014 constitution has eliminated the novelties introduced by the 2012 constitution regarding the Supreme Constitutional Court. Indeed, the new text does not specify the number of justices sitting on the court (it only states that the court is composed of a president and a "sufficient" number of members), and does not provide for *ex ante* constitutional review of electoral laws. In addition to these amendments—which are clearly aimed at restoring the previous order of the SCC—the 2014 constitution assigns to the court some very important powers. Indeed, besides deciding on the constitutionality of laws and regulations, the court is now "solely competent […] to interpret legislative provisions, and to adjudicate on disputes pertaining to the affairs of its members, on jurisdictional disputes between judicial bodies and entities that have judicial jurisdiction […]" as well as other types of dispute (Article 192 of the constitution).

The cases of Morocco, Tunisia, and Egypt mentioned above refer to the *strengthening* of constitutional courts; however, it is worth noting that Jordan, on the contrary, is an interesting case of *emergence* of a constitutional court following the Arab upheavals. In fact, despite recurrent calls for the setup of a similar body,[35] Jordan did not have a constitutional court. This demand was finally addressed in 2011, as one of the measure of a larger packet of constitutional reforms. Despite some concerns regarding the independence of this body (for example, Article 58 of the constitution states that all the justices will be appointed by the king), the establishment of a constitutional court has to be welcomed. This new body has the power to check the constitutionality of laws and regulations, as well as the right to interpret the provisions of the constitution if so requested either by virtue of a decision of the Council of Ministers or by a resolution taken by the Senate or the Chamber of Deputies passed by an absolute majority (Article 59). The parties who have the right to challenge the constitutionality of laws and regulations are the Senate, the Chamber of Deputies, and the Council of Ministries. Interestingly enough, even Jordan introduced concrete constitutional review.[36]

At the apex of the trend of emergence and strengthening of constitutional courts, one can find an interesting and curious proposal made by the Tunisian president Mohamed Moncef Marzouki to set up an International Constitutional Court. Marzouki, a former political exile, proposed the creation of such a body in his speech to the UN General Assembly on September 27, 2012, and then at the African Union Summit in January 2013. According to Marzouki, the International Constitutional Court would represent a further step in the journey towards the elimination of dictatorships. While the International Criminal Court tackles crimes only *after* they have been committed, the International Constitutional Court would have the task of *preventing* all forms of abuses, working as a "deterrent weapon against any despot and tyrannical regime."[37] The proposal made by Marzouki at the UN General Assembly is as follows:

> The UN Charter, the Universal Declaration of Human Rights, the charter, and a great many international conventions backed up by GA resolutions are all texts which could be deemed to be humanity's, mankind's [constitution], and the only thing missing is an implementation mechanism. For this reason, the Tunisian republic wishes to make a proposal for

> the creation of an International Constitutional Court, one similar to the ICC, a court which could be seized either to denounce certain constitutions or illegal charters or illegal or fraudulent elections. And this court would be competent to consider a number of disputes of issues, to rule on the legality or illegality of elections which are not in line with the United Nations and its charter. So all systems and all democratic systems will be faced with a clear duty of being recognized by this tribunal. This mechanism must also make the necessary recommendations and provide the necessary advice to all those who request it.[38]

Interestingly enough, Marzouki denounced some practices often followed by despots in the Arab world. These consist not only of organizing fraudulent elections, but also of trying to achieve undemocratic goals in the respect of the legal system. The latter is the case of Tunisia and Algeria, where Ben Ali and Bouteflika amended the constitutions (respectively in 2002 and 2008) in order to eliminate the provisions that limited the number of presidential mandates.[39] Arab autocrats, even when pursuing an undemocratic aim, "want to comply with the system,"[40] and this is precisely what Marzouki wants to fight against.

Preventing dictatorship and despotism through a judicial mechanism sounds very fascinating and intriguing. Obviously, many questions (and perplexities) arise when passing from words to deeds. Who would appoint the members of the court? What would form the parameter of review? Who would have standing to lodge a claim before the court? How wide would the jurisdiction of the court be? How would the decisions of the court be enforced? Moreover, the proposal touches a sensitive contemporary debate in international law, i.e., whether or not there is an international right to democracy. Overcoming all the theoretical and practical difficulties that the establishment and the functioning of the International Constitutional Court would involve will not be easy.

To talk of a new "wave"[41] of constitutional justice would not be correct, however the emergence and strengthening of constitutional courts in the MENA region confirms the fact that constitutional adjudication has become a *condicio sine qua non* for a country to be considered a real democracy even in the Arab world.

Learning from past experiences: constitutional courts in transitional countries

"Revolutions are not friendly times for courts, constitutions, and the rule of law. Indeed, it is far from certain that Egypt's judicial framework will emerge from the revolutionary tumult unscathed. But it is still remarkable how much a judicial actor was able to play a pivotal role in such an unfriendly environment."[42] These were the words used by Nathan Brown in his chapter to describe the crucial role played the Egyptian Supreme Constitutional Court in the transition from Mubarak's regime. Indeed, the decisions made by the

SCC strongly affected both the constituent process and the outcome of the transition itself. In June 2012 the court declared parts of the law governing the parliamentary elections unconstitutional and this led to the dissolution of the parliament; at the end of November 2012 President Morsi, who feared unfavorable judgments from the SCC, issued a constitutional declaration that had the effect—*inter alia*—of rendering immune the constitution-making process from judicial oversight, and he pushed ahead to get the constitution ratified the following month; in June 2013 the SCC overturned the electoral law for the upper house and the law governing the constituent assembly, and also overturned a provision of the country's emergency law.

It should be noted that Arab constitutional courts can draw inspiration and learn important lessons from their counterparts in other countries that underwent a transition from authoritarian rule.[43] For example, in some countries constitutional courts were created even before the new constitutions were adopted, and they deeply influenced the constitution-making processes. In Poland during the long process (1989–97) that led to the adoption of a new constitution, the Constitutional Court (that was set up in 1985, under the previous regime) established some fundamental democratic principles, such as the independence of judicial review and the separation of powers.[44]

In Albania the 1991 Law on the Major Constitutional Provisions (known as "Provisional Constitution"), represented a clean break with the totalitarian past, since it foresaw political pluralism, separation of powers, and protection of fundamental rights. The following year, for the first time in the country's history, a constitutional court was set up. During the period that goes from 1992 to 1998 (when the new constitution came into force), this body issued important judgments concerning the due process and the transitional justice, focusing in particular on the constitutional legitimacy of the "lustration laws"[45] adopted in the country.[46]

However, the most notable example of a constitutional court that actively participated in the constitution-making process is to be found in South Africa, where the Constitutional Court played a fundamental role in the very drafting of the new constitution. Set up in 1993, it was vested with the task of verifying that the final constitution was not in contrast with the 34 constitutional principles aimed at guiding the constituent assembly. The justices did not certify the first constitutional text and forced the constituent assembly to amend it on the basis of the 34 principles. The court facilitated the transition from Apartheid by also issuing a number of very important judgments that abolished the death penalty, prohibited inhuman or degrading treatments, and declared the unconstitutionality of corporal punishments.[47]

Even when constitutions have been promulgated, problems often arise in transitional countries with regard to the validity of the laws issued under the previous authoritarian regime. Italy is emblematic from this point of view. Although the Italian constitution came into force in 1948, the Constitutional Court only started its activity in 1956. During these eight years, instead of the constitutional provisions, several statutes from the fascist period that were in contrast with the constitution continued to be enforced, the most important being the 1931 Unified Code on Public Security, the 1930 Code of Criminal Procedure, and the 1930 Criminal Code. These texts have been labeled "the three fundamental texts of the Fascist tyranny."[48] To put it differently, between 1948 and 1956, many provisions of the Italian constitution remained "frozen." The first judgment of the Constitutional Court (no 1/1956) undoubtedly represents a milestone in the history of Italian constitutional justice and marks a turning point in the country's democratic transition. In fact, the court claimed the power to review the constitutionality of pre-constitutional statutes. Since its first "revolutionary" judgment, the Constitutional Court never looked back, and up until the end of the 1960s, it focused on eliminating the fascist legislation that still limited civil, political, religious and social rights and freedoms.

Turning back to the MENA region, it is interesting to note that Morocco presents some analogies with the Italian case. For example, the Criminal Code, which came into force in 1962 under the authoritarian regime of Hassan II, contains a number of provisions that are in contrast with the 2011 constitution, as well as with international human rights treaties. For instance, until recently, Article 475 provided a prison term of one to five years for a person who "abducts or deceives" a minor, but prevented the prosecutor from charging him if he then married the minor. According to rights activists in Morocco, courts have applied Article 475 even in cases of rape, thus allowing rapists to escape prosecution.[49] Another example is given by Article 496, which criminalizes the harboring of a married woman who leaves her husband. The Criminal Code also prohibits apostasy (Article 220), the ostentatious break of fast in a public space during Ramadan (Article 222), homosexual relations (Article 489), as well as sexual relations between individuals of opposite sexes who are not religiously married (Article 490). Even some of the provisions of the Code of Criminal Procedure fail to comply with democratic standards.[50] The introduction of concrete constitutional review may increase the chances that the Constitutional Court will rule on the constitutionality of the abovementioned articles.

Another field in which constitutional courts can play a fundamental role refers to the territorial organization of the state. Even though federalism is a plant that hardly takes roots in the Arab world, there are, however, some exceptions—at least from a formal point of view, such as Iraq and the United Arab Emirates[51]—and others may come in the near future. In Libya, one of the most sensitive decisions that the constituent assembly will have to make refers to the territorial organization, i.e., whether to create a centralized or a decentralized state. In fact, while the majority of the people of Tripolitania oppose the idea of creating a federal state, "federalists in eastern Libya expect a decentralized form of government to be adopted, or at least recognition of the autonomy of Cyrenaica. They favour an arrangement similar to that enjoyed by Kurdistan in Iraq."[52]

If a decentralized system were to be adopted, the setup of a constitutional court (together with other means such as the creation of a second chamber representing the subnational entities or the tribes or the ethnic/religious subgroups) would be crucial.

Again, a comparison with past transition proves this point. Indeed, Spain offers a clear example. In this country the actual decentralization of the state was considered a *condicio sine qua non* for a real transition from the authoritarian regime to a democratic form of state, especially because of the "Catalan and Basque issues." The Spanish Constitutional Court played a key role in the territorial organization of the state. The court, in its decisions on conflicts arising over the allocation of powers between the state and the regions, and through the interpretation of constitutional provisions regarding Part VIII of the constitution (which deals with the territorial organization of the state) guaranteed a rational functioning of the "*Estado autonómico*" (autonomous state). Many therefore refer to a "*jurisdictional* construction of the Autonomous State" (emphasis added).[53] In particular, the court contributed enormously to the *peaceful* resolution of the territorial disputes. Since the territorial organization of the state was one of the most sensitive issues in the country, it is probable that without the possibility of lodging a claim before the court, these political disputes would have increased.

Another issue that countries undergoing a transition from authoritarian rule often have to address is "dealing with the past," thus facing a number of sensitive issues regarding transitional justice. Again Arab constitutional courts could play a pivotal role. Transitional justice involves a wide range of mechanisms that vary from country to country. For example, some countries involved in the Arab uprisings have already adopted "political isolation laws" (PILs), which prohibit certain individuals who are deemed to have been previously associated with the former regimes from occupying political posts and holding public functions for a certain period of time. In Egypt the "political isolation law," which was adopted in 2012, was declared unconstitutional by the Supreme Constitutional Court. After long and bitter debates, Libya also introduced a PIL in spring 2013.[54] However, the amendments to Libya's Constitutional Declaration have included a provision that eliminates judicial review of the constitutionality of this law. As denounced by Lawyers for Justice in Libya, this provision "violates citizens' rights and the separation of powers […] Without allowing the ability to challenge the law on constitutional grounds individuals will not have a meaningful basis to defend themselves from decisions made pursuant to the PIL."[55] Even in Tunisia, the adoption of a "Political Isolation Law" represented one of the most sensitive issues at the heart of political debate. The new electoral law (adopted on May 1, 2014), however, rejected the proposed political exclusion of members of the *ancien régime.*[56]

Similar measures, called "lustration laws,"[57] were adopted in Central and Eastern Europe after the fall of the Berlin Wall, and the constitutional courts had to decide on their constitutional legitimacy.[58] It should be noted that although the decisions made by these courts were extremely divisive and differ significantly from country to country,[59] they were respected by the people, and the reason is that they came from impartial bodies that enjoyed a great support among the people.

So to sum up, constitutional courts are often "leading actors"[60] in transitions from authoritarian rule. However, one should not forget that these bodies *per se* do not guarantee the success of the democratization process. Indeed, they can contribute to

> the transition to liberal constitutional democracy if, but only if, a nation has already made a good start in that direction. An independent and vigorous constitutional court is the child of liberal democracy, and without that kind of polity, a constitutional court cannot function effectively.[61]

Unfortunately, at present this precondition is to a large extent missing in the Arab world. This means that the challenges that the newly established constitutional courts will have to face will be even more difficult.

The resistance of Arab monarchies to the wind of change

Sean L. Yom and F. Gregory Gause III have rightly pointed out that the "Arab Spring" might just as well be called the "Arab *Republics*' Spring."[62] As a matter of fact, while several long-lasting authoritarian presidents in the MENA region (Ben Ali in Tunisia, Qaddafi in Libya, Mubarak in Egypt and Saleh in Yemen) have been overthrown, Arab monarchs have so far survived the Arab uprisings.

Besides mere repression, the literature[63] has highlighted a number of other factors that explain why the eight Arab monarchies (Morocco, Jordan, Kuwait, Saudi Arabia, Oman, Qatar, United Arab Emirates (UAE), and Bahrain) have managed to resist to the wind of change that has been blowing in the Arab world since December 2010.

First and foremost, one should not forget the high degree of religious or tribal legitimacy enjoyed by Arab monarchs. The Hashemite House of Jordan and the Alaouite Crown of Morocco claim direct descent from the Prophet Mohammed. King Abdullah of Saudi Arabia is often referred to as "Custodian of the Two Holy Mosques," Mecca and Medina.[64] The royal families in Bahrain, Kuwait, Oman, Qatar, Saudi Arabia, and the UAE command authority and respect among the tribal confederations in their societies.

Second, Arab kings and emirs are often considered the effective guarantors of social and political stability. In Morocco, one of the main reasons why Mohammed VI was not called into question is because the people think that without the king and his "unifying role" the country would be ungovernable.[65] In Jordan, the monarchy serves as a "security blanket for all Jordanians regardless of their origins, providing protection for the country's various ethnic groups."[66] Moreover, "in times of unrest, crowds are more likely to protest for legislative change than for the abandonment of the monarchy."[67]

Third, Arab monarchs "don't dirty their hands" in everyday politics. This gives them a twofold advantage: first, when things go wrong, they lay all the blame on the politicians; second, when they are put under significant pressure by the population, they can initiate political, economic and constitutional changes so as to appear as the real reformers in the country. As we will see, this is precisely the strategy followed by Mohammed VI in Morocco and Abdullah II in Jordan.

Fourth, access to oil rents continues to be a fundamental means for "petro-monarchies" to prevent dissent and to calm down protests.[68] In fact, in order to appease the public's dissatisfaction, oil-rich monarchies have used the revenues deriving from oil reserves to give state employees pay rises, welfare payouts, creation of jobs, loan benefits, and costly price subsidies. It should be noted that "oil rents easily recirculate across borders in the form of aid,"[69] and therefore even nonoil countries (such as Jordan and Morocco) have benefited from economic assistance from the wealthier monarchies such as Saudi Arabia, Kuwait, Qatar, and the UAE.

Fifth, Arab monarchs can count on "foreign patrons":[70] the Unites States in Jordan and in the Gulf monarchies, and France in Morocco are probably the most evident examples. These close relations were of fundamental importance even during the Arab uprisings in order to constrain "Western calls for change."[71] In Bahrain, given the presence of the US Fifth Fleet, the United States' criticism of the gross violations of human rights by the police during the 2011 February protests was very limited. In much the same way, former French president Nicolas Sarkozy did not call for regime change in Morocco; on the contrary, he defined the reform process carried out by Mohammed VI as "exemplary."[72]

As far as external interventions are concerned,[73] the survival of the monarchies was also guaranteed through the military intervention of the Gulf Cooperation Council (GCC). This happened in Bahrain, which is the only Arab monarchy to have experienced large-scale protest demonstrations similar to those that took place in the republics. The GCC's action was crucial to calm down the situation.

"Surviving constitutionalism"

Despite the fact that *all* the Arab monarchies have managed to resist to the wind of change, one cannot deny the fact that the Arab upheavals have produced some significant political and constitutional changes. Of course, a distinction should be drawn between the Gulf monarchies, on the one hand, and Jordan and Morocco, on the other hand. Indeed, if the former managed to preserve the status quo and were forced to introduce only extremely limited changes,[74] the latter tried to compensate for the lack of oil reserves with political and constitutional reforms. It should be noted that both Mohammed VI and Abdullah II played an important role in the reform processes. In Morocco, the new 2011 constitution was "granted" by the king, and did not result from a democratically elected constituent assembly. Indeed, the constituent process was driven by Mohammed VI: "it was he who decided to engage in far-reaching constitutional reform, to identify the 'key elements' on which that reform was to be based, to appoint the Commission on Constitutional Reform, and finally to grant his approval to the draft presented to him by Mennouni [President of the Commission on Constitutional Reform]."[75]

In Jordan, in spring 2011 the king appointed two committees: the National Dialogue Committee to propose changes to the voting system, and the Royal Committee on Constitutional Amendments to propose reforms to the 1952 constitution. The packet of constitutional reforms was adopted in September 2011, while, after months of bitter debate, in June 2012 the parliament passed the new electoral law, which partially amended the "single non-transferable vote" system in place since 1993.

In Morocco, the 2011 constitution introduced a number of significant novelties, such as the strengthening of the head of government's and parliament's powers, a more independent judiciary, the strengthening of the protection of fundamental rights, the supremacy of international conventions over domestic laws, the recognition of *Amazigh* as an official state language, and the duty of the king to appoint the head of government from the party that wins the most seats in the elections to the House of Representatives.[76]

In Jordan, the constitutional reforms—which were much more limited compared to Morocco—included the prohibition of any form of torture; a partial enhancement of fundamental rights; the establishment of a constitutional court; the creation of an independent electoral commission (which replaced the Ministry of Interior in organizing elections); the judicial oversight of the elections of the members of the Chamber of Deputies (which replaced the Chamber of Deputies' right to determine the validity of the election of its members); a partial strengthening of judicial independence; a partial limitation of government's power to issue temporary laws when parliament is not in session.

Having said that, it should be noted that the changes introduced in Morocco and Jordan do not mark a real discontinuity with the past. The most important powers are still in Mohammed VI's and Abdullah II's hands. The Moroccan king continues to be the key figure in determining political direction and adopting decisions of strategic importance for the country. Moreover, he is still the "Commander of the Faithful," the president of the Higher Council of the Judicial Power, Supreme Commander of the Royal Armed Forces, and president of the Supreme Security Council. Even the Jordanian Sovereign has been almost immune to constitutional reforms. It is true that he has lost the power to indefinitely postpone elections, however—significantly enough—Chapter 4, Section I of the Constitution, devoted to "The King and His Prerogatives," has been left intact. Moreover, the reform of the electoral law did not produce any real change, since most of the seats are still elected through the "single non-transferable vote" system, which "systematically disadvantage[s] opposition by preventing the formation of the new opposition parties and stymieing Islamic predominance."[77]

The impression is that Mohammed VI and Abdullah II gave rise to what can be defined as "surviving constitutionalism": indeed, both the 2011 Moroccan constitution and the amendments to the Jordanian constitution mainly responded to the need to appease people's discontent so as to ensure the regime's stability and continuity. The two kings allowed constitutional reforms to take place as long as their key powers and prerogatives were not questioned: their main purpose was not to democratize the country, but to guarantee their own survival. We are therefore dealing with the paradox according to which constitutionalism—which should be aimed at limiting arbitrary power—is used as a means to maintain and strengthen authoritarian/semi-authoritarian regimes.

It is accepted that Mohammed VI and Abdullah II have so far achieved their aim: both monarchies continue to be *executive* monarchies, and the countries have remained authoritarian/semi-authoritarian regimes. Initially, one may be tempted to think that the two kings can "sleep easy." The novelties introduced in the Moroccan and Jordanian constitutions do not seem to represent (at least up to the present time) a real threat to the monarchies. Indeed, constitutions in authoritarian/semi-authoritarian contexts are often considered "paper tigers." This assumption is true in most cases, *but not always*. In fact, a comparison with other past non-democratic regimes shows that it is far from certain that "surviving constitutionalism" will work in the long run.

In his book *Constitutionalism and Dictatorship: Pinochet, the Junta and the 1980 Constitution*,[78] Robert Barros has shown that even an autocratic regime can be bound by a constitution of its own making. According to Barros, in 1980 the regime of General Pinochet "introduced and sustained a constitution which set into operation institutions that limited the dictatorship's power and prevented it from unilaterally determining the outcome of the October 5, 1988 plebiscite which triggered the transition to democracy in 1990."[79] In particular, the Constitutional Court (which was set up by the very constitution of 1980) played a fundamental role in determining the legal framework of the presidential plebiscite: the court required that the Electoral Court (Tribunal Calificador de Elecciones) be fully in place for the plebiscite, and it struck down provisions that restricted free political competition or that gave the opportunity for arbitrary intervention in the political process. Thus, the court was crucial in assuring that the plebiscite "would be a fair contest and a valid expression of the popular will."[80] Pinochet was defeated in the plebiscite, as 55 percent of the voters did not want to grant him another term in office.

Egypt is another interesting case. President Sadat, who pushed for economic liberalization in the country, decided to create a Supreme Constitutional Court (SCC) at the beginning of the 1970s so as to attract private investments. Indeed, in his opinion investors wanted a court that would effectively protect property rights.[81] Mubarak, who succeeded Sadat in 1981 following the assassination of the latter, was in favor of this policy. The SCC started to hear cases only in 1980: at the beginning, the court focused its activity on the protection of economic rights, thus fulfilling the expectations of Sadat and Mubarak. However, by 1985 the SCC began to grant people not only economic rights, but also civil and political rights. In this way, the court directly confronted the executive, which was opposed to political liberalization. As Clark Lombardi put it:

> by the mid-1980s the SCC was demonstrating a willingness to check the executive when it seemed unambiguously to violate explicit constitutional limitations on executive power – even if their decision touched upon sensitive issues. The SCC confronted the executive as early as 1985, when it issued a starting ruling setting limits on the executive's emergency powers.[82]

Thus, in the period from 1985 to the end of the 1990s, the Supreme Constitutional Court, which had been conceived as an ally of the executive, turned into a body capable of limiting the authoritarian power.

The cases of Chile and Egypt show that the novelties introduced in the constitutions of Morocco[83] and Jordan[84] should not be underestimated, since they may become effective constraints of authoritarian power in the future. Thus, "surviving constitutionalism," that has served to appease public's dissatisfaction in the short term so as to ensure the regimes' stability and continuity, may boomerang in the medium- and long-term.[85]

King Juan Carlos and the Spanish lesson

To date, no Arab king or emir has decided to start a process of transition to democracy. Even Mohammed VI—the Arab monarch who has introduced the highest number of reforms—"has taken his country only *halfway* along the route of democratic transition: in fact, under [his reign], Morocco has ceased to be an autocratic regime and turned into a hybrid regime, although not a democracy."[86]

History, however, has shown that in some cases monarchs may be crucial in guaranteeing the success of democratization processes. Spain is undoubtedly one of the best examples: in fact, King Juan Carlos played a pivotal role in conveying his country from the authoritarian regime of Franco towards a full-fledged democracy.

First of all, one has to remember that in the immediate aftermath of Franco's death, Carlos Arias Navarro was appointed as head of government. He was a Francoist politician who belonged to the most reactionary sector of the regime: he "never accepted the idea of transforming the inherited regime into a pluralistic democracy";[87] on the contrary, his will was the "preservation *post-mortem* of the Franco regime."[88] King Juan Carlos, who had made explicit in a speech before the United States Congress his desire for Spain to move towards a parliamentary democracy, forced the resignation of Arias

Navarro and replaced him with Adolfo Suarez Gonzalez, who became one of the most important protagonists of the "*cambio*" (change).

The king of Spain (who is the head of the armed forces) also contributed to the process of democratic transition and consolidation by making sure that the armed forces would accept some of the consequences of the "*cambio*," in particular those concerning the territorial decentralization of the state.[89] Indeed, in the years following the entry into force of the constitution, Basque terrorism reached its highest peak, with a shocking series of murders and attacks. Many of these attacks were directed at the members of the armed forces themselves.

Furthermore, one should not forget the king's intervention in the attempted *coup d'état* that occurred on February 23, 1981, in the Spanish Congress of Deputies. On that day, Colonel Antonio Tejero Molina entered the congress with some Guardia Civil soldiers and held the deputies hostage until the following day. Moreover, Captain General Jaime Milans del Bosch put tanks on the streets in Valencia and declared a state of emergency. King Juan Carlos, however, did not support the coup. He assured himself of the fidelity of military leaders, and decided to make a speech to the nation. At 1.15am on February 24, he appeared on television in military uniform, positioned himself against the rebels and defended the Spanish constitution. He declared: "The crown, symbol of the permanence and unity of the Nation, cannot tolerate, in any form, actions or attitudes attempting to interrupt with force the democratic process provided for by the Constitution, which was ratified by the Spanish people in the referendum." The intervention of the king determined the failure of the attempted coup.[90]

Rebus sic stantibus, it is very improbable that Arab monarchs will act as "transitional figure[s]"[91] in the way King Juan Carlos did. Very improbable, however, does not mean impossible. Again, the comparison with Spain is of great interest. In fact, one should not forget that when Juan Carlos became king of Spain, his key role in the democratic transition was anything but taken for granted. Indeed, some elements might have led to the conclusion that the monarch would have preserved the continuity of the previous autocratic regime. One just has to think of the speech made by the Caudillo on July 22, 1969 before the Spanish parliament when Juan Carlos was appointed as his successor:

> The decision we shall take today should contribute, in a major way, to everything being secured and well secured for the future [*a que todo quede atado y bien atado para el futuro*] […] It must be clear and well understood by Spaniards of today and of future generations that this Monarchy is the one […] that was instaurated through the Law on Succession approved on July 7, 1947 […] This is the Monarchy of the National Movement, the perennial continuator of its principles, institutions and of the glorious tradition of Spain. For this reason, and in order to implement the provisions on the succession, when the day shall come,

> the Crown shall be instaurated through the person we are presenting today as the successor […][92]

Following that speech, Juan Carlos went down on his knees and took an oath of allegiance to the then head of state (Franco), to the Principles of the Movimiento Nacional and to the Fundamental Laws of the Realm.[93]

Given that situation, one could hardly have expected that the King would have become "*el piloto del cambio*" (the pilot of the change).[94] On the contrary, the "great paradox" was that "the king used the absolute powers inherited by General Franco to dismantle the regime and build a new democratic and parliamentary system."[95] This behavior was due to the fact that the king immediately understood that "the Crown would have been much more vulnerable in an autocratic regime with no separation of powers, than in a democratic Monarchy […] As surprising as it may sound, the more the King sacrificed his powers, the more he became free, and the more he moved away from political responsibilities, the more he strengthened his institutional role."[96] Thus, in only three years (1975–8) Spain turned from a "Francoist monarchy" to a democratic parliamentary monarchy, provided for by the 1978 constitution.

It is evident that now more than ever Arab monarchs have to face what Samuel Huntington defined as the "King's dilemma."[97] To date, despite the uprisings, kings and emirs in the MENA region have managed to preserve their near-absolute power. However, the transformation of their authoritarian monarchies into democratic parliamentary monarchies where "the king reigns but does not rule" may, one day, become the only way to guarantee their own survival.

External variables: influencing the transitions in the MENA region from outside

Besides the role played by internal actors and factors, the outcome of the processes of transition from authoritarian rule often depends on a number of external variables. From this point of view, the transitions in North Africa and in the Middle East following the Arab upheavals are not an exception. In the following paragraphs, three of these variables will be examined: military intervention, the role played by the Venice Commission in the processes of constitution-building, and the "*Zeitgeist*."

Military intervention

The most evident form of external participation in the MENA region was military intervention. The case of Libya is emblematic. As pointed out by Karim Mezran and Eric Knecht, "while the war was undoubtedly won by Libyans, it must be recognized that the revolution's success was largely determined by the intervention of a diverse set of foreign actors motivated by myriad interests but united by the strong desire to see a world without Qaddafi."[98] Indeed, the UN Security Council Resolution (UNSCR) 1973 (which authorized all necessary means to protect civilians and allowed for a no-fly zone), the NATO mission led by US, UK, and France, as well the military, financial, and strategic support provided by Qatar and Sudan to the anti-Qaddafi forces, were all crucial in overthrowing the Brother Leader.

Another example of military intervention is Bahrain. The protests and the demonstrations that broke out in February 2011, "proportionately to the size of the population, were the largest any Arab country has experienced in the current wave of unrest."[99] The protesters called for the election of a constituent assembly to draft a new Basic Law, and for the transition from a monarchy to a republic. Since the situation was getting out of control, the intervention of the Gulf Cooperation Council troops—led by Saudi Arabia—was crucial to help the royal family to suppress the revolt.[100] This action "sent the message that any attack on one Gulf Arab ruling family would be considered an attack on all."[101]

In Syria, the European Union and the United States imposed sanctions on the regime, while a military intervention has been so far only threatened. The strong suspicion that Syrian president Bashar al-Assad had authorized the use of chemical weapons caused the reactions of several Western and non-Western countries (United States, France, Turkey, Saudi Arabia, Qatar …), which were willing to attack Syrian military targets. Several factors—among which the Russian diplomatic initiative—contributed to avert a military strike. In the end, Assad's government agreed to destroy its chemical weapons stockpile and to sign on to the United Nations' Chemical Weapons Convention.

Constitution-building processes: the role of the Venice Commission

In some cases, external intervention may even concern constitution-making and implementation processes. Japan and Germany are two interesting cases in which the respective constitutions were—to a certain extent—imposed by foreign powers. In Japan, the Allied Forces wrote the draft of the constitution, reducing, in particular, the emperor's power and imposing a parliamentary form of government,[102] while in Germany the winning powers required the constituent assembly to establish a federal state and to provide for a strong protection of fundamental freedoms.[103] More recently, several transitions were "guided" by international organizations. In the case of Bosnia, Kosovo, East Timor, Cambodia, and Sierra Leone, for example, "military and political actors such as NATO, the United Nations, international NGOs as well as single foreign states exercised pressure, imposed time frames, and delivered technical and financial support in order to produce new constitutions."[104]

Even in the case of North Africa and the Middle East following the Arab upheavals, some external actors—although in a much more limited manner compared to the abovementioned experiences—intervened in the constitution-building processes. In particular, it is important to mention the role played by the European Commission for Democracy through Law—better known as the Venice Commission—which is the Council of Europe's advisory body on constitutional matters. While maintaining its main focus on Europe, the commission has, since the adoption of its revised statute in 2002, become increasingly active outside Europe. Following the Arab uprisings, the commission has started very important cooperation with some countries in the MENA region in the field of the building of democratic institutions, constitutional justice and electoral issues. Jordan and Libya, despite not being members of the Venice Commission, in 2012 engaged in a dialogue with the commission on cooperation in the field of constitutional justice (in the case of Jordan) and in the processes of drafting and adopting a new constitution (in the case of Libya).[105]

In Morocco, member of the Venice Commission since 2007, focus was put on constitutional implementation. For example, in October 2012, the Moroccan minister for solidarity, women, family, and social development, requested the Venice Commission's assistance to set up the Authority for Parity and Fight against Discrimination as well as the Advisory Council for Family and Childhood, bodies that are foreseen by the new constitution (Articles 164 and 169). Moreover, the commission participated in some exchanges of view with the members of Moroccan parliament during workshop and seminars concerning, for instance, the responsibility of the government before the parliament, or the preparation of the future organic law on the protection of the Amazigh language.[106]

The country that has benefited the most from the assistance of the Venice Commission is Tunisia. The cooperation included the process of constitution-making, the reform of the judiciary, as well as the improvement of the electoral legislation and practice. As far as electoral issues are concerned, it should be noted that the commission organized training seminars for judges and lawyers on electoral disputes with a view to the elections of the Constituent National Assembly (CNA), that were held on October 23, 2011. Moreover, the commission provided legal assistance to the Parliamentary Assembly of the Council of Europe missions in the framework of the elections of the CNA.[107] Furthermore, in 2012 the Constituent National Assembly and the Venice Commission opened a dialogue to discuss the issue of electoral systems and to explore possible ways to improve the electoral legislation and practice in the country.[108]

One should also remember, as underlined above, that the commission started an intensive cooperation with the CNA regarding the constitution-making process, and that the speaker of the National Constituent Assembly requested the opinion of the Venice Commission on the final draft Constitution of Tunisia.

The decision to request the opinion of the Venice Commission confirms the tendency that has been developing in the last decades, i.e., the constitution-makers' will to try to comply with international standards and comparative best practices. Indeed, as highlighted by Andrea Lollini and Francesco Palermo,

> even though the rhetoric of constitutional discourse survives, underlying the absolute freedom of constitution-givers in determining the contents of a constitution, all recent constitution-formation processes and increasingly even the very texts of new constitutions tend to make reference to their embedment into international law and comparative standards […] The international community and (sometimes vague) comparative standards are being considered as a source of legitimacy in a way that becomes increasingly similar to the internal political process.[109]

"Zeitgeist": ***democracy, authoritarian monarchy, and Islamic fundamentalism***

Another external variable that may significantly affect a transition from authoritarian rule is given by the "*Zeitgeist*," which derives from the German tradition of the history of ideas, and means "spirit of the times." According to Juan J. Linz and Alfred Stepan, "when a country is part of an international ideological community where democracy is only one of many strongly contested ideologies, the chances of transiting to […] democracy are substantially less than if the spirit of times is one where democratic ideologies have no powerful contenders."[110] According to the two eminent scholars, the effect of a "*Zeitgeist*" favorable or unfavorable to democracy can be easily understood if one compares Europe between the two world wars (when democracy was only one of several contested ideologies, such as communism, fascism, authoritarian constitutional monarchy, and Catholicism) with Europe during the 1970s and the 1980s (when the democratic ideal had almost no real contenders).

If transitions to democracy in North Africa and in the Middle East following the Arab uprisings are facing so many difficulties and obstacles, it is also because the MENA region seems much more similar to Europe between the two world wars than to Europe during the 1970s and the 1980s. In fact, on the one hand, it is true that the democratic ideal is consolidating itself more and more among the Arab people (the upheavals are a clear demonstration of this tendency), on the other hand, however, the Arab world is still influenced by non-democratic ideologies, such as authoritarian monarchy and Islamic fundamentalism. Indeed, Arab monarchs, despite holding quasi-absolute powers, are often not called into question by the people, since they enjoy a high degree of religious or tribal legitimacy, they are considered the effective guarantors of social and political stability, and they "don't dirty their hands" in everyday politics. Islamic fundamentalism, which is still a very strong and diffuse ideology in the Arab world,[111] is notoriously at odds with the secular and democratic state, characterized by equality between men and women, separation between religion and state, and the protection of fundamental rights, such as free speech and freedom of religion.

Turning from authoritarian to democratic parliamentary monarchies, as well as marginalizing Islamic fundamentalism represent two of the most important challenges for the countries involved in the Arab uprisings in order to establish democratic forms of government.

When conserving is better than changing

In June 2011 American sociologist and political scientist, Jack Goldstone observed:

> The greatest risk that Tunisia and Egypt now face is an attempt at counterrevolution by military *conservatives*, a group that has often sought to claim power after a sultan has been removed. This occurred in Mexico after Diaz was overthrown, in Haiti after Jean-Claude Duvalier's departure, and in the Philippines after Marcos' fall. And after Suharto was forced from power in Indonesia, the military exerted its strength by cracking down on independence movements in East Timor, which Indonesia had occupied since 1975 [emphasis added][112]

Of course, with regard to Egypt, Goldstone's predictions proved to be absolutely right because the Morsi government was indeed toppled by the army on July 3, 2013. But in part the reason for this was the fact that most of the powers of the military had been conserved despite the revolution. This is demonstrated by the much criticized constitution-making process followed by the Muslim Brotherhood that we illustrated above. The choice of using the 1971 constitution as the basis for drafting the new fundamental law was in itself an act of *conservation* rather than *change*. Moreover, where changes were made when it came to the military the new provisions that were introduced clearly had the aim of safeguarding a main actor of the *ancien régime*. Let us turn briefly to the text of the 2012 constitution to see how the army came out as a "winner" of the constitution-making process.[113]

Beginning with the preamble of the Morsi constitution we can see that rather surprisingly the army is included among those actors who supported the revolution that overthrew Mubarak:

> We the People of Egypt, in the name of God, the Merciful, and with His assistance, state: This is our Constitution, the document of the revolution of January 25, 2011, which our youth began, around which our People gathered, *and with which our armed forces sided* [emphasis added].

As Tom Ginsburg has underlined "the armed forces stayed in their barracks knowing that no matter what happened they would maintain their privileged status under the new constitution."[114] The fact that the army was considered among the winners of the revolution by the Morsi government is confirmed by reading other articles of the constitutional text.

Very briefly, the new fundamental law established that the minister of defense be a military officer and the National Defense Council be split into two separate organs: the National Security Council, a mainly civilian body, and a *new* defense council, with a majority of military officers. Again in terms of *conservation* of power, this novelty was important in ensuring the army's control over the military budget: in fact it is the defense council, dominated by the military, that decides on military budgetary matters.

The concessions granted by Morsi to the armed forces did not, however, stop there, given that the National Defense Council has to be consulted not only on bills concerning the army, but also in the case of declarations of war or deployment of troops abroad. In geopolitical terms, it is evident that this provision would have prevented, for example, the Muslim Brotherhood, while they were in power, from unilaterally declaring war on Israel on the basis of their parliamentary majority.

Of course given that six months later the army toppled the Morsi government one cannot reason in terms of a mere will of the Muslim Brotherhood to preserve the powers of the military. The truth of the matter is that, during its period in government, the Muslim Brotherhood was not able to fully exercise its power due to the hostility of the army, but also of other institutions of the state. In other words the Muslim Brotherhood did want *change* rather than *conservation* but they did not have the power to implement this fully. In mid-2012, as Nathan Brown illustrates in his chapter, "the leaders of Brotherhood specifically began to sense a coordinated effort to bring them down"[115] therefore, on one hand, Morsi in November 2012 speeded up the constitution-making process so as to immunize it from judicial review, on the other, important concessions were made to the armed forces in order to keep the military on his side, a move that in the short term seemed to work, but in the long run did not.

Still referring to Goldstone's prediction, but turning now to Tunisia one can observe that there are of course military conservatives in this country as well and therefore the risk of a *coup d'état* cannot be excluded altogether, but Tunisia's armed forces appear to have a less prominent role compared to Egypt. At present, the risk that Tunisia appears to run is not related to resistance of the conservatives (military and non), but to the ambiguities pertaining to the semi-presidential form of government introduced in the 2014 Constitution, which could potentially jeopardize Tunisia's transition to democracy and lead to a return to a form of authoritarianism albeit of a different nature with respect to the Ben Ali regime. We previously underlined how Al-Nahda's compromises have driven Tunisia's constitutional bargain. One compromise is its omission of *sharia* from the constitution, but another compromise is its acceptance of a semi-presidential form of government and this is where, potentially, a storm could be brewing.

Historically semi-presidentialism has long sparked debate among scholars,[116] however, the majority of authors is against its adoption in "new democracies" and this is where Al-Nahda's decision to accept a compromise with respect to its initial proposal to adopt a parliamentary form of government (which many consider the preferable option for a transitional country) should be critically examined. In opting for a semi-presidential system there are fundamentally three possible problems: first, the potential challenge to the rule of law stemming from the election of a populist candidate; second, the issue of "cohabitation"; third the fragility of the system in the case of a "divided minority government."

The first problem concerns the direct election of the president. In a transition process such as that of Tunisia having a populist leader who personalizes his/her power could be a risk. His/her authority could end up being even more potent than that exerted by a head of state and government in a presidential system especially if he/she is also supported by a large majority in parliament.[117]

The second problem that may arise in semi-presidential systems is the simultaneous presence at the top of the executive of two different opposing powers where the president may decide to challenge the legislature with regard to the appointment of the prime minister. As Pickard clearly illustrates, the secular forces in Tunisia have been pushing for a directly-elected president through a two-round voting system because they believe that in a run-off election the majority of Tunisians would choose the non-Islamist candidate, but this implies that they acknowledge the fact that Al-Nahda will continue to be the party with a relative majority in parliament. It goes without saying that in a constitutional phase of transition authoritarian ambitions might, once more, play a major role in defining the institutional framework and in the Tunisian context this may fuel the possibility of a return to some form of authoritarianism. In any case, as Linz points out, the compromise between the opposite forces may imply Machiavellian machinations or contradictory policies to the detriment of the effectiveness of the decision making process.[118]

Last but not least, there is the hypothesis put forward by Cindy Skach in the case "neither the president nor the prime minister, nor any party or coalition, enjoys a substantive majority in the legislature."[119] The consequences of such a situation are evident: legislative deadlock, government instability and therefore the president's propensity to act by decree so again, imagining the adoption of this form of government in Tunisia, there is a risk of a shift back to authoritarianism.[120]

There are some provisions that have been included in the new constitution of Tunisia that are a cause of concern. The president clearly combines the role of head of state and head of government as emerges from Article 77 that, on one hand, establishes that the president of the republic is responsible for representing the state (a function typical of a head of state) but, on the other, also asserts that he/she is responsible for determining the general state orientations with regard to defense, foreign relations, and national security related to protecting the state and the national territory from all internal and external threats (a power typically exercised by a head of government). The diarchal character of the executive is confirmed by Article 91, which states that "The

Head of Government determines the state's general policy, *taking into account the provisions of Article 77*, and shall ensure its execution" (emphasis added). The uncertainty as to who is the chief of the executive is further corroborated by Article 93, which first states that "The Head of Government chairs the Council of Ministers," but it then goes on to assert that "it is mandatory for the President of the Republic to preside over the Council of Ministers in issues relating to defence, foreign policy, and national security […]. The President may also attend the Council of Ministers' other meetings, and if so, he/she presides over the meeting."[121]

Article 101 of the 2014 constitution goes on to stipulate that the Constitutional Court has the function of resolving conflicts between the president and prime minister over their respective powers. Again, potentially, these provisions could be a recipe for institutional deadlock, a deadlock that in transitional countries is often broken by a return to authoritarianism. Frankly this would be a dismal outcome for a constitution-making process that has justly deserved the praise of many observers and a paradoxical boomerang for a governing party, Al-Nahda, that has so far adopted a spirit of collaboration and compromise as a way of realizing the hopes that emerged with the Jasmine Revolution.

Having said this there are also provisions that clearly have the aim of avoiding a shift to authoritarianism and that should be judged as extremely positive. Based on the negative experience of other countries with presidential or semi-presidential regimes the last two paragraphs of Article 75 of the constitution establish that no one can be elected as president for more than two full terms and that this limit applies regardless of whether the two terms are consecutive or separate (thus avoiding a Putin–Medvedev-style "job swap"). Last but not least, the constitution may not be amended to increase the number or the length of presidential terms (again in an attempt avoid ploys used in other countries such as Venezuela or, again, Russia).[122]

We have seen that in Egypt there has already been a counterrevolution by military conservatives and in Tunisia the seeds that could lead to a return to authoritarianism have been planted in the 2014 constitution, but of course these are countries where a revolution took place. On the contrary, Morocco and Algeria are two examples of where conservation has so far prevailed over change.

As we explained above, in Morocco (and also Jordan) the main instrument that has been used to preserve the existing system of government is what we have defined as "surviving constitutionalism," i.e., these countries have used constitutional reforms as an attempt to *conserve* the existing regime. Strictly related to constitutional reform is of course "electoral engineering" and indeed both Morocco and Jordan, together with several other countries in the Arab world, have adopted electoral systems and organized elections in such a way as to resist to the wind of change.[123] Indeed "in the decades preceding the 2010–11 Arab uprisings, authoritarian regimes organized elections to co-opt the opposition and expand political participation, but to avoid democratization."[124] For example in Morocco in 2007 King Mohammed VI demonstrated his skills in "distorting the link between the ballot box and the parliament chamber, making each new government look much the same as the one before."[125]

But there is a factor of conservation that goes beyond surviving constitutionalism and electoral engineering because when the Islamist movement Parti de la justice et du développement (PJD) won the elections in Morocco it avoided a confrontation with the king, evidently because the party wanted to be accepted as a legitimate political player and to become fully integrated into the *existing* political-institutional system.[126] This acknowledgement of the king's role is a clear demonstration of how the conservative forces are still very powerful.

Another instrument that the conservative forces can of course resort to is rentier and resource politics. As John Entelis explains with great clarity in his chapter, this is one of the factors that has determined the conservation of the authoritarian regime in Algeria. However, alongside the plentiful hydrocarbon resources and the central role played by Sonatrach, another factor that has so far convinced the majority of Algerians that "conserving is better than changing" is the fear of a return to the terrible bloodshed of the 1990s. Finally, still with regard to Algeria, other factors that have contributed to the preservation of the present regime is the geopolitical diversity of the country (especially compared to Tunisia and Egypt) and the diffused power balance among the ruling elites that makes Bouteflika's presidency different to that of Ben Ali, Qaddafi, and Mubarak.

Uncertainty continues to reign

In choosing the title of this book we intentionally decided not to use expressions and terms such as "Arab Spring," "Arab Awakening," "Fourth Wave of Democratization," "Transitions to Democracy," and so forth because they are based on the presumption that the outcome of the process of transformation that is affecting the countries in Northern Africa and beyond will be the instauration of a democratic regime. This is essentially the reason why we have simply used the expression "transition" (*Political and Constitutional Transitions in North Africa: Actors and Factors*). Indeed, it is common knowledge that a transition may consist of abandoning the previous autocratic regime in order to establish a democratic form of state, but also a shift from one form of autocracy to another.

As each of the chapters of this volume demonstrates, the outcome of the transitions in the countries under examination is characterized by a very high degree of uncertainty therefore as of this writing it is extremely difficult (if not impossible) to predict what will happen not only in the medium and long term, but also in the short term. One just has to think of what is happening in Egypt where in the space of two years we are already in the midst of a "second" transition, going from the authoritarian regime of Mubarak to the government of the Muslim Brotherhood led by President Mohammed Morsi and then to a new government led by General Abdel Fattah el-Sisi.

It is not by chance that, with regard to the uncertainty that characterizes transitions, nearly 30 years ago Guillermo O'Donnell and Philippe C. Schmitter in their seminal book *Transitions from Authoritarian Rule* observed that:

> the high degree of indeterminacy embedded in situations where unexpected events (*fortuna*), insufficient information, hurried and audacious choices, confusion about motives and interests, plasticity, and even indefinition of political identities, as well as the talents of specific individuals (*virtù*), are frequently decisive in determining the outcomes.[127]

Thus in the light of this uncertainty and indeterminacy, the only prediction that we are prepared to make is the fact that the wind of change in the MENA region has been so profound that we believe that a return to the specific type of regime that existed for such a long time in this area is highly improbable. The impression is that an equilibrium that lasted for many decades has been broken given the fact that the young populations of North Africa are no longer prepared to accept and support highly personalized autocratic regimes such as those of Ben Ali, Mubarak, and Qaddafi.

Beyond that, the only other certainty is that uncertainty continues to reign.

References

Abu-Karaki, M., "Democracy and Judicial Controlling in Jordan: A Constitutional Study," *Journal of Politics and Law*, vol. 4, no. 2, 2011.

Al-Ali, Z., "Constitution Drafting and External Influence," in T. Ginsburg and R. Dixon (eds.), *Comparative Constitutional Law* (Cheltenham: Edward Elgar, 2011).

——, "Constitutional Legitimacy in Iraq: What Role Local Context?," in R. Grote and T.J. Röder (eds.), *Constitutionalism in Islamic Countries. Between Upheaval and Continuity* (Oxford: Oxford University Press, 2012).

——, *The New Egyptian Constitution: An Initial Assessment of its Merits and Flaws*, www.opendemocracy.net/zaid-al-ali/new-egyptian-constitution-initial-assessment-of-its-merits-and-flaws.

Al-Ali, Z. and Ben Romdhane, D., *Tunisia's New Constitution: Progress and Challenges to Come*, https://www.opendemocracy.net/arab-awakening/zaid-al-ali-donia-ben-romdhane/tunisia%E2%80%99s-new-constitution-progress-and-challenges-to-, 2014.

Alarabiya.net, *GCC Troops Dispatched to Bahrain to Maintain Order*, Alarabiya.net, March 14, 2011, www.alarabiya.net/articles/2011/03/14/141445.html

Barros, R., *Constitutionalism and Dictatorship: Pinochet, the Junta and the 1980 Constitution* (Cambridge: Cambridge University Press, 2002).

Bernoussi, N., "La Constitution de 2011 et le juge constitutionnel," in Centre d'Études Internationales (ed.), *La Constitution marocaine de 2011: Analyses et commentaires* (Paris: LGDJ, 2012)

Biagi, F., "Le Corti costituzionali nelle transizioni democratiche: i casi dell'Italia, della Spagna e della Repubblica ceca," *Annali on-line – Pubblicazioni dello IUSS*, vol. 5, no. 1, 2011, http://annali.unife.it/iuss/article/view/685/594.

——, "Three Generations of European Constitutional Courts in Transition to Democracy," *Diritto pubblico comparato ed europeo*, no. 2, 2014 (forthcoming).

——, "Will Surviving Constitutionalism in Morocco and Jordan Work in the Long Run? A Comparison with Three Past Authoritarian Regimes," *Cambridge Journal of International and Comparative Law*, vol. 3 (3), 2014 (forthcoming).

Blount, J., Elkins, Z., and Ginsburg, T., "Does the Process of Constitution-making Matter?," in T. Ginsburg (ed.), *Comparative Constitutional Design* (Cambridge: Cambridge University Press, 2012).

Brewer-Carías, A.R., *Judicial Review in Comparative Law* (Cambridge: Cambridge University Press, 1989).

Brown, N., "Judicial Review and the Arab World," *Journal of Democracy*, vol. 9, no. 4, 1998.

Brynen, R., Moore, P.W., Salloukh, B.F., and Zahar, M-J., *Beyond the Arab Spring: Authoritarianism and Democratization in the Arab World* (Boulder: Lynne Rienner Publishers, 2012).

Brzezinski, M., *The Struggle for Constitutionalism in Poland* (London: Macmillan, 2000).

Burgis, M.L., "Judicial Reform and the Possibility of Democratic Rule in Jordan: A Policy Perspective on Judicial Independence," *Arab Law Quarterly*, no. 21, 2007.

Calamandrei, P., "La Costituzione e le leggi per attuarla," *Dieci anni dopo 1945–1955* (Bari: Laterza, 1955).

Cappelletti, M., *Il controllo giudiziario di costituzionalità delle leggi nel diritto comparato* (Milano: Giuffrè, 1968).

Cercas, J., *The Anatomy of a Moment* (London, Berlin, New York and Sidney: Bloomsbury, 2011).

Cruz Villalón, P., *La curiosidad del jurista persa, y otros estudios sobre la Constitución* (Madrid: Centro de estudios políticos y constitucionales, 1999).

Dado, N., *Growing Violence against Minorities Threatens Future of Christians in Syria and across Muslim World*, www.arabamericannews.com/news/index.php?mod=article&cat=Community&article=7560, 2013.

de Vergottini, G., "Costituzionalismo europeo e transizioni democratiche," in M. Calamo Specchia, M. Carli, G. Di Plinio, and R. Toniatti (eds.), *I Balcani occidentali. Le costituzioni della transizione* (Turin: Giappichelli, 2008).

——, "Foreword," in J.O. Frosini, *Constitutional Preambles: At a Crossroads between Politics and Law* (Rimini: Maggioli, 2012).

Eljarh, M., "A Bad Omen for Libya," www.foreignpolicy.com, 2013.

Ellis, M.S., "Purging the Past: The Current State of Lustration Laws in the Former Communist Bloc," *Law and Contemporary Problems*, vol. 59, no. 4, 1996.

Fabbrini, F., "Kelsen in Paris: France's Constitutional Reform and the Introduction of A Posteriori Constitutional Review of Legislation," *German Law Journal*, vol. 9, no. 10, 2008.

Favoreu, L., *Les Cours Constitutionnelles* (Paris: Presses Universitaires de France, 1986).

Friedrich, C.J., "Rebuilding the German Constitution," *American Political Science Review*, 1949.

Frosini, J.O., *The Egyptian Revolution Left the Army Untouched*, www.viasarfatti25.unibocconi.eu/notizia.php?idArt=11781, 2013.

Frosini, J.O. and Pegoraro, L., "Constitutional Courts in Latin America: A Testing Ground for New Parameters of Classification?," *Journal of Comparative Law*, vol. 3, no. 2, 2008.

Gallala-Arndt, I., "Constitutional Jurisdiction and its Limits in the Maghreb," in R. Grote and T.J. Röder (eds.), *Constitutionalism in Islamic Countries: Between Upheaval and Continuity* (Oxford: Oxford University Press, 2012).

Ginsburg, T., Melton, J., and Elkins, Z., "On the Evasion of Executive Term Limits," *William and Mary Law Review*, vol. 52, 2011.

Goldstone, J.A., "Understanding the Revolutions of 2011," *Foreign Affairs*, vol. 90, no. 3, 2011.

Grote, R., "Models of Institutional Control. The Experience of Islamic Countries," in R. Grote and T.J. Röder (eds.), *Constitutionalism in Islamic Countries. Between Upheaval and Continuity* (Oxford: Oxford University Press, 2012)

Human Rights Watch, *Human Rights Watch 2013 World Report*, www.hrw.org/sites/default/files/wr2013_web.pdf.

——, *"Just Sign Here": Unfair Trials Based on Confessions to the Police in Morocco*, June 2013, www.hrw.org/sites/default/files/reports/morocco0613webwcover.pdf.

——, *Morocco: Human Rights at a Crossroads*, October 2004, www.hrw.org/print/reports/2004/10/20/morocco-human-rights-crossroads.

Huntington, S.P., *Political Order in Changing Societies* (New Haven: Yale University Press, 1968).

Imholz, K., "A Landmark Constitutional Court Decision in Albania," in N.J. Kritz (ed.), *Transitional Justice: How Emerging Democracies Reckon With Former Regimes*, vol. 2 (Washington, DC: United States Institute of Peace Press, 1995).

——, "States of Emergency as Pretexts for Gagging the Press: Word Play at Albania's Constitutional Court," *East European Constitutional Review*, vol. 6, no. 4, 1997.

International IDEA, *Constitutional Courts after the Arab Spring: Appointment Mechanisms and Relative Judicial Independence*, Spring 2014, http://constitutionaltransitions.org/publications/constitutional-courts-after-the-arab-spring.

Keyman, A., "The Resilience of Arab Spring Monarchies," *e-International Relations*, April 2012, www.e-ir.info/2012/04/02/the-resilience-of-arab-monarchies-in-the-arab-spring/#_ftn1.

Klug, H., "South Africa's Constitutional Court: Enabling Democracy and Promoting Law in the Transition from Apartheid," *Journal of Comparative Law*, vol. 3, no. 2, 2008.

"Les grandes décisions de la jurisprudence du Conseil Constitutionnel [1994–2013]," *Revue marocaine d'administration locale et de développement*, no. 31, 2013.

Le Roy, T., "Constitutionalism in the Maghreb: Between French Heritage and Islamic Concepts," in R. Grote and T.J. Röder (eds.), *Constitutionalism in Islamic Countries. Between Upheaval and Continuity* (Oxford: Oxford University Press, 2012).

Lijphart, A., "Constitutional Design for Divided Societies," *Journal of Democracy*, vol. 15, no. 2, 2004.

Linz, J.J., "Presidential or Parliamentary Democracy: Does It Make a Difference?," in J.J. Linz and A. Valenzuela (eds.), *The Crisis of Presidential Democracy: The Latin American Evidence* (Baltimore and London: Johns Hopkins University Press, 1994).

Linz, J.J., and Stepan, A., *Problems of Democratic Transition and Consolidation. Southern Europe, South America, and Post-Communist Europe* (Baltimore and London: Johns Hopkins University Press, 1996).

Lollini, A. and Palermo, F., "Comparative Law and the 'Proceduralization' of Constitution-Building Processes," in J. Raue and P. Sutter (eds.), *Facets and Practices of State-Building* (Leiden and Boston: Martinus Nijhoff Publishers, 2009).

Lollini, A., *Constitutionalism and Transitional Justice in South Africa* (New York and Oxford: Berghahn Books, 2010).

Lombardi, C., "Egypt's Supreme Constitutional Court: Managing Constitutional Conflict in an Authoritarian, Aspirationally 'Islamic' State," *Journal of Comparative Law*, vol. 3, no. 2, 2008.

Maravall, J.M. and Santamaría, J., "Political Change in Spain and the Prospects for Democracy," in G. O'Donnell, P.C. Schmitter, and L. Whitehead (eds.), *Transitions from Authoritarian Rule. Southern Europe* (Baltimore and London: Johns Hopkins University Press, 1986).

Matsui, S., *The Constitution of Japan: A Contextual Analysis* (Oxford and Portland: Hart Publishing, 2011).

Mekki, N., *Tunisia's New Election Law and the Consolidation of a New Constitutional Order*, www.constitutionnet.org.

Mezran, K. and Alunni, A., "Power Shifts in the Arab Spring: A Work in Progress," *The Bologna Center Journal of International Affairs*, vol. 15, spring 2012.

Mezzetti, L., *Teoria e prassi delle transizioni costituzionali e del consolidamento democratico* (Padua: Cedam, 2003).

Morodo, R., *La transición política* (Madrid: Tecnos, 1985).

Moustafa, T., *The Struggle for Constitutional Power: Law, Politics and Economic Development in Egypt* (Cambridge: Cambridge University Press, 2007).

Noueihed, L., and Warren, A., *The Battle for the Arab Spring: Revolution, Counter-revolution and the Making of a New Era* (New Haven: Yale University Press, 2012).

Ottaway, M., *Bahrain: Between the United States and Saudi Arabia*, http://carnegieendowment.org/2011/04/04/bahrain-between-united-states-and-saudi-arabia/2tzk#.

Ottaway, M. and Muasher, M., "Arab Monarchies: Change for Reform, Yet Unmet," *The Carnegie Papers*, 2011, http://carnegieendowment.org/files/arab_monarchies1.pdf.

Pasquino, G., "Semi-presidentialism: A Political Model at Work," *European Journal of Political Research*, vol. 31, 1997.

Powell, C.T., *El piloto del cambio. El rey, la monarquía y la transición a la democracia* (Barcelona: Planeta, 1991).

Sadurski, W. (ed.), *Constitutional Justice, East and West. Democratic Legitimacy and Constitutional Courts in Post-Communist Europe in a Comparative Perspective* (The Hague: Kluwer Law International, 2002).

Sánchez Navarro, Á.J., *La transición española en sus documentos* (Madrid: Centro de estudios políticos y constitucionales, 1998).

Sartori, G., *Comparative Constitutional Engineering. An Inquiry into Structures, Incentives and Outcomes*, 2nd edition (London: Macmillan, 1997).

Sbailò, C., "'Primavera araba', 'risveglio islamico', 'deriva autoritaria'. Mutamenti costituzionali nel Nord Africa a tre anni dall'inizio delle rivolte," *Diritto pubblico comparato ed europeo*, no. 1, 2014.

Schwartz, H., *The Struggle for Constitutional Justice in Post-Communist Europe* (Chicago: University of Chicago Press, 2000).

Sebhallah, E.R., "Bilan du Conseil constitutionnel marocain (1994–2011)," in *Cinquante ans de vie constitutionnelle au Maroc. Quel bilan?*, Publications de l'Association marocaine de droit constitutionnel, 2013.

Tajadura Tejada, J., "La legitimidad de la Monarquía parlamentaria," in C. León Bastos and V.A. Wong Meraz (eds.), *Homenaje al Doctor Jorge Carpizo en Madrid* (México: Porrúa, 2010).

The Venice Commission of the Council of Europe, *Annual Report of Activities 2011*, Council of Europe, 2012, www.venice.coe.int/webforms/documents/?pdf=CDL-RA (2011)001-e.

WBEZ Worldview, "Tom Ginsburg Discusses the Draft Egyptian Constitution," December 13, 2012, www.law.uchicago.edu/news/tom-ginsburg-discusses-draft-egyptian-constitution-worldview.

Yetiv, S.A., "Oil, Saudi Arabia, and the Spring that Has Not Come," in M.L. Haas and D.W. Lesch (eds.), *The Arab Spring: Change and Resistance in the Middle East* (Boulder: Westview Press, 2013).

Yom, S.L., "Jordan: The Ruse of Reform," *Journal of Democracy*, vol. 24, no. 3, 2013.

Yom, S.L. and Guase III, F.G., "Resilient Royals: How Arab Monarchies Hang On," *Journal of Democracy*, vol. 23, no. 4, 2012.

Zovatto, D., *Latin America Suffers Reelection Fever*, www.idea.int/americas/latin-america-suffers-reelection-fever.cfm.

Notes

* This article is the result of the combined efforts of both authors, however paragraphs "The Rise to Power of the Islamist Parties and their Approaches to Constitution-making" and "When Conserving is Better than Changing" were written by Justin O. Frosini, while the others were written by Francesco Biagi. The premise and the last paragraph are by both.

1 See G. de Vergottini, "Costituzionalismo europeo e transizioni democratiche," in M. Calamo Specchia, M. Carli, G. Di Plinio, and R. Toniatti (eds.), *I Balcani occidentali. Le costituzioni della transizione* (Turin: Giappichelli, 2008), p. 3 ff.; L. Mezzetti, *Teoria e prassi delle transizioni costituzionali e del consolidamento democratico* (Padua: Cedam, 2003), pp. 5–6.

2 "When there are profound differences about the territorial boundaries of the political community's State and profound differences as to who has the right of citizenship in that State, there is what we call a 'stateness' problem" (J.J. Linz and A. Stepan, *Problems of Democratic Transition and Consolidation. Southern Europe, South America, and Post-Communist Europe* (Baltimore and London: Johns Hopkins University Press, 1996), p. 16).

3 See paragraph "'Zeitgeist': Democracy, Authoritarian Monarchy and Islamic Fundamentalism."

4 K. Mezran and A. Alunni, "Power Shifts in the Arab Spring: A Work in Progress," *The Bologna Center Journal of International Affairs*, vol. 15, spring 2012.

5 The most significant constitutional changes in North Africa since the beginning of the Arab uprisings are analysed by C. Sbailò, "'Primavera araba', 'risveglio islamico', 'deriva autoritaria'. Mutamenti costituzionali nel Nord Africa a tre anni dall'inizio delle rivolte," *Diritto pubblico comparato ed europeo*, no. 1, 2014, p. 3 ff.

6 D. Pickard, "Al-Nahda: Moderation and Compromise in Tunisia's Constitutional Bargain," in this volume.

7 … i.e., just six months before the Republican Constitution came into force.

8 See G. de Vergottini, "Foreword," in J.O. Frosini, *Constitutional Preambles: At a Crossroads between Politics and Law* (Rimini: Maggioli, 2012), p. 13.
9 D. Pickard, "Al-Nahda: Moderation and Compromise in Tunisia's Constitutional Bargain," in this volume.
10 Z. Al-Ali, *The New Egyptian Constitution: An Initial Assessment of its Merits and Flaws*, p. 1, www.opendemocracy.net/zaid-al-ali/new-egyptian-constitution-initial-assessment-of-its-merits-and-flaws (accessed May 25, 2014).
11 Ibid.
12 Ibid., p. 6.
13 Ibid., p. 2.
14 The six-month deadline was always going to be extremely problematic, which is why President Morsi should have revisited the March 2011 interim constitution as soon as he assumed his powers in June 2012.
15 See N. Brown, "Egypt: A Constitutional Court in an Unconstitutional Setting," in this volume.
16 See www.venice.coe.int/WebForms/pages/?p=03_neighbours (accessed May 25, 2014).
17 The observations of the commission are available at www.venice.coe.int/webforms/documents/?pdf=CDL(2013)034-e (accessed May 25, 2014). On the role played by the Venice Commission also see the paragraph "Constitution-building Processes: The Role of the Venice Commission."
18 WBEZ Worldview, "Tom Ginsburg Discusses the Draft Egyptian Constitution," 13 December 2012, www.law.uchicago.edu/news/tom-ginsburg-discusses-draft-egyptian-constitution-worldview (accessed May 25, 2014).
19 See J. Blount, Z. Elkins, and T. Ginsburg, "Does the Process of Constitution-making Matter?," in T. Ginsburg (ed.), *Comparative Constitutional Design* (Cambridge: Cambridge University Press, 2012), p. 41.
20 Z. Al-Ali and D. Ben Romdhane, *Tunisia's New Constitution: Progress and Challenges to Come*, p. 2, https://www.opendemocracy.net/arab-awakening/zaid-al-ali-donia-ben-romdhane/tunisia%E2%80%99s-new-constitution-progress-and-challenges-to- (accessed May 25, 2014).
21 See International IDEA, *Constitutional Courts after the Arab Spring: Appointment Mechanisms and Relative Judicial Independence*, spring 2014, http://constitutionaltransitions.org/publications/constitutional-courts-after-the-arab-spring/ (accessed May 25, 2014). It should be noted that judicial review, generally in the form of constitutional courts, was a common feature in the Arab world even before the Arab uprisings. However, "only a few of the bodies charged with the task [were] viewed as effective defenders of constitutionalism" (N. Brown, "Judicial Review and the Arab World," *Journal of Democracy*, vol. 9, no. 4, 1998, p. 85 ff). On the models of constitutional review in the Islamic world see R. Grote, "Models of Institutional Control. The Experience of Islamic Countries," in R. Grote and T.J. Röder (eds.), *Constitutionalism in Islamic Countries. Between Upheaval and Continuity* (Oxford: Oxford University Press, 2012), p. 221 ff.
22 In fact, Article 133 provides that "the Constitutional Court shall have competence to look into an exception of unconstitutionality raised in the course of a trial, when one of the parties argues that the law on which depends the outcome of a trial undermines the rights and freedoms guaranteed by the Constitution."
23 See F. Biagi, "The Pilot of *Limited* Change: Mohammed VI and the Transition in Morocco," in this volume.
24 I. Gallala-Arndt, "Constitutional Jurisdiction and its Limits in the Maghreb," in R. Grote and T.J. Röder (eds.), op. cit., p. 254.
25 Ibid., pp. 254–5.
26 This was the metaphore used by Robert Badinter, cited by N. Bernoussi, "La Constitution de 2011 et le juge constitutionnel," in Centre d'Études Internationales (ed.), *La Constitution marocaine de 2011. Analyses et commentaires* (Paris: LGDJ,

2012), p. 211. On the contrary, the council has been very active in the field of electoral justice (see E.R. Sebhallah, "Bilan du Conseil constitutionnel marocain (1994–2011)," in *Cinquante ans de vie constitutionnelle au Maroc. Quel bilan?*, Publications de l'Association marocaine de droit constitutionnel, 2013). A collection of the most important decisions of the Moroccan Constitutional Council between 1994 and 2013 can be found in "Les grandes décisions de la jurisprudence du Conseil Constitutionnel [1994–2013]," *Revue marocaine d'administration locale et de développement*, no. 31, 2013.

27 It should be noted that according to Article 158(7) of the new constitution, a provisional authority in charge of determining the constitutionality of laws had to be set up in the first three months following the promulgation of the constitution. This body was established by organic law no. 14/2014 of April 18, 2014, and will carry out its functions until the set up of the Constitutional Court, which has to be created within a maximum of one year from the first legislative elections.

28 Gallala-Arndt, op. cit., p. 246.

29 On the impact of the French heritage on the Maghreb countries see T. Le Roy, "Constitutionalism in the Maghreb. Between French Heritage and Islamic Concepts," in R. Grote and T.J. Röder (eds.), op. cit., p. 109 ff. On the introduction of the *ex post* constitutional review in France see F. Fabbrini, "Kelsen in Paris: France's Constitutional Reform and the Introduction of A Posteriori Constitutional Review of Legislation," *German Law Journal*, vol. 9, no. 10, 2008, p. 1297 ff.

30 See M. Cappelletti, *Il controllo giudiziario di costituzionalità delle leggi nel diritto comparato* (Milano: Giuffrè, 1968); A.R. Brewer-Carías, *Judicial Review in Comparative Law* (Cambridge: Cambridge University Press, 1989).

31 C. Lombardi, "Egypt's Supreme Constitutional Court: Managing Constitutional Conflict in an Authoritarian, Aspirationally 'Islamic' State," *Journal of Comparative Law*, vol. 3, no. 2, 2008, p. 242.

32 Ibid.

33 N. Brown, "Egypt: A Constitutional Court in an Unconstitutional Setting," in this volume.

34 Ibid.

35 See M.L. Burgis, "Judicial Reform and the Possibility of Democratic Rule in Jordan: A Policy Perspective on Judicial Independence," *Arab Law Quarterly*, no. 21, 2007, pp. 162–3; M. Abu-Karaki, "Democracy and Judicial Controlling in Jordan: A Constitutional Study," *Journal of Politics and Law*, vol. 4, no. 2, 2011, p. 180 ff.

36 "In pending cases, any party to the lawsuit may argue that a law is not in conformity with the Constitution. In case the relevant court finds that the plea has merit, it must refer the matter to the court specified by the law for the purposes of examining the referral of such to the Constitutional Court" (Article 60).

37 The video of Marzouki's speech addressed to the UN General Assembly is available at http://webtv.un.org/watch/tunisia-general-debate-67th-session/1864492175001/ (accessed May 25, 2014).

38 http://webtv.un.org/watch/tunisia-general-debate-67th-session/1864492175001/ (accessed May 25, 2014).

39 Eliminating the constitutional provisions that limit the number of presidential mandates is a practice followed also by many Latin American leaders (see D. Zovatto, *Latin America Suffers Reelection Fever*, www.idea.int/americas/latin-america-suffers-reelection-fever.cfm (accessed May 25, 2014). On this issue see also T. Ginsburg, J. Melton and Z. Elkins, "On the Evasion of Executive Term Limits," *William and Mary Law Review*, vol. 52, 2011, p. 1807 ff.).

40 Le Roy, op. cit., p. 112.

41 See L. Favoreu, *Les Cours Constitutionnelles* (Paris: Presses Universitaires de France, 1986).

42 N. Brown, "Egypt: A Constitutional Court in an Unconstitutional Setting," in this volume.
43 On the role played by constitutional courts in transitions to democracy see F. Biagi, "Le Corti costituzionali nelle transizioni democratiche: i casi dell'Italia, della Spagna e della Repubblica ceca," *Annali on-line – Pubblicazioni dello IUSS*, vol. 5, no. 1, 2011, http://annali.unife.it/iuss/article/view/685/594 (accessed May 25, 2014); F. Biagi, "Three Generations of European Constitutional Courts in Transition to Democracy," *Diritto pubblico comparato ed europeo*, no. 2, 2014 (forthcoming).
44 See M. Brzezinski, *The Struggle for Constitutionalism in Poland* (London: Macmillan, 2000).
45 See below.
46 See K. Imholz, "A Landmark Constitutional Court Decision in Albania," in N.J. Kritz (ed.), *Transitional Justice: How Emerging Democracies Reckon With Former Regimes*, vol. 2 (Washington, DC: United States Institute of Peace Press, 1995), p. 729 ff.; K. Imholz, "States of Emergency as Pretexts for Gagging the Press: Word Play at Albania's Constitutional Court," *East European Constitutional Review*, vol. 6, no. 4, 1997.
47 On the role played by the South African Constitutional Court in the transition to democracy see H. Klug, "South Africa's Constitutional Court: Enabling Democracy and Promoting Law in the Transition from Apartheid," *Journal of Comparative Law*, vol. 3, no. 2, 2008, p. 174 ff.; A. Lollini, *Constitutionalism and Transitional Justice in South Africa* (New York and Oxford: Berghahn Books, 2010).
48 P. Calamandrei, "La Costituzione e le leggi per attuarla," *Dieci anni dopo. 1945–1955* (Bari: Laterza, 1955), p. 253.
49 Human Rights Watch, *Human Rights Watch 2013 World Report*, p. 591, www.hrw.org/sites/default/files/wr2013_web.pdf (accessed May 25, 2014). The part of Article 475 that prevented the prosecutor from charging the person if he then married the minor was repealed at the beginning of 2014 by Law 15–14.
50 See Human Rights Watch, *Morocco: Human Rights at a Crossroads*, October 2004, www.hrw.org/print/reports/2004/10/20/morocco-human-rights-crossroads (accessed May 25, 2014); Human Rights Watch, *"Just Sign Here": Unfair Trials Based on Confessions to the Police in Morocco*, June 2013, www.hrw.org/sites/default/files/reports/morocco0613webwcover.pdf (accessed May 25, 2014).
51 The 2006 Iraqi Constitution speaks of Iraq as a federal state and establishes three main levels of government: the federal government in Baghdad, regional governments and provinces (Art. 116). See Z. Al-Ali, "Constitutional Legitimacy in Iraq. What Role Local Context?," in R. Grote and T.J. Röder (eds.), op. cit., pp. 652–62. Art. 1 of the Constitution of the United Arab Emirates (UAE) describes itself as a federal state. Both the Federal Supreme Court of Iraq and the Supreme Court of the Union in the UAE have been expressly given the power of adjudication of center-periphery disputes (see R. Grote, *op. cit.*, p. 233). In practice, however, a *real* decentralisation of the country can be found only in democratic states, and this is not the case of Iraq and UAE.
52 M. Eljarh, *A Bad Omen for Libya*, www.foreignpolicy.com (accessed May 25, 2014).
53 P. Cruz Villalón, *La curiosidad del jurista persa, y otros estudios sobre la Constitución* (Madrid: Centro de estudios políticos y constitucionales, 1999) p. 459.
54 See K. Mezran and E. Knecht, "Actors and Factors in Libya's Revolution," in this volume.
55 www.libyanjustice.org/news/news/post/91-political-isolation-law-which-violates-human-rights-must-be-applied-with-restraint (accessed May 26, 2014).
56 N. Mekki, *Tunisia's New Election Law and the Consolidation of a New Constitutional Order*, www.constitutionnet.org (accessed May 26, 2014).
57 These laws were aimed at preventing former communist leaders, party officials, as well as suspected collaborators, from holding high public positions.

58 See W. Sadurski (ed.), *Constitutional Justice, East and West: Democratic Legitimacy and Constitutional Courts in Post-Communist Europe in a Comparative Perspective* (The Hague: Kluwer Law International, 2002).

59 For example, the lustration laws were considered legitimate by the Constitutional Court of the Czech and Slovak Republic and by the Constitutional Court of the Czech Republic, while the Hungarian Constitutional Court—as well as many other constitutional courts in the region—declared these measures unconstitutional (see M.S. Ellis, "Purging the Past: The Current State of Lustration Laws in the Former Communist Bloc," *Law and Contemporary Problems*, vol. 59, n. 4, 1996, p. 182 ff.; Sadurski (ed.), op. cit., p. 163 ff.).

60 Biagi, "Three Generations of European Constitutional Courts," op. cit.

61 H. Schwartz, *The Struggle for Constitutional Justice in Post-Communist Europe* (Chicago: University of Chicago Press, 2000), p. 226.

62 S.L. Yom and F.G. Guase III, "Resilient Royals: How Arab Monarchies Hang On," *Journal of Democracy*, vol. 23, no. 4, 2012, p. 74.

63 See Yom and Guase III, op. cit.; R. Brynen, P.W. Moore, B.F. Salloukh and M-J. Zahar, *Beyond the Arab Spring. Authoritarianism and Democratization in the Arab World* (Boulder: Lynne Rienner Publishers, 2012), p. 173 ff.; M. Ottaway and M. Muasher, "Arab Monarchies: Change for Reform, Yet Unmet," *The Carnegie Papers*, 2011, http://carnegieendowment.org/files/arab_monarchies1.pdf (accessed May 25, 2014); L. Noueihed and A. Warren, *The Battle for the Arab Spring: Revolution, Counter-revolution and the Making of a New Era* (New Haven: Yale University Press, 2012), p. 245 ff.; A. Keyman, "The Resilience of Arab Spring Monarchies," *e-International Relations*, April 2012, www.e-ir.info/2012/04/02/the-resilience-of-arab-monarchies-in-the-arab-spring/#_ftn1 (accessed May 25, 2014).

64 Keyman, op. cit.

65 See F. Biagi, "The Pilot of *Limited* Change: Mohammed VI and the Transition in Morocco," in this volume.

66 Ottaway and Muasher, op. cit., p. 9.

67 J.A. Goldstone, "Understanding the Revolutions of 2011," *Foreign Affairs*, vol. 90, no. 3, 2011, p. 13.

68 See S.A. Yetiv, "Oil, Saudi Arabia, and the Spring that Has Not Come," in M.L. Haas and D.W. Lesch (eds.), *The Arab Spring. Change and Resistance in the Middle East* (Boulder: Westview Press, 2013), p. 97 ff. It should be noted, however, that oil rents play a key role not only in the monarchies, but also in the republics, such as in Algeria (see J. Entelis, "Algeria: The Outlier State?" in this volume).

69 Yom and Guase III, op. cit., p. 83.

70 Ibid, p. 84.

71 Brynen, Moore, Salloukh and Zahar, op. cit., p. 187.

72 See www.lemonde.fr/afrique/article/2011/06/18/la-france-salue-les-reformes-annoncees-par-le-roi-du-maroc_1538011_3212.html (accessed May 25, 2014).

73 On the external intervention in transition processes also see the section "External Variables: Influencing the Transitions in the MENA Region from Outside."

74 In Saudi Arabia, for example, the king announced that women will be allowed to vote and run for office in the next municipal elections (2015); in Oman the powers of the Shura Council were strengthened; in the UAE the electorate for the Federal National Council was expanded (see Brynen, Moore, Salloukh and Zahar, op. cit., p. 173 ff.; Ottaway and Muasher, op. cit., p. 14 ff.).

75 F. Biagi, "The Pilot of *Limited* Change: Mohammed VI and the Transition in Morocco," in this volume.

76 This practice had already been followed on two occasions (following the 1997 and 2007 elections), although since it had no constitutional status it could be disregarded at any time. On the novelties introduced by the 2011 Constitution, see

F. Biagi, "The Pilot of *Limited* Change: Mohammed VI and the Transition in Morocco," in this volume.

77 S.L. Yom, "Jordan: The Ruse of Reform," *Journal of Democracy*, vol. 24, no. 3, 2013, p. 135.

78 R. Barros, *Constitutionalism and Dictatorship: Pinochet, the Junta and the 1980 Constitution* (Cambridge: Cambridge University Press, 2002).

79 Ibid., p. 1. The plebiscite was on whether President Augusto Pinochet should remain in office for a further eight years.

80 Barros, op. cit., p. 305.

81 See T. Moustafa, *The Struggle for Constitutional Power: Law, Politics and Economic Development in Egypt* (Cambridge: Cambridge University Press, 2007).

82 Lombardi, op. cit., p. 243.

83 Such as the duty of the king to appoint the head of government from the party that wins the most seats in the elections to the House of Representatives, the supremacy of international conventions over domestic laws, the introduction of concrete constitutional review, the strengthening of judicial independence …

84 Such as the set up of a Constitutional Court, the establishment of an independent electoral commission to supervise the electoral process, the judicial oversight of the elections, the king's loss of the power to indefinitely postpone elections …

85 On the concept of "surviving constitutionalism" in Morocco and Jordan see also F. Biagi, "Will Surviving Constitutionalism in Morocco and Jordan Work in the Long Run? A Comparison with Three Past Authoritarian Regimes," *Cambridge Journal of International and Comparative Law*, vol. 3 (3), 2014 (forthcoming).

86 F. Biagi, "The Pilot of *Limited* Change: Mohammed VI and the Transition in Morocco," in this volume.

87 J.M. Maravall and J. Santamaría, "Political Change in Spain and the Prospects for Democracy," in G. O'Donnell, P.C. Schmitter, and L. Whitehead (eds.), *Transitions from Authoritarian Rule. Southern Europe* (Baltimore and London: Johns Hopkins University Press, 1986), p. 81.

88 R. Morodo, *La transición política* (Madrid: Tecnos, 1985), p. 96.

89 See C.T. Powell, *El piloto del cambio: El rey, la monarquía y la transición a la democracia* (Barcelona: Planeta, 1991), p. 280.

90 With regard to this fundamental moment in the history of Spain see J. Cercas, *The Anatomy of a Moment* (London, Berlin, New York and Sidney: Bloomsbury, 2011).

91 Brynen, Moore, Salloukh, and Zahar, op. cit., p. 188.

92 This passage by Franco was translated by the authors.

93 The speech of Franco and the oath of Juan Carlos can be found in Á.J. Sánchez Navarro, *La transición española en sus documentos* (Madrid: Centro de estudios políticos y constitucionales, 1998), p. 171 ff.

94 Powell, op cit. The title of Biagi's chapter ("The Pilot of *Limited* Change. Mohammed VI and the Transition in Morocco") was clearly inspired by Powell's book.

95 J. Tajadura Tejada, "La legitimidad de la Monarquía parlamentaria," in C. León Bastos and V.A. Wong Meraz (eds.), *Homenaje al Doctor Jorge Carpizo en Madrid* (México: Porrúa, 2010), p. 932.

96 Powell, op. cit., p. 18.

97 S.P. Huntington, *Political Order in Changing Societies* (New Haven: Yale University Press, 1968).

98 K. Mezran and E. Knecht, "Actors and Factors in Libya's Revolution," in this volume.

99 M. Ottaway, *Bahrain: Between the United States and Saudi Arabia*, http://carnegieendowment.org/2011/04/04/bahrain-between-united-states-and-saudi-arabia/2tzk# (accessed May 25, 2014).

100 See *GCC Troops Dispatched to Bahrain to Maintain Order*, March 14, 2011, www.alarabiya.net/articles/2011/03/14/141445.html (accessed May 25, 2014).
101 Noueihed and Warren, op. cit., p. 156.
102 See S. Matsui, *The Constitution of Japan: A Contextual Analysis* (Oxford and Portland: Hart Publishing, 2011), pp. 3–18.
103 See C.J. Friedrich, "Rebuilding the German Constitution," *American Political Science Review*, 1949, p. 465 ff.
104 A. Lollini and F. Palermo, "Comparative Law and the 'Proceduralization' of Constitution-Building Processes," in J. Raue and P. Sutter (eds.), *Facets and Practices of State-Building* (Leiden and Boston: Martinus Nijhoff Publishers, 2009), p. 314. On external intervention in constitution-making processes see also Z. Al-Ali, "Constitution Drafting and External Influence," in T. Ginsburg and R. Dixon (eds.), *Comparative Constitutional Law* (Cheltenham and Northampton: Edward Elgar, 2011), p. 77 ff.
105 See www.venice.coe.int/WebForms/pages/?p=03_neighbours (accessed May 25, 2014).
106 Ibid.
107 The Venice Commission of the Council of Europe, *Annual Report of Activities 2011*, Council of Europe, 2012, pp. 73–5, www.venice.coe.int/webforms/documents/?pdf=CDL-RA(2011)001-e (accessed May 25, 2014).
108 See www.venice.coe.int/WebForms/pages/?p=03_neighbours (accessed May 25, 2014).
109 Lollini and Palermo, op. cit., p. 306.
110 Linz and Stepan, op. cit., p. 74.
111 As witnessed—*inter alia*—by the growing violence against Christian minorities in the Arab world. See N. Dado, *Growing Violence against Minorities Threatens Future of Christians in Syria and across Muslim World*, available at www.arabamericannews.com/news/index.php?mod=article&cat=Community&article=7560 (accessed May 25, 2014).
112 J.A. Goldstone, "Understanding the Revolutions of 2011," *Foreign Affairs*, vol. 90, no. 3, 2011, pp. 8–16.
113 J.O. Frosini, *The Egyptian Revolution Left the Army Untouched*, www.viasarfatti25.unibocconi.eu/notizia.php?idArt=11781 (accessed May 25, 2014).
114 WBEZ Worldview, "Tom Ginsburg Discusses the Draft Egyptian Constitution", 13 December 2012, www.law.uchicago.edu/news/tom-ginsburg-discusses-draft-egyptian-constitution-worldview (accessed May 25, 2014).
115 See N. Brown, "Egypt: A Constitutional Court in an Unconstitutional Setting," in this volume.
116 Among the most renowned supporters of the semi-presidential system are Giovanni Sartori and Gianfranco Pasquino. See G. Pasquino, "Semi-presidentialism: A Political Model at Work," *European Journal of Political Research*, vol. 31, 1997, pp. 128–37, and G. Sartori, *Comparative Constitutional Engineering. An Inquiry into Structures, Incentives and Outcomes*, 2nd edition (London: Macmillan, 1997), p. 135.
117 A. Lijphart, "Constitutional Design for Divided Societies," *Journal of Democracy*, vol. 15, no. 2, 2004, p. 102.
118 J.J. Linz, "Presidential or Parliamentary Democracy: Does It Make a Difference?," in J.J. Linz and A. Valenzuela (eds.), *The Crisis of Presidential Democracy: The Latin American Evidence* (Baltimore and London: Johns Hopkins University Press, 1994), p. 55.
119 C. Skach, *Borrowing Constitutional Designs: Constitutional Law in Weimar Germany and the French Fifth Republic* (Princeton: Princeton University Press, 2005), p. 17.
120 Skach is such a sceptic that not only does she discourage semi-presidential forms of government in nascent democracies but she also pushes for abolishing those that already exist. See Skach, op. cit., p. 17.

121 Note that the English translation uses two difference verbs, i.e., "chairs" and then "presides over," whereas in the French version the expression used is always "*préside.*"

122 This provision is of particular significance especially if one makes a comparison with democratic transitions elsewhere: for example, tampering with the Constitution in order to be elected for a third term has been defined as an "obsession" for many leaders in Latin America. See J.O. Frosini and L. Pegoraro, "Constitutional Courts in Latin America: A Testing Ground for New Parameters of Classification?," *Journal of Comparative Law*, vol. 3, no. 2, 2008, p. 61.

123 For an exhaustive description and explanation of past electoral waves in the Arab world and the electoral engineering of authoritarianism see the chapter "Electoral Politics" in Brynen, Moore, Salloukh, and Zahar, op. cit., pp. 147–72.

124 Brynen, Moore, Salloukh and Zahar, op. cit., p. 158.

125 See M. McFaul and T. Cofman Wittes, "The Limits of Limited Reform," *Journal of Democracy*, vol. 19, no. 1, 2008, p. 20, and Brynen, Moore, Salloukh, and Zahar, op. cit., p. 159.

126 See F. Biagi, "The Pilot of *Limited* Change: Mohammed VI and the Transition in Morocco," in this volume.

127 G. O'Donnell and P.C. Schmitter, *Transitions from Authoritarian Rule. Tentative Conclusions about Uncertain Democracies* (Baltimore and London: Johns Hopkins University Press, 1986), p. 5.

Index

Note: Italicized numbers indicate a figure; n indicates a chapter endnote

For Product Safety Concerns and Information please contact our EU
representative GPSR@taylorandfrancis.com
Taylor & Francis Verlag GmbH, Kaufingerstraße 24, 80331 München, Germany

www.ingramcontent.com/pod-product-compliance
Ingram Content Group UK Ltd.
Pitfield, Milton Keynes, MK11 3LW, UK
UKHW022125190926
475702UK00013B/1663
9780815348887